Early praise for How to be a Ch

"There has never been a better tim
officer, but at the same time, press
role are increasing exponentially, and there has historically been a
lack of definition and professional consistency in the way the role
and remit of the function is envisaged in corporations. In this
indispensable book, the authors gather the latest thinking and cut
through the confusion to provide a deeply practical, constructive
and realistic guide to navigating through these pressures and
becoming more effective and empowered in the process."

- **Alison Taylor**, Executive Director at Ethical Systems and
author of "Higher Ground: How Business Can Do the Right
Thing in a Turbulent World"

"From your first day in the role to making the role a long-term
success, the authors provide a much-needed dose of reality about
being a CSO, setting out the day-to-day challenges as well as the
broader ever more challenging environment this vital role sits in.
Whether you work in a highly ambitious company or one that is
just getting started on sustainability, with the world's eyes on your
company, this book is for you."

- **Nadine Smith**, Director of Government and Enterprise at
Social Finance UK

"Anna and Jennifer have done the difficult job of bringing
complex sustainability and ESG concepts together in a very
accessible way. The book synthesizes years of development into a
few chapters and brings out the essence. Reading it also feels like
a journey of recognition. This is a really useful guide for CSOs
and anyone who wants to understand the corporate sustainability
profession and industry."

- **Hero Boonstra**, VP Sustainability/ESG at VTTI

HOW TO BE A CHIEF SUSTAINABILITY OFFICER

ANNA KROTOVA

JENNIFER GEARY

Cover design: Tehsin Gul and Cassie Björck
Editors: David Woods-Hale and Kriti Toshniwal
Copyright © 2024 Anna Krotova and Jennifer Geary. All rights reserved.
Published by Kindle Direct Publishing

For more information about the authors and further materials, visit www.coo-author.com

ISBN: 978-1-9997683-6-2 (print)
ISBN: 978-1-9997683-7-9 (e-book)

Dedications

To Sam. I love you, thank you for everything.

Anna

In memory of my Dad, Declan Kiely.

Jenny

About the authors

Anna Krotova is a sustainability leader with 15 years of experience in the subject. She has held sustainability roles across various sectors, from non-profits and international development organisations to consulting and private sector companies. Over the years, she has built unique insights about the sustainability field, the ecosystem of its many actors, and how they all relate and interact with each other. In her positions at the International Finance Corporation, Metabolic, Global Reporting Initiative, and private sector companies, Anna has helped organisations improve their sustainability practices, usher in impactive changes in company operations and culture, and encourage meaningful reflection around sustainability issues. She holds an MA in Environmental Policy from Moscow State University as well as an MSc in Industrial Ecology from Delft University of Technology, and she serves in various capacities across the sustainability community. She lives in Amsterdam with her husband and son.

Jennifer Geary is a senior executive with more than 25 years of experience in finance, technology, risk, and legal, across diverse industries from finance to not-for-profit. She has poured that deep and diverse experience into authoring a range of bestselling business books. Jennifer is also a facilitator, speaker, and advisor to emerging businesses and serves as a mentor on the Enterprise Ireland Scale programme. She has qualified as a chartered accountant, PRINCE 2 practitioner, CISA and CISSP and holds a certificate in Sustainable Finance and ESG Investing from NYU Stern School of Business, and a certificate in Ethics and AI from the CISI. She lives in London with her husband, two children and two cats. This is her fourth book.

Table of Contents

Introduction

Why this book is needed

Over the next few years, thousands of professionals will be entering sustainability roles as organisations start to catch up with environmental, social and governance (ESG) regulations, and face systemic risks to their operations.

Within sustainability, there is a profound paradox. For as long as we have had commercial enterprises, economic growth has been the imperative that defined how businesses operated and how they were rewarded. There seemed to be an apparently infinite supply of resources at our hands to create what we wanted.

Sustainability has changed those fundamental assumptions. It has introduced the idea of constraints: we do not have infinite supplies of everything.

Growth can still be the goal, but not always, not at all costs, and only when the benefits it brings are shared. A blind pursuit of growth – of an unsustainable strategy – has become a path to irrelevance.

And so Chief Sustainability Officers (CSOs) are being brought on board to help companies navigate this paradigm shift. They are asked to find new pathways to pursuing the economic objectives of the company while operating within an environmentally and socially safe space. This is an incredibly complex task for one corporate function to address. To be effective, CSOs need to be proficient in sustainability theory and its foundational concepts, understand the industry they're in, and be skilled at navigating organisational dynamics – all while constructively challenging the status quo and effecting change. It is also a function that comes laden with risk – of greenwashing, of legal penalties, and of sending us backwards.

Yet, practical information about how to run corporate sustainability at this expected level of quality is hard to come by. In the past, only a handful of companies have had a defined corporate sustainability role while others treated it as an extension to public affairs, HR or marketing functions. Today, the CSO role has evolved to being a key member of the leadership team who helps to shape major decisions about company strategy and operations and supports all functional areas of the business. Thought-leading sustainability academics, consultancies and think tanks have published articles, reports and white papers that address elements of the job but – as with the previous books in the 'How to be a…' series – we saw a gap in the market for a practitioners' handbook that would bring all these pieces together and speak to the real experience of the job.

With this book, we wanted to provide an accessible read that covers the breadth and the challenges of the CSO function and offers a technical toolkit and a hands-on guide for leading the transformation towards a sustainability-aligned business.

What sustainability is all about

Organisations operate within the broader economic, natural and social environment, and are deeply intertwined with it. They need energy, materials, water and other resources to deliver their products and services; they rely on people, infrastructure and public institutions to operate. In turn, companies satisfy public needs and demands through products and services, create jobs and contribute to economic development.

In an ideal world, the 'taking' and the 'giving' is in balance. The resources that companies take are replenished and converted into goods with minimum waste, pollution and other negative consequences on the natural environment and its living beings; people are offered safe and decent working conditions and fair remuneration for the labour, skills and time they provide to the organisation; and local communities, economies and governments receive back the value of the enabling conditions they provide for companies to operate, in the form of affordable and quality products and services, ethical governance practices and taxes.

However, too often, this balance is broken. Companies continue to profit through depleting and damaging their surrounding environment. By now, we all know what the damage is: climate change, biodiversity loss, the waste crisis, water pollution and water scarcity, 'forever' chemicals, inequalities across global regions, classes, and genders, as well as the rise of corrupt institutions and kleptocracies.

For many years, this debt was tucked away in different corners of the world, but today we have much more access to information about environmental degradation and social injustice, and their consequences for the long-term well-being of society. Our greater collective awareness about this debt and the physical impacts themselves are starting to affect the ways in which companies operate. There are fewer resources to extract and at higher cost, more disruption to supply chains, and growing distrust in companies from current and prospective employees, communities and governments.

Sustainability is about trying to rebalance the scales. It starts with acknowledging that any business decision you make will have an impact on the natural environment and people far and wide, for better or for worse; admitting that profitability should rely on responsible and equitable approaches to workers, communities, and the natural environment; and then reflecting that in corporate values, practices, decisions, and policies.

Who this book is for

We wrote this book to serve as a practical guide for anyone who has found themself to be responsible for the sustainability function, in enterprises large and small. It's addressed to Chief Sustainability Officers, but many companies will hire sustainability leads several tiers down the C-suite – Sustainability VPs, Directors, Heads, and Sustainability Managers, this book is for you too. It's also for CEOs who have hired – or are thinking of hiring – a CSO, so they can understand what they can, and cannot, expect of this role.

This book will also be useful for:

- those aspiring to a corporate sustainability role, whether you're starting your career, switching roles or industry, or progressing forward in your current role – this book will give you a set of tools, help set expectations, and help inventorise skills and knowledge gaps;
- board executives who are charged with ESG oversight mandates and want to understand more what the CSO role is;

- recruiters who seek to better understand the CSO / Head of Sustainability profile; and
- members of the academic community who wish to draw on practical experiences of running a corporate sustainability function and embed their insights in sustainability learning programmes.

This book is primarily intended for CSOs in commercial organisations, though our hope is that it has resonance for any organisation setting foot on the sustainability transition pathway – governmental, not for profit and for profit alike. We have used the word 'organisations' to cover this entire spectrum and the word 'companies' and 'business' where we are referring to commercial enterprises.

Section One is about setting you up for success. We cover what the role is about, key relationships of the CSO in the organisation, and foundational concepts in sustainability. We decipher what a sustainability-conducive culture is, guide you through markers of a strong sustainability strategy, and explain the steps to develop one.

Section Two covers the technical components of the role. We explore key sustainability impacts and the tools and frameworks to manage them. We explain how to develop policies and make them work, how to report and the internal controls this process requires, how to incorporate sustainability into risk management and build a credible investor relations strategy, and how to communicate your sustainability work to stakeholders accurately and impactfully.

Section Three brings it all together and this is where we discuss practicalities. We look at how to set you up for strategy execution – including drawing up a sustainability budget, designing incentives mechanisms, and structuring reporting lines.

We explore approaches to build your sustainability team and embed it in the organisation, and how to navigate and procure technology solutions. We conclude by offering words of advice from sustainability practitioners as you step into the role and look ahead at what's next for sustainability.

Given it's an emerging role, there isn't a defined path to becoming a CSO, but the mandate, responsibilities and required qualities to succeed in the role are becoming clearer over time. In the past, one would find their way into a sustainability role through in-house mobility or by volunteering for additional responsibility, for example, combining a business development, strategy or marketing role with sustainability tasks. Some CSOs come from the existing C-suite – candidates are appointed from existing senior leadership for their knowledge of the business, internal relationships and strategic foresight. If this is your scenario, you're likely well versed in how your organisation works and what your business is trying to achieve but you're probably new to the sustainability world. Other professionals switch to CSO roles from partner roles in consulting, senior level roles in high-profile NGOs and international organisations, or governmental agencies. They are experts in sustainability or one of its topics but may be new to the corporate world.

We have tried to adapt the book to CSOs at all of these different levels of maturity and professional background.

We have structured most chapters to give you a short background on how this functional area relates to sustainability, what a CSO is aiming to achieve and what good looks like. We then offer practical guidelines of where to start when building or improving on this functional area, whether that's embedding sustainability in the culture of your organisation or developing sustainability policies. We offer standards, best practices and examples from the industry for you to build on and integrate in your work. Finally, we offer warning signs – a list of possible blockers or distractions that can set you off track, and checklists to make sure you reach for maximum impact.

We hope you find this book helpful, and we would love to hear your feedback and continue the dialogue. You can reach us via LinkedIn, visit Anna's website at www.annakrotova.com or contact Jenny at jennifer@coo-author.com.

SECTION ONE: THE FOUNDATIONS

Chapter 1

The role of the CSO

If you have chosen a career in sustainability and aspire to being a CSO, you have chosen a dynamic, fulfilling and challenging profession.

It is still a relatively new and evolving corporate role, and you have the opportunity to shape and improve it, adding to the growing body of knowledge and ways of working that will ultimately make our organisations more responsible, more efficient and more resilient. It also means that you have seen and worry deeply about the direction our world is taking and want to make it your life's work to do something about it.

In its short life so far, the expectations of the sustainability function have evolved along with our understanding of the complexity of the sustainability transition, and the demands to deliver on it fully. Investors are more attentive to the sustainability credentials of companies they manage, and regulators have raised the bar on sustainability performance and transparency. Company leadership is expected to have its finger on the pulse about what's happening in the farthest corners of their organisations, and to anticipate impacts far in the future, to mitigate the risk of losing access to capital and the license to operate.

Today, the CSO acts (or has the potential to act) as a strategic advisor to the organisation – one who ensures that everything the company does adds up to long-term value creation, while at the same time setting standard operating procedures for the organisation, running a portfolio of their own projects, and being the centre of expertise for the company on sustainability topics.

What a CSO does day-to-day

The CSO responsibilities will vary depending on the company sector, size, and established organisational capabilities, but a common mandate of the CSO today includes:

- Strategy – Ensuring alignment between company strategy and sustainability; identifying and assessing sustainability impacts, risks and opportunities; directing the organisation to focus on a core set of the most material issues; setting targets and drawing up project roadmaps; setting accountability with respective teams; and overseeing execution.
- Setting up sustainability governance and change management – Reviewing the organisation's policies and procedures, risk management framework, internal controls, culture, behaviour, and level of awareness on sustainability topics among employees, board, and senior management. Reviewing data systems and tooling and embedding sustainability accountability across the entire organisation.
- Reporting – Overseeing the full life cycle of the reporting process, from planning, to setting up data management systems, to eventually coordinating production or writing (parts of) the report; aligning financial and sustainability

reporting; and providing input to the annual reporting process.

- Running a portfolio of projects – Planning coordinating, troubleshooting, course-correcting and tracking results; the CSO often acts as a sustainability programme management office to the rest of the organisation, ensuring that company initiatives are set up for success and are on track.
- Monitoring the space – Keeping abreast of regulatory, scientific, technological, public and competitor sustainability and ESG developments, and actioning or directing relevant updates to respective teams; anticipating impacts from these developments on the company and its sustainability work.

What makes a good CSO

The scope of the CSO role requires left-side and right-side brain functions. You need to be analytical and focused on execution and at the same time, you need to excel at communication skills, people management and diplomacy, and draw on your creative skills to find solutions to non-standard problems. A rare person will come to the CSO role fully formed and you will lean on the support of the broader sustainability team, and the wider organisation, to fill in on some of the aspects. However, below are a few critical characteristics any CSO should have to be successful.

Systems thinker

You need to be able to see the big picture, both in terms of how the activities and decisions of your company impact the world around it, and how everything in your company adds up to either support or hinder the sustainability transition. Systems thinking is about understanding the connections and relationships between things so that you can see how the system works[1] – in your case, the organisation and its internal and external environment. For example, if the company is launching a new product line, what impacts downstream and upstream will that create across the life cycle of the product? What if you produce this product in great quantities over the years? Or if the CFO has the target to reduce capital expenditures (CapEx) while you have the target to decarbonise the business and need to invest in new energy-efficient technologies, how will these two targets interact?

Exceptional communicator

Communication is at the centre of the CSO's remit, with skilful diplomacy needed across activities such as:

- translating and contextualising big, complex sustainability issues into concepts your organisation will understand;
- forming internal partnerships and alliances, getting buy-in, and advocating for change;
- motivating and inspiring others around you to act;
- facilitating project groups with people from differing technical backgrounds;
- developing and delivering presentations and reports to get the message across to executives;
- representing your organisation in external industry groups, high-level forums and conferences; and
- managing relations with regulators, investors, employees, activist groups and NGOs.

CSOs often rely on their personal influence and leadership to get the job done, so communication is their main tool. You need to be able to switch between communicating information in a factual, analytical and direct manner; and being a storyteller who calls on people's imagination, shared experiences and feelings. You need to adapt your language to each person's level of knowledge of the subject, their professional background, competing priorities, political views (yes, you will also have to work with people who think 'climate change is a hoax' or that it's 'hippie tree-hugging stuff'), or even their mood! You're also validating marketing messages and external communication for factual accuracy and compliance, while maintaining your company's unique copywriting style. Taken together, these activities require an exceptional combination of communication styles and techniques.

Intrapreneur

A lot of your work will be about creating a blueprint for what's not there yet, charting new territory in the organisation, connecting the dots and building ecosystems. You will often work without complete direction from the top and be expected to navigate ambiguity, bringing structure to it. You will be suggesting new processes, operating principles and products, as well as nurturing the culture of sustainability. You will be connecting departments that work in silos and reaching out to the farthest corners of the organisation. This will require proactivity, creativity and courage. You will need to have the ability to see gaps and opportunities quickly – and act upon them – and build connections across the entire organisation and its ecosystem.

As Hero Boonstra, VP of Sustainability & ESG at a global privately-owned energy service company, tells us: "I spend a lot of time understanding what is on people's agendas (board level, department, division level) and where there are useful common denominators and people need to cooperate in order to succeed. Bringing people together around a topic and integrating often separated interests and concerns seems to be more important in this role than ever before."

Programme manager

You will be running multiple sustainability projects and initiatives at the same time. These will be wildly different in terms of characteristics and time investment required – from coordinating the work of the team, to deep analytical work, to quick troubleshooting and subject-matter plug-ins. Your ability to plan, prioritise, coordinate, deliver, and keep cool in the process is essential.

Beyond overseeing your own portfolio of projects, you will be the go-to person for all things sustainability in the organisation – quick advice on an employee initiative, a quick slide or two for a meeting with potential investors, a last-minute invitation to speak at an event… you have to be ruthless with what you decide to grant your attention to. You will learn to estimate how much time various tasks require as they land on your desk and know when to say 'no' so you can remain focused on the execution of key goals.

Finally, you will be setting up a lot of programmes from scratch and will need to be able to source funding, develop roadmaps and workplans, set up a programme office, plan resources and appoint people, troubleshoot and move things forward.

Resilience

Most people who come to a CSO role are driven by genuine interests to make the world a better place. You know the science and where we're headed, and you want to make your contribution through the corporate platform. But a company is not a philanthropic organisation – its purpose can be as simple as offering a product or service people want to buy, earning a return for shareholders in the process. This creates the infamous dichotomy for sustainability professionals: on the one hand you're ultimately serving growth objectives and on the other, you're charged to minimise the negative impacts of that growth. Not everyone in your organisation will appreciate that the two must be complementary, and a win-win will not always be possible.

This dichotomy can manifest itself in conflicts at work and you have to be prepared to face them calmly, pick your battles wisely, and keep moving things forward enthusiastically. You also need to recognise when a person, or an organisation, is not going to get there and to have the strength to step away with your values intact.

Patience

Transitions take time. People might not be ready for the message – maybe they need to reflect on what you said, consult others, or really 'see' the problem to connect with it. For example, a conversation about emissions reductions might be received better after a heatwave. Sometimes senior executives are so overwhelmed with their responsibilities that they simply don't have space in their agenda or in their mind – you will learn to recognise when it's the right time to bring a message across. This can be frustrating, but these are the boundaries that you have to respect and be patient about and adjust your planning and priorities accordingly. You also need the patience to allow any new processes to root themselves and give results. Remember, you're challenging something that's been done a certain way for years and change takes time.

When a CSO role may not be the right fit for you

What personality traits are not a good fit for the CSO? Below are some red flags that may indicate your career match lies elsewhere. They also serve to remind us to temper our own impulses on those challenging days.

Impatient, driven by spectacular, early results: change is painful, non-linear and takes time. Quick wins and 'ta-da' moments will be few and far between. The value in this role is the patient and repeated application of the activities in this book. You plant lots of seeds and it can take time for them to bloom.

Needing validation: this is not a role for someone who lives off regular and frequent praise and approval. You may spend a lot of your time being told that people don't have time, that sustainability goals are unrealistic, that the situation is hopeless, or ridiculous, or both. You need to source your energy from well-held internal beliefs and a strong sense of your own 'why'. You also want to shower others with praise when things go well – this will encourage others but means that you're not often in the spotlight.

Overly draconian or singularly focused: in our experience, the more successful CSOs are those who understand – and believe in – the business they are trying to reform. They view the mission of the organisation in a positive way and give credit to the rest of the organisation for doing a tough job. They acknowledge the challenges and empathise with the trade-offs that people make, but they still persist, gently, with the need to adapt. They are able to move freely between different sentiments in the organisation without becoming embroiled in them, and they are certainly not there to drive their own personal or political sustainability convictions. These CSOs are likely to be viewed much more positively than those that set themselves against the organisation, when every day can feel like a battle.

If you're transitioning to the role from another business function

If you've been with the business for a while and are transitioning to the CSO role, inventorise what transferable skills you bring – you may have more than you think.

For example, if you have worked in finance, your analytical skills, financial audit and control experience, understanding of the budgeting process and finance structuring, and knowledge of the annual reporting process will be highly valuable in making the business case for sustainability with your CFO, building a solid sustainability control environment and reporting process, and managing investor relations. Your financial analysis skills will be relevant to assessing and quantifying sustainability-related risks and opportunities during the materiality assessment.

If you're coming from investor relations, your understanding of financial markets and investment analysis, will help you align sustainability initiatives with investor expectations and communicate these alignments effectively.

If you're transitioning from HR, your people management skills will support you in managing wider stakeholder relations, drive change across the organisation and grow a sustainability culture.

If you're transitioning from legal and compliance, your knowledge of the policy space and ability to navigate and interpret regulation will be highly relevant in adapting company processes in a timely and comprehensive manner, anticipating regulatory change and driving high-quality responsible business practices. Your 'lawyer's lens' will help de-risk corporate sustainability communications and avoid greenwashing.

If you're coming from supply chain, your knowledge of industry and technology will be invaluable in finding effective and innovative solutions to decarbonisation and building more resilient supply chains.

As one of the experts whom we have interviewed for this book told us: "We need more business experts – IT, procurement, real estate, finance, operations, etc. – who are upskilled in sustainability versus only the people on the CSO's team. The 'us / them' approach doesn't work as we become the morality police, and it also removes the accountability from the rest of the organisation to make the company sustainable."

Key relationships of the CSO

A well-defined and organised sustainability function will have an impact across the whole organisation. The type and size of your organisation, and your material topics, will determine the departments with which you will work more closely – but, in general, you will work with all of them. Some of the key dynamics with the other senior disciplines you will encounter – perhaps for the first time – are outlined below, including touchpoints and synergies between your function and theirs; possible contradictions between your objectives, behaviours and processes; and ways to approach leaders in these functions.

CSO and the Board

The Board is the governing body of the organisation. It provides insight, advice, and leadership to the company so as to protect the interests of shareholders (i.e., maximise the value that shareholders receive for their investment), manage risk, and ultimately ensure the prosperity of the company. Boards bring outside-world expertise to organisations and, in the context of sustainability, their role is to screen and translate how these issues affect the business and take corrective action. At the same time, sustainability expertise on boards is often lacking, which can confine the role, for example, to ticking boxes on investor questionnaires. If this is your situation, your goal is to get the topic of sustainability on the board agenda early and do the educational work to help the board comprehend how it connects to the business strategically.

The board is also involved in making decisions on corporate governance issues, an important element of responsible business. There are several areas in which the CSO can offer advice on best practice, including the way the governance of the organisation is structured, how the board is evaluated, who is appointed into executive roles, how management is compensated and incentivised, and how conflicts of interest are addressed. At a minimum, the CSO is usually responsible for documenting these factors in the annual sustainability report.

CSO and the Chief Executive Officer

The CEO's main responsibilities are to set the strategic direction of the company, make major corporate decisions, manage the operations and resources of the organisation, liaise between the board of directors and corporate operations, and represent the company to the public. Their attitude to sustainability is critical to your success and whether your role will be treated as symbolic or strategic.

Many visionary CEOs, who understand the global sustainability context, hire CSOs to work with them on business transformation, but many more hire CSOs to perform minimum compliance in response to sustainability regulations, without being familiar with the full scope of the position. Understand from the CEO what they want to achieve with sustainability for the organisation and discuss how you will bring the different aspects of the CSO role in scope. Consider what characteristics of an organisation or

CEO would make you not want to work for them – and hold true to those principles.

CSO and the Chief Financial Officer

The CFO is the gatekeeper of a company's capital management. They are responsible for treasury, investor relations, credit risk, financial planning and financial reporting, accounting, and tax. Their objective is to secure financing and reduce the cost of funds. The CFO can be one of your biggest allies, but you need to approach the relationship pragmatically. Many CFOs see sustainability as a source of cost without a visible return on investment. Change that perception by raising awareness of the costs of inaction and by quantifying opportunities related to a sustainability-aligned business. In more mature organisations, you will jump directly to working with the CFO on sustainability valuation models and controls, as well as capital structuring and sourcing in order to finance the sustainability transition of the business.

You will also work closely with the CFO on sustainability reporting and auditing, which is becoming just as regulated and just as mature as financial reporting. In fact, a strong trend we see in the market today is that CFOs are rapidly becoming owners of sustainability reporting and performance while the CSO acts a centre of expertise and support on the matter. Either way, CFOs own the company audit and assurance process, and you want to use those established relationships to set up group reporting and accounting processes and controls. Depending on the sustainability reporting regime to which you are subject, assurance of publicly disclosed sustainability data may be mandatory, so this is a cost item for which you'll need to establish a process and discuss early.

CSO and the Chief Operating Officer

The COO oversees the day-to-day operational and administrative functions of the business and is usually someone who 'gets things done' in the company. They have a wide knowledge of the organisation, and their mandate can encompass operations, supply chain management, procurement, and, in some organisations, also finance, technology and people. Sometimes they are tasked to lead a specific strategic initiative, such as a change management process, an expansion, or a restructure.

The COO's main objectives revolve around delivering the organisational strategy, improving efficiency, and minimising costs. There should be a natural synergy with sustainability because resource efficiencies that sustainability aims for should ultimately result in cost reductions. If you're operating in resource-intensive sectors, talk to your COO about physical and transition risks from climate change. These could include increased costs of raw materials, supply chain disruptions, increasing prices for energy and carbon taxes, greater regulation of existing products and services. Equally, sustainability practices can also lead to opportunities that may be of interest to your COO, such as access to subsidies and investment to transition to low-emission technologies, or greater supply chain resiliency.

Work with them on a cost-benefit analysis of reducing environmental impacts or decarbonising various areas of the business based on what your material topics are.

CSO and the Chief Legal Officer / General Counsel

The CLO (or General Counsel or GC) is the company in-house lawyer who is responsible for identifying and mitigating legal issues across the company. In their capacity as company secretary, they gatekeep access to the board and oversee corporate governance affairs, such as remuneration policies for the C-suite and board, nominations of the highest governing body, or appointments of committees. Sometimes the CLO oversees the risk and compliance functions too.

You may depend on the CLO to access the board and get sustainability on their agenda. Talk to them about the changing regulatory landscape in this topic – the swath of laws adopted recently on greenwashing and supply chain due diligence, sustainability reporting regulation and mandatory assurance. Show statistics on real litigation cases in your sector due to irresponsible business conduct. Regulators are lowering the thresholds for suing board members for sustainability-related issues – it is your job to ensure the board is competent, educated and aware of its ESG responsibilities and potential consequences of decisions. Work with your CLO to establish a sustainability oversight mechanism and an approach to how you will support the board (see chapter 12).

You will also work closely with the CLO on sustainability reporting and corporate communications. The legal team will want to review and sign off on any public statements you are publishing, and they will also provide you with much of the content about company corporate governance practices.

Finally, the CLO will be your ally in interpreting and operationalising regulation as it relates to sustainability.

CSO and the Chief People Officer / Chief Human Resources Officer

The CPO is responsible for ensuring that the organisation has the human resources to support the execution of its strategy. They oversee the full life cycle of an employee experience in the company, starting from attraction, recruitment, and retention, all the way through to development and exit. They are responsible for the employee value proposition (EVP) and making the company an attractive, safe, and fair place to work. They should have the formal mandate concerning employee social impacts. They usually own the policies and practices concerning labour arrangements; remuneration, collective bargaining and diversity, equity, and inclusion (DEI). Sometimes volunteering and philanthropic activities might fall under their wing as a way to maintain an attractive employer brand.

The CPO is a critical partner in your efforts to: (1) drive sustainability culture, as they usually oversee and manage processes related to evolving and safeguarding company values, (2) deliver the annual reporting process as they hold all employee-related data and often they will have their own data management systems in place, and (3) introduce innovation and best practices on social impact topics as they are the ultimate decision-maker on what gets prioritised for the people strategy.

People and sustainability functions have a strong synergy. A company's response to sustainability challenges is a major factor in people's decision-making about their place of work, especially for the younger generation for whom climate change and social injustice have been the major backdrop of their upbringing. Use this argument to secure the CPO's support for your programmes, show numbers about your company's demographics and their values from both the current and targeted talent pool. Look into employee survey results – what do people say about sustainability and purpose? What 'demand' exists for these topics internally?

Another strong touchpoint for partnership is sustainability reporting. It's likely your company is (or will soon be) subject to regulatory sustainability reporting. For those subject to the EU reporting regime, labour-related requirements are extensive, even for companies with prior experience of sustainability reporting.

These requirements will involve a substantial volume of data points across the workforce – from employees on the payroll to those outsourced. As an experiment, ask your people team if gender pay gap data is readily available and if discrepancies exist, why and what is the plan to address them. Run a workshop with the CPO and their leadership team about reporting expectations, identify gaps in data availability and gaps in performance (e.g., existence of certain policies or processes), identify priorities and chart a plan forward. In the end, the CPO is responsible for managing people topics, so build a relationship with them early on.

CSO and the Chief Marketing Officer

The CMO is responsible for developing and executing marketing strategies to promote the company's products and services to future and existing customers, increasing brand awareness, boosting sales, and driving customer engagement.

Marketing has a huge impact on sustainability. The global impact of 'advertised emissions' – emissions that result from the uplift of sales generated by advertising – has been calculated at 208 million tonnes of CO_2 in 2022.[2] Talk to your CMO about responsible marketing practices. Inspire them to take a leading role in the industry with your company's marketing practices – very little is currently done in this space. Discuss with them their adherence to the International Chamber of Commerce (ICC) Advertising and Marketing Communications Code[3] and map your current practices against the ICC's principles.

You will also work closely with the CMO on consumer research, external sustainability communications and asset production (e.g., the sustainability page on your company website, social media assets, white papers), speaking engagements and media relations. Discuss how you want to arrange responsibilities and the process for these areas of work, how you will share team resources and budget. Depending on how your organisation is structured, some of these responsibilities – like media relations – may also fall under the responsibilities of the Chief Communications Officer which we discuss below.

CSO and the Chief Risk Officer / Chief Compliance Officer

The CRO ensures that there is an effective system of controls in place to manage strategic, reputational, operational, financial, or technology-related risk. They are a critical partner when it comes to sustainability risk management. At a minimum, you will work with the CRO to: (1) introduce a sustainability risk register in the Enterprise Risk Management Framework, and (2) include sustainability responses in your Request for proposal / Request for information systems.

Generally, the CRO and their team will own the process of escalating and reporting risks, but you have to discuss how to set responsibilities around sustainability risk oversight – a matter of capacity and sufficient level of understanding of sustainability risks by the CRO. You might decide on a cadence where you flag and discuss sustainability risks with the CRO, or you agree on a list of risks that the risk team takes responsibility for monitoring.

CSO and the Chief Communications Officer

The Chief Communications Officer is responsible for the internal and external communications system and tools, content production and general company tone, and occasionally public affairs. They are a great partner in telling the sustainability story internally and in most cases will happily support you. Ask them to walk you through your company's internal communication system and agree where and how to plug in sustainability content. Get creative.

If your Chief Communications Officer is also responsible for public affairs, discuss a process for responding to stakeholders – you would want to formulate key points in your responses / statements before handing off to the CCO to package up and polish. The legal team will need to sign off as well. We discuss external communications in chapter 11.

These are just some of the key relationships for the CSO and you might work with other functions too. If you need to innovate and redesign your products, you will likely work with the Chief Product Officer and their team on research and development, and later with the Chief Commercial Officer to work out a commercial strategy for these products. Almost every organisation needs to manage digital security (a sustainability reporting topic if material) led by the Chief Information Security Officer, and you will often find an ally in the CISO.

C-suite mapping exercise

You will need to educate key decision-makers in the organisation on sustainability and get their buy-in. Maybe you're joining a company with a long record of sustainability work and a strong sustainability culture, where the necessity for sustainability is well understood and shared by the majority, and the roles and accountabilities are set. Or you might be joining a company where the decision to open a sustainability role originated from investor concerns, which prompted the leadership to act, but where most decision-makers are new to the domain. They might be completely open and ready to absorb your recommendations, or they might have their own views and ideas about the topic. Use this stakeholder mapping exercise adapted from project management theory[4], to map internal stakeholders from the C-suite. It is geared to help you identify key internal stakeholders, map out their interests, and define the tactics to work with them.

Step 1. Identify internal stakeholders

Write down the names and titles of key decision-makers in executive management, senior leaders, and their responsibilities. Your organisation may have other roles or call them differently, so this can be adapted to your context.

Step 2. Identify pain points

Write down key pain points and goals of the decision-makers outlined above, as they relate to the organisation as a whole. For example:

Table 1. Key stakeholders, responsibilities, and pain points

Stakeholder	Responsibilities	Pain points
Shareholders	Portfolio management	• Achieve highest possible return on investment (ROI) • Mitigate risks
Co-Founder / President and CEO	Strategy, business execution and compliance	• Improve group's profitability • Mitigate risks
Chief Financial Officer	Treasury, investor relations, credit risk, planning, financial reporting, accounting, and tax	• Secure financing • Reduce cost of funds
Chief Legal Officer	Legal affairs, compliance, insurance, company secretary	• Mitigate legal and compliance risks
Chief Commercial / Chief Revenue Officer	Commercial, marketing	• Increase revenue
Chief Operations Officer	Operations, IT, EHS	• Decrease operating expenses • Improve operational efficiency
Chief Product Officer	Product development, innovation	• Deliver best performing product • Innovate
Chief People Officer	People and employee communications	• Attract and manage talent • Protect workforce
Chief Information and Security Officer	Information technology and security	• Digitise operations • Mitigate digital security risks
Regional Vice Presidents	Regional strategy execution	• Improve region's profitability

Step 3. Qualify internal stakeholders

Plot decision-makers on a four-quadrant graph based on two criteria: their influence in the organisation; and their interest in sustainability.

'Interest' can mean both stakeholders' general motivation for the topic but also the strength of synergy between their pain points and how you can help address them through sustainability (your shared interest).

'Influence' refers to stakeholders' power to influence major company decisions.

Figure 1. Internal stakeholder mapping based on influence in an organisation and interest in sustainability

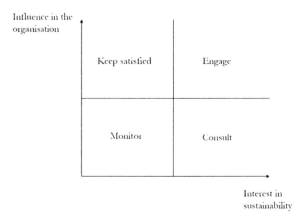

What does your graph look like? Is everyone somewhere in the centre or spread across? Who ended up in your upper right quadrant? Are they who you expected them to be?

Step 4. Determine how to act

When you've analysed your graph, you can adopt different tactics to approach internal stakeholders based on their positions on the graph:

- Engage – Manage these stakeholders closely. They are your key players with whom engagement is absolutely necessary because of the influence they have on the organisation and the impact you can achieve together if you're addressing their pain points and bringing value to their work.
- Keep them satisfied – With these stakeholders, maintain their level of comfort and confidence in your work. This group needs to understand and see the value of sustainability for the company even though it might not be directly relevant to their objectives. You want to build a relationship with this group where you can call on them for advocacy and support because of their high influence in the organisation or – at a minimum – you need them not to detract from your work.
- Consult – This is a good group of stakeholders to fall back on for information, insights, and ideas. They might not have the same influence as other C-suite members, but they could generate ample insight relevant to your work and be the first to put their hand up to support. Consult them for their views on ideas, concerns you have or things you want to pilot and keep them informed about progress.
- Monitor – Establish an infrequent cadence of check-ins with these stakeholders to monitor any sentiments and changes.

You might still run into detractors – stakeholders who, for whatever reason, are not on board. This could be an investor who's dragged into an ESG culture war and sees it as a threat or part of a 'woke agenda', or an executive who paints a binary, black and white picture of sustainability. Most likely you won't change their views, and engagement may only have a negative effect. Focus on what you can control and offer clear, evidence-based statements about the sustainability work of the company. Don't engage in arguments over points of view. Instead do your homework and, if confronted, have all your numbers at hand.

The example above has executive management as the primary internal stakeholders. Adapt this to a group that works for your context. For example, you may wish to add the board, employees, your existing team, middle management and other personas.

Summary

The role of CSO is challenging but fulfilling. It's not for everyone. You should now have a sense of the job and have considered how it maps to your own personal traits and attributes. You understand how the CSO role typically interacts with the rest of the C-suite. You have mapped your key stakeholders and have a plan for how to engage with them. You can see the difference in what is expected of you as you step up from sustainability executive into the most senior sustainability role in the organisation. Hopefully, you are still feeling motivated about the role. If so, read on to understand some key concepts underpinning sustainability.

Chapter 2

Sustainability vocabulary

Executives use a common financial vocabulary that everyone understands – 'profit and loss' (P&L), 'liability', 'return on investment' (ROI) – these are all set concepts necessary to understand the organisation's financial performance and inform sound decision-making. Likewise, sustainability operates by its own vocabulary. Let's unpack the key concepts in corporate sustainability that your organisation needs to be proficient in.

Sustainability, ESG and CSR

Sustainability, ESG and CSR are the three terms at the top of CSO vocabulary and you will often hear them used interchangeably. People like to contrast and compare them, but don't let that distract you – they all have their unique history and place.

Sustainability

As a normative concept, 'sustainability' comes from 'sustainable development', a term introduced by Norwegian politician Gro Harlem Brundtland and the United Nations in their 1987 report for member states: Our Common Future. It stands for "development that meets the needs of the present without compromising the ability of future generations to meet their own needs".[1]

Our Common Future (or The Brundtland Report) was a landmark document that introduced the idea that economic development, environmental issues, and social well-being are interconnected issues and should be addressed by governments as such when they formulate policies and country development plans. The Brundtland Report laid the groundwork for several major forums that moved the sustainability discussion forward significantly. These include the UN Earth Summit in 1992 and the adoption of Agenda 21 (the predecessor to the UN's Sustainable Development Goals). These initiatives led to sustainable development being crystallised as the UN's global policy objective.

The report also addressed private enterprises, calling on their possibilities for "bringing about far-reaching changes and improvements".[2] This was the first reference and appeal to the role of business in sustainability at a political level.

From this, the concept of sustainability came to be formalised and understood as the end-goal state in which the economy operates in line with ecological limits and social well-being, as it meets human needs. In the business context, consider sustainable development as a framework that invites an evolution in the way we manage business, at the core of which is the recognition that profitability relies on responsible and equitable approaches to workers, communities, and the natural environment.

ESG

Environmental, social and governance (ESG) are three groups of issues on which investors screen the company's non-financial performance. ESG originated as a risk proxy for investors who use it to understand whether the financial performance of companies they are invested in (income statements and balance sheet items such as assets, liabilities, and capital) might be at risk from poor management practices. For example, if a company disposes of its hazardous waste properly and sets up strong health and safety practices at the workplace, it is less likely to be subject to fines from regulators or reputational damage from employees and the public. If it relies on scarce natural resources to produce its products, it might run into supply intermittency and commodity cost spikes, leading to delays in production and higher commodity costs.

Investors know these links and want to have the confidence that a company is addressing risky issues that might affect its bottom line and prevent it from delivering on its responsibilities to shareholders. They are interested in these impacts insofar as their implications have positive or negative financial repercussions on the company. ESG is therefore an investor lens into some sustainability concepts, but from the point of view of financial performance.

ESG originated in the early 2000s when a group of officials in the UN Environment Programme's Finance Initiative (UNEP FI) set out to devise how to make institutional investors consider sustainability as part of their investment decision-making. Back then, ethical investing was largely an exclusionary process centred on personal ethics – pension funds and other long-term owners of financial assets would remove the obviously 'unethical firms' from their portfolio but the action would stop there.[3]

In 2004, UNEP FI released two key reports that introduced the ESG concept[4]: Who cares wins[5] and The Materiality of Social, Environmental, and Corporate Governance Issues to Equity Pricing.[6] In the latter, authors argued that "the long-term protection of shareholder value rests on rigorous integration of environmental, social and corporate governance issues in the valuation process", and that ignoring it "may expose investors and companies to unnecessary risk. Those who wish to create the foundation for, and then realise, long-term shareholder value, must fully integrate ESG considerations into the market, investment, and board room considerations".[7]

After the publication of these reports, a chain of events followed that helped to take ESG into the mainstream of the investment world. In 2005, UNEP FI released the Freshfields Report, in which a group of lawyers challenged the then prevalent view of investors and asset managers that the exclusive focus of fiduciary duty is on financial returns and made the legal case for the integration of ESG considerations in investment policy and practice.[8]

Several months later, the United Nations launched the UN Principles for Responsible Investment (UN PRI) stipulating six principles for responsible investing and thereby bridging the worlds of capital markets and multilateral organisations through a language that both could understand. Responsible investing split into many directions (e.g., socially responsible investing, thematic investing, impact-first investing), but fast forward several years to 2020 and ESG investing became mainstream. In that one year, the European Commission[9], the International Organization of Securities Commissions (IOSCO)[10], the International Financial Reporting Standards (IFRS)[11], and the US Securities and Exchange Commission (US SEC)[12] all made major announcements that led to a surge of ESG regulation on sustainable finance and transparency globally. This was a watershed moment, after which ESG trickled down to companies via investor relations, finance, and legal departments because institutional investors and regulators started to demand more transparency on how these issues are managed.

Critically, ESG does not offer a methodology to assess what's important for the company to focus on as part of its sustainability strategy to be resilient long-term. However, once a company has defined its key material topics and impacts and sustainability strategy, ESG metrics can be chosen to monitor how the organisation is performing and progressing in those areas.

Different standards offer a menu of ESG topics and metrics organisations can use. Here, we leverage the McKinsey & Company definitions where, in broad terms, the three ESG categories cover the following:[13]

- The 'E' in ESG – environmental topics – measured through the energy and other resources your organisation consumes, the waste it generates, and the consequences on living beings as a result. Every organisation uses energy and resources; every organisation affects, and is affected by, the environment. The issues under 'E' that investors might look for include climate change and emissions, air and water pollution, energy consumption, waste management, water management, materials use and the circular economy, and biodiversity.
- The 'S' in ESG – social topics – measured through the quality of the relationships your organisation has and the reputation it fosters with people and institutions in the communities where you do business. Every organisation operates within a broader, diverse society and affects real human beings and their human rights. The issues under 'S' can include employee health and safety; diversity, equity

and inclusion; labour standards; human rights; privacy and data security; community relationships and procurement practices.

- The 'G' in ESG – governance – the internal system of practices, controls, and procedures your organisation adopts in order to govern itself, make effective decisions, comply with the law, and meet the needs of stakeholders. Every company, which is itself a legal creation, requires governance. The issues under 'G' can include board composition, corporate ethics, executive compensation, incentives, bribery and corruption, and lobbying.

Corporate Social Responsibility

A lot of sustainability debate today is about the purpose of business in the world. The origins of this discussion go back to US academic circles in the 1950s. Back then, a group of economists was questioning the purpose of companies in corporate America as they become institutional powers, with enormous impacts on society and the ecological environment around them. In 1953, American economist Howard R. Bowen published the book The Social Responsibilities of the Businessman in which he introduced the term 'corporate social responsibility' (CSR) and explored "whether and how CSR can help business reach the goals of social justice and economic prosperity while creating welfare for a broad range of social groups, beyond the corporations and their shareholders".[14]

The CSR concept was hotly debated by then academics and economists like Jules Backman, Keith Davis, Richard Eells, Milton Friedman, Henry Manne, Joseph McGuire, George Steiner, Clarence Walton and others, with several major schools of thought arguing that the social responsibility of business is anything and everything from sole profit maximisation to running the business ethically and within legal frames, to being a purely voluntary pursuit in whatever form.[15]

In 1971, the US Committee for Economic Development introduced the idea of a 'social contract' between business and society, or what we commonly refer to today as the business's 'social license to operate'.[16] The social contract is based on the idea that business functions because of 'public consent', therefore business has an obligation to serve the needs of society constructively. The Committee defined those responsibilities to be: (1) provision of jobs and economic growth through well-run businesses, (2) running the business fairly and honestly regarding employees and customers, and (3) becoming more broadly involved in improving the conditions of the community and environment in which it operates.

There were several iterations of these responsibilities, with the most notable one by Archie Caroll, Professor of Management Emeritus in the Terry College of Business, University of Georgia, in 1979[17] (republished in 1991) in which he separated CSR into four layers of a pyramid:

- Economic responsibilities – being profitable;
- Legal responsibilities – obeying laws and regulations;
- Ethical responsibilities – doing what is just and fair, avoiding harm; and
- Philanthropic responsibilities – being a good corporate citizen.

Most of the companies we look up to today for their pioneering sustainability work have been inspired by the principles and philosophy of CSR. At the same time, as a management framework, CSR lacked the specificity to measure impacts and performance, plus many companies have flipped Caroll's pyramid and have put too much emphasis on philanthropic responsibilities. These are some of the reasons why CSR is often dismissed, and unfairly so – the breadth and quality of intellectual thought on which CSR is predicated is must-read homework for CSOs.

To summarise the relationship between sustainability, ESG and CSR: they neither contradict nor compete with each other but rather all have their own place and role. Sustainability is a north star for organisations to aspire to if they want to continue creating value long-term and responding to the needs of society. CSR is the intellectual framework to help business define their broader purpose in society. ESG is a tool to help organisations measure how well they're performing on various indicators as they step onto the path of sustainability transformation.

Impact

Sustainability revolves around managing impacts. So, what is impact?

The Global Reporting Initiative (GRI) defines impact as the "effect an organization has or could have on the economy, environment, and people, including effects on their human rights, as a result of the organization's activities or business relationships".[18] In other words, impact is the "change in an aspect of people's well-being or the condition of the natural environment caused by an organisation".[19]

GRI further defines that:

> Impacts can be actual or potential, negative or positive, short-term or long-term, intended or unintended, and reversible or irreversible. Through the type of impacts the organization makes, it contributes negatively or positively to sustainability. Impacts are usually split into three meta-groups – impacts on the economy, environment and people.

Impacts on the economy

These are impacts an organisation has on the economic systems and on its stakeholders at the local, national and international levels. An organisation can impact the economy through various practices, such as its competition practices, procurement practices, pricing, and the taxes and other payments it makes to governments – topics that are usually covered under the 'G' of ESG.[20]

Think about tax. Going back to the basics, taxes are a source of revenue for the government – they are levied to finance the state such that it can maintain public infrastructure and invest in public services like healthcare and education, or to finance defence. They are central to the fiscal policy and macroeconomic stability of countries and are acknowledged by the UN to play a vital role in achieving the SDGs.[21]

Taxes encapsulate the financial value of the many factors upon which company's profitability depends – access to educated and healthy workers, markets, public infrastructure and services, natural resources, and a public administration.[22] So, taxes are a key mechanism for companies to contribute to the economies in which they operate. At the same time, the world is set to lose USD 4.7 trillion in the next decade if companies continue to avoid their tax obligations – an equivalent to losing a year of worldwide spending on public health.[23]

Impacts on the environment

These refer to an organisation's impacts on natural elements: air, land, and water, and the ecosystems they are part of, which include living organisms. An organisation impacts the environment through its use of natural and other resources, such as energy, land, water, as well as through its practices in relation to safety and waste disposal – the 'E' of ESG.[24]

Direct impacts (e.g., soil erosion due to overgrazing by livestock or deforestation), almost always leads to indirect impacts, the effects of which transgress the local boundaries of where the initial impacts occurred. For example, the impact of decreased soil health further reduces the capacity of the soil to sustain plant and animal productivity, and store CO_2 and water. In the case of deforestation, the reduced capacity to store CO_2 further exacerbates climate change. You will need to study the many inter-linkages between local impacts and their global effects to arrive at a complete understanding of your organisation's impacts.

Impacts on people

These are an organisation's impacts on individuals and groups, such as its employees, the communities where it operates its businesses, vulnerable groups, and society at large. These include impacts on human rights. An organisation can impact people through its employment practices, such as its wages and employee benefits, its supply chain working conditions, and the accessibility and safety of its products and services – the 'S' of ESG.[25]

Many companies have adopted the view that impacts on people refer to effects on their employees exclusively. However, it's important to emphasise that 'people' is a much broader concept and can refer to society at large. For example, when a company emits greenhouse gases, it has an impact on the climate system and contributes to climate change, but this matters because climate change then affects people's well-being through extreme weather events, water shortages and biodiversity loss that in turn disrupt food production for the population.

Consider employment practices. When a company hires people from a small village and offers them a decent wage, it helps improve the individual's financial situation, and at the same time, contributes to the economic security of the whole village because people are now able to save for a rainy day, pay for learning opportunities for their children, and access better medical care.

(Double) Materiality

In general terms, materiality is "a measure of how important a piece of information is when making a decision".[26] In corporate sustainability, the concept of materiality originated in 2006 when GRI introduced the 'materiality principle' in its G3 Guidelines (a precedent to the GRI Standards). A year earlier, UNEP FI introduced the materiality concept for investors and GRI helped move it into the corporate world.

GRI defined materiality as the principle to help companies determine which topics are "sufficiently important"[27] to report on because they reflect the organization's economic, environmental, and social impacts, or influence the decisions of stakeholders.

Failure to take materiality into account could lead an organisation to focus on the wrong things too much and ignore the right ones – or greenwash – by reporting on initiatives that have little real value to sustainability, while ignoring the great harms it is doing elsewhere.

Together with the materiality principle, GRI introduced guidance on how to determine material impacts, and very quickly this took a life of its own and turned into what's known today as a 'materiality assessment' (also, 'materiality analysis'). The materiality assessment is at the heart of both strategy and reporting, steps that sit on opposite ends of the corporate sustainability management life cycle. After all, reporting is an account of how the organisation has managed its impacts, so whatever issues it decides to report on are what is material to its sustainability transformation in the first place. We cover how to conduct a materiality assessment in chapter 5.

Financial materiality and impact materiality

It's crucial to understand the difference between application of materiality in financial reporting as opposed to sustainability reporting. In financial reporting, 'financial materiality' was and is used to determine financial impacts on an organisation (also, 'single materiality' or 'outside-in' materiality). In sustainability reporting, materiality is about the impacts of the organisation on the world around it, i.e., "the economic, environmental, and social impacts of an organisation that cross a threshold in affecting the ability to meet the needs of the present without compromising the needs of future generations" – an explanation grounded on the definition of sustainable development and what came to be referred to as 'impact materiality' (also, 'inside-out' materiality).

The materiality approach that an organisation must use depends on where it operates and the reporting obligations in that jurisdiction. At the time of writing this book, two leading regulatory regimes have formalised their positions on an approach to materiality in non-financial reporting:

- Companies who prepare reports in the US must use the financial materiality approach mandated by the US Securities and Exchange Commission (US SEC).
- Companies that operate in the EU and meet certain thresholds must use a double materiality approach under the EU Corporate Sustainability Reporting Directive (EU CSRD).

In addition, the International Accounting Standards Board (IASB) is a non-profit organisation that, for decades, has developed the International Financial Reporting Standards (IFRS) – a global baseline for financial accounting. In 2021, the IASB established the International Sustainability Standards Board (ISSB) to develop the IFRS Sustainability Disclosure Standards. Companies in countries whose jurisdictions prescribe using the International Financial Reporting Standards (IFRS) Standards to report financial information can use the IFRS Sustainability Disclosure Standards to report complimentary non-financial information. To date, this includes 144 countries, including markets in Asia and South America. IFRS Standards are used in the EU too, but the CSRD overrides them. The ISSB prescribes a single materiality approach.

Here's an example of how financial and impact material issues can interact:

Suppose a company draws water from an aquifer facing a medium level of water stress to produce a beverage, its main product line and source of revenue. But the company does this at a rate faster than the aquifer can replenish. At some point, the aquifer is depleted. This impacts the ecosystem around the aquifer, leading to desertification and low river flow (impact materiality: environmental impacts) and disrupting access to much-needed water for the community around the aquifer (impact materiality: social impacts) → this further leads to legal penalties for the company for infringing on the people's fundamental human right to access safe drinking water (financial materiality: financial damage from penalties) and forces the company to move operations to another location due to depleted stock of its main raw material (financial materiality: costs of relocation). This example can continue, including further knock-on effects such as loss of jobs in the community because of the company moving its operations, disruption of the water cycle, and so on.

There's a simple way to illustrate the three perspectives of materiality to understand them in a snapshot:

Figure 2. Double materiality illustration

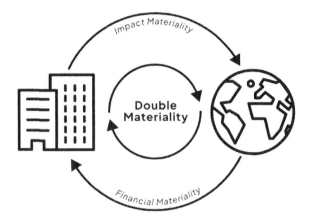

Often, perspectives on materiality between the organisation's different stakeholders differ and you will have to perform a delicate balancing act to make sure you're managing sustainability-related risks to financial value while also genuinely addressing your impacts on people and planet. Ultimately, your material impacts 'outwards' will almost always turn into material financial risks inwards to the company sooner or later. It is your job as CSO to educate stakeholders about the relationship between the two and ensure an appropriate response is formulated in your sustainability strategy.

Stakeholders

Organisations are open, dynamic systems that interact with the environment around them – they depend on it, they shape and influence it, and they are affected by it. To deliver on their goals effectively, organisations need to create a system of cooperation within and around them. Company management needs to be able to attract capital and convince the providers of that capital that their investment will see a return and is generally better than other investment opportunities; employees must be attracted to work for the company; suppliers must see a profitable and stable relationship with the business; finally, the business must provide goods and services that people want to buy. Profitability, in fact, poses a multidimensional problem in pleasing lots of people.[28]

In 1984 US philosopher and business professor R. Edward Freeman introduced Stakeholder Theory,[29] in which he widened the definition of an organisation's stakeholders to customers, suppliers, employees, communities and others who have a stake in the organisation. Building on this, Professor Nikos Avlonas, Founder & President at Centre for Sustainability and Excellence, explains that "a company's primary relation with society includes all the interactions with groups that result in its fulfilling its ultimate goal of producing goods and services for the customers."[30]

Think about the people whose land your organisation is using to extract resources, the investors who trust your business enough to give it their money to grow, the people who trust your organisation to employ them, or the customers who buy its product. Think about governments that paid for the education of people that your organisation employs, and that offer favourable economic conditions for the business to operate.

The success of the organisation depends on how well it knows and understands who its stakeholders are and their concerns – as well as where these concerns converge or diverge from those of the organisation. A successful organisation would anticipate and respond to these concerns before they turn into risks, and it would build networks and reciprocal relationships to find solutions to complex issues in order to stay resilient in turbulent times. Just like any of us have relationships with other human beings to achieve our goals, so do organisations. And, just like human beings, stakeholders will appreciate your organisation if you build relationships based on honesty, fairness, reciprocity, respect and transparency.

Who are the organisation's stakeholders?

Usually, stakeholders are separated into primary stakeholders – those critical to the organisation's survival and actions – the customers, communities, suppliers, employees and workers, and shareholders and investors; and secondary stakeholders – groups that have an interest in or can be affected by the organisation – the government, civil society organisations and activist groups, trade unions and future generations.[31]

Organisations depend on stakeholders to operate, while stakeholders depend on organisations to uphold their rights, minimise problems and / or achieve their interests.[32]

Here is an illustrative example of the many dependencies between the organisation and its stakeholders:

Table 2. Dependencies between stakeholders and the organisations

Stakeholder	Organisation's dependency on stakeholders	Stakeholders' dependency on organisations
Employees and other workers	Skills and labour	Pay, decent working conditions, job security
Consumers / customers	Sales / revenue	Safe, affordable and / or value-for-money products and services
Shareholders, investors and other financiers	Capital provision	Return on investments / steady flow of income, capital growth and business continuity, cash generation
Suppliers	Steady supply of goods or services at affordable price to support business continuity	Stable flow of orders and payments
Local communities, including vulnerable groups	Access to land, primary materials, workforce, local knowledge	Job security and employment, economic development
Business partners	Sales pipeline, brand and reputation	Revenue and commissions on sales and joint deals, access to new markets and customers
Governments	Tax breaks and other incentives, public infrastructure, public services such as higher education to future employees, product quality requirements and operating rules	Community investments and development, infrastructure development, economic development, reduction in unemployment and job market creation
Trade unions	Provision of safety nets and consultation on workers' issues	Access to consultation and decision-making forums to protect workers
Civil society organisations / non-governmental organisations	Brand and reputation, advice on subject-matter issues	Providing a valuable product or service to the community, employing staff in the community, paying tax
Future generations	License to operate expressed via agency of current generations (civil society, public institutions, NGOs and international organisations)	Existence and quality of life

Stakeholder engagement

As a CSO you will need to assess who the stakeholders of your organisation are and the multitude of dependencies and impacts you have on them, and to develop an engagement approach. You will need stakeholder engagement continuously throughout the year and for different goals:

- To complete / update the materiality assessment
- To develop insight into a high-stake issue and plan of action, e.g., entering a new market, developing a new product or service, understanding systemic issues and context when seeking to address / pivot on a material issue
- To manage long-term impacts
- To manage crises
- To build partnerships to advance a material topic
- To protect reputation and anticipate critique, i.e., screen for risks / keep the finger on the pulse about how the organisation continues to be perceived

These goals will also determine the type of engagement you need to build: a continuous, ongoing relationship via a governance mechanism, such as a stakeholder advisory board or external committee (e.g., with investors who are supporting you to an IPO event, or with local communities whose trust is critical to open a new facility), or a focused / short-term engagement (e.g., when sourcing employee views on a new policy, or when managing a crisis or change in regulation).

Purpose

The Oxford English Dictionary defines 'purpose' as "the reason for which something is done or created or for which something exists".[33]

What then is the purpose of business? Going back to the basics, businesses exist to deliver on the needs of society, earn a profit in return, and redistribute that profit in the form of salaries to workers, dividends to shareholders and investment in business growth, and taxes to the state. And, generally, businesses are expected to do all this in ways that meet legal obligations and don't make the public want to shut it down.

However, somewhere along the way, we have lost the connection between business generation of profit – its purpose – and the impact on the natural environment and societal well-being. As the most glaring example, climate change is the result of decades of 'free' pollution of the atmosphere with greenhouse gases which is now altering weather patterns, leaving governments and the public to pick up the bill after weather anomalies. Gig economies succeed partly because of their 'race to the bottom' where workers are paid a minimum wage with no provision of social security benefits, so when workers get sick from overwork or injuries, and can't afford medical care or extended leave without losing a job, society has to address the consequences.

Arguably, such pursuit of purpose without regard to its externalities is the result of society's own prioritisation – cheap food, cheap energy and cheap labour seemed to be necessary components to fuel global development at the speed it went in the past half a century. And, while it has brought immense benefits and advances in terms of education, health and life expectancy, the lack of connection between profit generation and societal well-being seems to have grown too.

Today, there is a sense that this is reaching its climax as we've come to know so much more about the physical state of our planet and the extent to which our economic activity has impacted our shared home. Unlike 20-30 years ago, a CEO cannot afford to ignore how they make profit. The global interconnectedness of our world and the literal transparency of where impacts occur thanks to technological developments,[34] have made it impossible to view business activities in isolation from the impacts these activities have on different stakeholders and the environment.

There's nowhere to hide in a world of hyper-transparency.

The very nature of challenges facing society has changed too – from climate change to societal polarisation and cybercrimes – we've transitioned to an era of systemic risks, in which cause-and-effect relationships are extremely complex to map out and the consequences can be sudden and detrimental.

In this context purpose can't be divorced from the conversation about resilience. For example, in the Netherlands, the Corporate Governance Code defines the responsibilities of the board as the continuation of the company and sustainable long-term value creation that should take into account the impact of the actions of the company on people and the environment.[35]

As such, a more contemporary approach to thinking about corporate purpose is to ask what is the relevance of sustainability to what the company does and how it does it?

Here are some related questions to consider:

- How does the company assist people, societies and nations in addressing the challenges they face – or simply, what is its wider contribution to public interests and societal goals?
- How do the business strategy and business model aim to prevent or minimise negative impacts and problems?
- How is it balancing the interests of different stakeholders?
- What are the short, medium and long-term vision and strategy to manage its impacts on the economy, environment and people, including impacts on their

human rights, across the organisation's activities and business relationships?

- What are the broader trends (e.g., macroeconomic, social, political) affecting the organisation and its strategy?

We're not advocating that companies reinvent themselves towards something they are not (unless their business model is actually being rendered irrelevant in the sustainability transition). We are, however, suggesting that companies widen their view so that what they do aligns with how the world around them is changing and the basic principles of responsible business conduct.

Summary

Sustainability operates by its own vocabulary, which CSOs need to be proficient in. Key terms include:

- Sustainability: an end-state in which the economy operates in line with ecological limits and social well-being, as it meets human needs.
  In the context of organisations, sustainability broadly is a north star to aspire to if they want to continue creating value in the long-term and constructively responding to the needs of society.
- ESG: an investor proxy to measure an organisation's exposure to risk and the amount of capital they would need to invest to mitigate it.
  In the context of organisations, ESG is a tool to help measure how well they're performing on various indicators as they step onto the path of sustainability transformation.
- Corporate social responsibility: a framework that introduced the idea of a 'social contract' – that companies' responsibilities include being profitable, respecting the law, doing no harm, and being a good corporate citizen.

- Impact: the effect of an organisation's activities and decisions on its external environment. Organisations impact the economy, the environment, and people and their human rights.
- Double materiality: a foundational tool for organisations to measure the relationships between the impact of their activities on external environment and on value creation, and a compass to help focus sustainability strategy.
- Stakeholders: individuals and groups whom the organisation depends on to operate. Successful organisations ground their stakeholder relations in respect, transparency and reciprocity.
- Purpose: the reason why your organisation exists, which can be as simple as producing a good product or service but must be grounded in respect for responsible business conduct, human rights and nature.

Now that we're clear on foundational concepts, it's time to address the two key pillars that will underpin your work: culture, which plays a critical role in the ability of the organisation to transform; and strategy, whereby we integrate sustainability considerations in all aspects of the mission.

Chapter 3

Fostering a sustainability culture

A great strategy will fall flat without a strong culture that supports its execution.

Edgar Schein, the founder of the discipline of organisational behaviour defined culture as "a system of shared assumptions, values and beliefs"[1] or, more colloquially 'how we do things around here'. He adds that culture is "what the group has learned in its efforts to survive, grow, deal with its external environment, and organise itself".[2]

Now imagine sustainability, where the core mandate of the CSO is to re-examine the status quo and transform the organisation. For years the company has done things a common way, geared to certain objectives – and now you come in to question those processes. You introduce new processes and new ideas, pioneer unconventional projects, start growing a community of people that rally around the topic… you shake things up!

Why do we start by looking at culture?

Culture is an organisation's hidden competitive advantage. It takes a long time to build, it's hard to replicate, and it either supports or undermines everything else – including strategy. A positive, reinforcing culture will be the tailwind to all your efforts. A negative culture will lead to resistance, token actions, failure and blame.

It follows that, if you as CSO can influence the culture positively, your efforts are more likely to succeed.

In your first 90 days in the role, devote as much effort into diagnosing the culture as you would put into developing the sustainability strategy, and do this in parallel. You need to understand what visible or subtle forces will hinder or support your work. Once you launch (or refresh) the sustainability strategy, your focus will shift to nurturing the culture you need to enable the sustainability transformation. You will have to embody sustainability values and foster norms around it and help the organisation turn them into shared rules of behaviour, so that sustainability becomes second nature.

What is a sustainability culture?

Author and speaker Matt Tenney says: "A culture of sustainability, or sustainable business culture, is one in which all team members, from senior leaders to frontline people, are mindful of the effects the business has on its employees, the environment, and the long-term financial success of the business."[3]

How do you know if sustainability features at the very heart of your business, in your culture?

When company behaviour is consistent with a sustainability culture, everyone in the organisation considers the consequences of the decisions they make, and consciously strives to avoid negative impacts and align decision-making with positive outcomes for sustainability goals. People in the organisation take a holistic view on making decisions, big and small, and of every type – from corporate strategy to operations and processes, to the look and feel of their office and even the language they use.

The work to nurture the culture of sustainability starts with everyone – from the board and senior management who model the company values every day through their behaviours and actions, all the way to employees who, through a myriad of small actions, influence the whole.

As a CSO you have the tough job to align the company's purpose, vision, and values with sustainability, create a rational and an emotional response to the topic, update major processes and documents with sustainability principles, and create conditions for mindset shifts such that new – different – norms of sustainability behaviours emerge. Be prepared that, as with any change process, this will take time.

Culture diagnostic

Whether you're new to the organisation or new in the role as CSO, it can help to first diagnose the culture. Start by observing, talking, and researching. Look at the tangible manifestations of culture. Ask employees why things are done the way they're done. Challenge inconsistencies between what's being said and what's being done. Study historic company surveys. Look at the words people use in corporate communication channels. Company gossip and anecdotes that involuntarily land on your desk can expose information about company ethics and integrity.

Companies pride themselves on their unique culture but often they conflate "the 'fun' quotient of the working environment" with culture,[4] – like having a barista in the office or throwing extravagant company events – and forget to look at how various systems, norms and values actually interact to influence desired behaviour.

Explore to what degree sustainability culture might already exist in the company. Unless you're coming to an organisation with a long history of serious sustainability work, a sustainability culture may not yet be deeply embedded in the business. Assess whether your organisation has the following foundations to build a sustainability culture: [5]

- The level of knowledge people, at all levels of the organisation, have about the business and its purpose, how it intersects with sustainability, what damage it currently does through its operations, what the sustainability goals are, why those goals are important, and their role in achieving those goals. If you ask a board member or a colleague at the water cooler what the company's top sustainability goals are, will they know?
- The degree to which company leadership and employees behave in a way consistent with sustainability. For example, when faced with the decision to travel, do employees weigh carbon footprint implications? When the company sees red flags connected to environmental and social performance of suppliers, does it choose low margins over these negative impacts? Where sustainability issues are not regulated by a policy but people in the company know they exist, how do they choose to behave?
- The capabilities that exist to embrace change and to execute the company's sustainability strategy, such as board and management structures and processes, people educated on sustainability, and other resources that enable the company to implement change and embed sustainability into day-to-day operations.
- How the company communicates – how do employees learn about major sustainability updates in the company?

Is there a cadence of townhalls, CEO or leadership updates, Slack newsletters? Do employees know where to look up the organisation's sustainability strategy?

- Do people have a sense of ownership? The personal responsibility and accountability that people across the company feel for achieving its purpose.

- The company's history, from its founding principles to mergers and acquisitions in the recent past. What was the story behind starting the company and is it an inspiring one? Can you leverage the history of the organisation for sustainability? How old is the organisation and what kind of experiences and learnings has it shared? How long has current management been around? What 'organisational baggage' is the organisation carrying that may weighing it down in its transition to a sustainability culture?

- Who are the employees? Why do people come to work and why this place in particular? What do they value? Where do they come from and what's their demographic? Is sustainability important to them? What social norms and experiences do people bring from their culture across the organisation? Which is a dominant culture? INSEAD professor Erin Meyer wrote an exceptional book The Culture Map, decoding how people "think, lead, and get things done across cultures".[6]

- The company's management style – is it top-down, bottom-up, or a partnership? How do managers and leaders show up and treat others in the organisation? How do they get things done together? How do they take responsibility for failure? This can determine whether leaders will think along with you to solve challenges, be your sounding board, and take accountability, or whether they will leave you to swim on your own.

Positive culture traits

A positive, resilient culture is a general precursor to business success. It also serves the sustainability agenda well. Below are some positive traits and how they impact sustainability.

1. Collaborative culture, predicated on teamwork – Delivering sustainability improvements is a team sport, requiring cross-functional collaboration and systems thinking. Organisations that know how to come together in loosely coupled teams, work a problem, and deliver it, will find it easier to effect change.
2. Positive role models – Where the leadership team openly embraces and supports sustainability, and they truly model it in the decisions they make (even if it costs them or causes inconvenience), stories of these totemic actions will trickle through the organisation and embed themselves in the culture.
3. A growth mindset, curiosity, and the ability to learn from mistakes – No organisation is perfect and there will be some mistakes in our long road to a sustainable future. The organisation that recognises this honestly, bounces back from mistakes, acknowledges them, and learns from them will fare better in the long run.
4. A transparent, empowered culture – One where employees feel able to speak up, make suggestions, call out issues and take actions. This sort of culture will help surface issues and find solutions more quickly.
5. Innovation, agility, and creativity – An organisation that is pre-disposed to innovation is more likely to come up with creative solutions to knotty problems, and to know how to test them and put them into action quickly.
6. Respect for legal, risk and compliance – A risk-aware culture is less likely to act recklessly and do damage in the first place, will generally make better decisions and will

be more pre-disposed to comply with new practices and standards.

7. Accountability – An organisation that takes responsibility, that commits to realistic timelines and keeps to them in its general business, will likely also commit seriously to sustainability actions.

What can limit change?

If your work is going to be about transformation and change, you have to understand how the people in your organisation are 'wired' and the negative or positive effects this can have on your change mandate.

Beware of these common psychological blockers to sustainability change:

Power structures and perceived loss of power

Who might lose because of your transformational agenda? Who might feel threatened because of the growing influence of the sustainability agenda? For example, are you spearheading the discussion on DEI topics that should normally be owned by the People team? Are you introducing innovations that should have originated in the research and development department? For the CSO who is simply trying to get the job done, this seems needlessly defensive, but power structures can be a major blocker if you ignore them. Be very clear with your stakeholders about what you are, and are not, there to do.

Fear

Fear of change, of the unknown, of being exposed to gaps, of failure, of admitting we've been doing things wrong and taking responsibility for it, of public censure in a hyper-transparent world. Confront fear by acknowledging that all great challenges have solutions and break down the path towards them into small, digestible steps.[7] Reassure stakeholders that others are doing this well and you can too. Show them that you're not naïve about the risks and have plans to work around them.

Social norms

The informal rules that govern behaviour in groups and societies. They can be explicit (obvious) and implicit (unspoken), and they often transfer between people in subtle ways through social cues of what is appropriate in that group. Social norms are so powerful because we all have an intrinsic desire to 'fit in' and be accepted by the group around us which is why we will replicate the accepted social norms.[8] For example, a company might have a policy of ethical conduct but the actual social norm could be bullying, expressed through derogatory comments, jokes, or body language toward minority groups that nobody ever calls out. Work with your leaders and culture carriers to role model the desired behaviour to shift social norms.

Cognitive biases

Mistakes in reasoning and cognitive decision-making – there are more than 100 of them[9] – can affect the outcomes of your discussions significantly. A fellow sustainability practitioner was contracted by a company to research sustainable packaging options. The company that hired her was leaning towards paper packaging initially. She performed a life cycle assessment – an analysis that measures the impacts on the environment associated with the life cycle of a product – which revealed, ironically, that polystyrene foam packaging was much better from an environmental perspective than paper packaging in this case. However, the company was dead set on paper – something that it perceived to be an environmentally friendly option – and was reluctant to look at the evidence.

As the CSO, you may have to draw on all of your research, influence, and storytelling to dispel myths and point towards a better way.

Fatigue

People might simply not have the energy and mental space for sustainability. Maybe the company is getting back on its feet after a restructure or a merger / acquisition. Perhaps an individual has personal things going on in the background. Maybe they've heard the same message too many times but seen little action and lost the enthusiasm. Change fatigue is real. Feel out the atmosphere in the organisation and adjust your approach and timing accordingly.

Values, framing, and personalities

These are by far the most challenging factors. Where the majority of people in the organisation believe in the need for sustainable operations and this is already part of the language in the organisation, your role will be easier. But in many organisations, this is still not the case. People might associate it with politics or think it's hippy tree-hugging stuff. Some might see sustainability as a risk to their freedom of choice, lifestyle, and even personal finance. You might work in a company where the CEO has a particular view on sustainability, which doesn't align to yours, and has the final say. Understand who is in front of you, what they care about and what they value, the biases they may be harbouring, and find the arguments and the framing that are considerate of this and bring your message effectively.

Dysfunctional or weak culture

The organisation that is working against itself or lacks clarity on accepted norms and behaviours. A dysfunctional culture may take root in a lack of ethics and integrity – something that sits at the heart of sustainability and that you can try to leverage to lift culture to a better standard. Be a role model for the change you want to see. Be consistent and persistent, reinforce the right messages and ensure your team does too.

Building a sustainability culture

Growing and embedding a sustainability culture is a process that will run parallel to strategy execution and setting internal controls. Business consultancy McKinsey argues that organisations need to create four basic conditions for employees to change their behaviour. These are: the story you tell, role modelling, reinforcing mechanisms, and capacity building.[10]

We have broken down what that means in practice and added a couple of other steps from our own experience.

Raise awareness

Awareness is the very first step in any change management and transformation process. People need to understand why sustainability is important in the first place, what it is, and what it is not. Most people would have heard about sustainability; however, their knowledge and understanding of it will vary wildly, and they might come with pre-conceptions.

Try to get everyone to at least a baseline level of knowledge early – this can be done through a sustainability course (discuss with management whether to make this mandatory), offsite sessions with the board and senior leaders, and one-to-one conversations with key stakeholders. Make a plan for how the organisation can become a place of continuous learning.

Are people clear about the role their organisation plays, and the impacts it is causing? Do they know the facts? While it can be daunting to lay out the facts – especially for leaders – it's important to speak uncomfortable truths. This can elicit emotions of all kinds, including dismissive and hostile reactions from people who don't want to hear them. Most people, however, will appreciate the transparency around what's really going on and it will help them understand why you're calling on them to act. To begin to change, people must perceive a need to change and that comes with understanding the gap between where we are today, where we want to go and why.

Tell a story

Think about what you want people to think, feel and do when you craft a sustainability narrative to compel the organisation to join on the journey. And think about the differing motivations of your audience and how you can appeal to each. Are you saving the planet – is that not a task too daunting? Are you calling on the good nature of people to care? How are you balancing the negative and positive framing of the problem – are you creating a sense of hope or hopelessness? In the sustainability movement, we're tired of both the doom and gloom but also of fake optimism and glossy images of a world that doesn't exist – people disengage from such narratives – so aim to find the right balance of pragmatism and positivity.

Speak in a simple language to which people can relate. A lot of corporate sustainability narratives justify sustainability through 'leaving a great legacy behind', 'being on the right side of history', 'positive impacts for all'... these are all good intentions, but they are too generic. Who are these 'all' and why should I care about them? What does 'the right side' mean in our particular context?

Talk about real lives, real people, real impacts, both positive and negative. Work with your communications and marketing team to deconstruct your sustainability strategy into clear and simple messages everyone can understand and engage with.

Use images to support your story but make sure they are directly relevant and communicate the life and the people that everyone can relate to – use photographs of real employees, real communities in your supply chain. Don't use images that are overly metaphoric or that negate basic laws of nature like plants growing out of money, it's really hard to take those seriously. Also, don't use clichés like 'sustainability is in our DNA' – phrases like this are overused and quickly become meaningless. Instead, show real results that will speak for you, your organisation and its people.

Find your influencers

Humans are social beings, and our norms are often shaped by the influence of others. David Attenborough, Greta Thunberg, Paul Polman – these are figures who have shifted tectonic plates of public opinion and moved the global discussion on sustainability topics forward more than 20 years of policy work combined.

Find the influencers in your organisation. Identify the role models and culture carriers who will be your allies in advocating for sustainability and co-create the plan of action with them. The CEO and the C-suite are an obvious choice because of their visibility and high profile, as well as their responsibility to safeguard company values, but it's often in middle management where you'll find some powerful influencers.

Role modelling is not sponsorship – the executive team has to demonstrate desired behaviours, not just endorse them on paper. If you're having a company group volunteering day, make sure an executive is present. If you're introducing a travel policy at work, ensure the leadership team also subscribes to it. You will see a shift in behaviour very quickly. A fellow sustainability practitioner was responsible for improving waste management in her office – she approached it holistically, but the favourite part was when she did a staged photoshoot of senior leaders using resources responsibly. In the first year of the programme, the recycling rate in the headquarters increased from 35% to 90%, and in year two the company saved a further USD 250,000 on supply purchases like paper and printer ink.

Beyond the executive group, you really need to study your organisation to find people others look up to – the culture carriers who can influence others. This can be an office manager who everyone appreciates for how attentive they are to employee needs, a quiet team member who everyone respects for the quality of their work, a team lead who is admired for their impeccable work ethic and integrity, a salesperson who sets the bar on closing deals for the rest of the organisation. There are various reasons that make us all tick, so find out what these are for different groups in your organisation and recruit the role models who embody these different values.

Build up sustainability knowledge and skills

An organisation can only grow as fast as its knowledge.[11] You need to build a solid fact base about material sustainability topics, so your work resonates with the organisation, teams don't default to incrementalism, and you don't lose time on explaining decisions. Don't stop at launching a sustainability course – there are so many ways to build up knowledge on this topic and get creative! Consider these other options:

- A sustainability book club
- Short summary notes from events and conferences you visit, shared in company communication channels
- An infographics library on the company intranet page (Visual Capitalist[12] is a fantastic resource)

- Brown bag lunches with external speakers
- Movie nights
- Sustainability news weekly round-up
- Outdoor activity days
- Thematic awareness campaigns celebrating key sustainability dates, like the World Environment Day

If you're managing a sustainability team, enrol them in a learning plan with an external provider or ask them to suggest a list of thematic conferences they would like to attend, if budget allows. If you're working with the board and the executive team, consider a powerful away-day offsite with external speakers or add a sustainability session to any existing offsites. Executives should also be the first to complete any sustainability courses you're launching for the organisation and take the lead in reinforcing the rest of the organisation to follow suit.

Many other things will compete with sustainability for your organisation's attention – you have to find an optimum format and frequency of communication. If the business is stable or growing, you may have more budget to invest in education and pioneer creative solutions. If your company is struggling, you might need to limit learning activities to those that don't demand active participation, like sharing sustainability news that employees can quickly scan, register in their minds, and move on from. Think about timing: what is your busiest quarter, when during the day are people's agendas packed with meetings, when is the organisation due to deliver on major projects? This is not to say that you should compromise on sustainability learning but that you should be conscious of timing when this content will be received best. People will appreciate your consideration of their timelines and you will generate more engagement this way.

Start a sustainability group

A group of sustainability champions is a fantastic resource to support the sustainability transformation –they are your sounding board, custodians of sustainability values and principles, an additional pool of help if you're running short of resources on your direct sustainability team, and the pioneers of any new changes you're introducing.

In our experience, most organisations will have at least 10-15% of staff who are already committed to sustainability in their private lives. A further 10-15% will often be curious about the topic and will be easy to engage. Identify a few of the most passionate individuals and empower them to start a community group. They don't need to sit on your sustainability team, in fact, it's better that they don't, so you don't confine sustainability to the boundary of your team, but you or someone on your team should help to manage the group.

Define a realistic scope of their responsibilities – remember they are 'volunteer' staff with full-time jobs – and ask for a plan of activities they'd like to own and coordinate. Set check-ins with this group – these are the most loyal supporters of your mandate and people who might be closer to the organisation than you are in some areas, so you want to keep a close relationship to understand how any projects and changes are resonating with the rest of the organisation. This is also a great group to involve in organising any awareness or volunteer days, so offer your group a budget and some autonomy and you will be surprised how far that can take sustainability engagement across the company.

Reinforce desired behaviours

You need to register and anchor the desired sustainability behaviours when you see them. Compliments and acknowledgements are a powerful instrument to shift behaviour – they act as cues on what's being appreciated and expected. They can take form in many ways – from verbal compliments from a senior leader to monetary and non-monetary incentives.

Consider the following options:

- Monetary rewards, e.g., performance cash bonuses, salary increases, profit sharing for individual contributions that support company sustainability goals and agenda.
- Non-monetary recognition awards, e.g., public recognition in company townhalls, awards, prizes, newsletters, team meetings, annual events, or during key sustainability dates like the World Environment Day.
- Employee benefits, e.g., an education award (e.g. professional development course at the expense of the organisation), time off for volunteering, green mobility schemes, train travel incentives.
- Professional development, e.g., promotions, inter-company mobility for sustainability assignments, an additional learning and training budget to improve sustainability competence.

Is it working?

How will you know that the culture is changing? As a CSO you will spot the changes quickly. Some of the most telling examples are when people come to you to talk about something they have achieved and feel proud of, something they started doing differently – big or small.

You can also try a more tangible way of measuring performance. Introduce sustainability questions in your annual employee engagement surveys or pulse surveys. Ask employees: (1) if they understand how sustainability relates to the organisation's activities and to their job, (2) how strongly they feel sustainability is embedded within the organisation, (3) whether they feel they are contributing to positive sustainability impacts, and (4) if they know where to find information about the organisation's sustainability work. The results of these surveys should, over time, indicate whether you're moving the needle.

Culture checklist

1. Be clear on what the organisation's purpose, business, and values are and communicate how they connect to sustainability.
2. Focus on three top sustainability priorities / goals (we will explore these further in the next chapter) and make sure everyone in the organisation – from board to workers on the floor – understands them, buys into them, and is clear about their role in achieving these goals.
3. Start at the top and move down – make sure senior leaders have the appropriate mindset, knowledge, capabilities, and behaviour before cascading this down throughout the organisation.
4. Bring in middle management who are close to business units, markets, customers, and partners and who build buy-in and participation as they translate company vision to day-to-day execution.
5. Build capabilities and create learning and upskilling opportunities for all levels in the organisation. Bring perspectives of internal and external stakeholders, create a knowledge hub. Start a community group and find your influencers. Grow employees into sustainability champions and sustainability leaders.
6. Communicate – talk about sustainability at townhalls, in company newsletters, tell a compelling story, and integrate the narrative across the organisation.

7. Reinforce desired behaviours to cement change. Celebrate successes, highlight positive stories from the front lines, acknowledge culture champions, and use rewards and incentives.
8. Trust your intuition about what you're seeing and feeling about the overall company culture and how sustainability is attaching to it.
9. Correct for blockers – power structures that can work against you; fear, fatigue, cognitive biases, or generally dysfunctional behaviours in your company culture.
10. Give it time and allow two years at least for change to be felt tangibly.

Summary

Culture is arguably the single most powerful element that will determine the success or failure of your sustainability endeavours. If you are aware of it, diagnose it, strengthen it where you can, correct for blockers, create operational alternatives to how things are done, you will give sustainability a fighting chance of success.

You now have the tools to examine your culture and to make the changes necessary. Next, we consider the simultaneously important, over-arching element of strategy and how to weave sustainability into it.

Chapter 4

Developing a strategy

Strategy is a prioritised set of actions to achieve long-term goals. It's a framework to help align and focus everything else in the organisation – finance and budgets, projects, people and talent plans, risk management, and so on. It helps everyone see the clear line between their daily job and the end game and – just as importantly – it clarifies what not to do.

Strategy answers three questions:

- The 'Why': why does the organisation exist and what is its mission?
- The 'What': what does the organisation need to do to succeed?
- The 'How': how will the organisation get there?

To be effective, sustainability has to interact with the organisation at a strategic level. As an incoming CSO, you will need to lead the effort to help the organisation answer how its purpose, business strategy, and business model align with sustainability. Depending on the ambition and sustainability maturity of your organisation, you will usually find yourself either:

1. Creating a standalone sustainability strategy – not linked to business strategy and normally a collection of compliance must-haves.
2. Adding a sustainability pillar to the corporate strategy – where responsibility for sustainability is recognised, but still where sustainability is not seen as a source of value creation.
3. Completely realigning the existing corporate strategy to sustainability – where sustainability adds to or carries the value proposition of the business, and where you can literally valuate sustainability aspects.

Most CSOs aspire to scenario #3. In reality, many CSOs and heads of sustainability will start off somewhere between scenarios #2 and #3. The challenge of the role is bringing the organisation closer to the first scenario, where that is possible. Sustainability strategy development is an opportune moment for a reset / setting a fresh direction and ambition, especially if the role is new.

The business case for sustainability

Your CEO doesn't need to be an idealist for you to 'sell' the business case for sustainability. In a world where resources are finite, ecological systems are weakened in their capacity to sustain economic activity in the volumes at the cost levels that we have been used to. The changing climate system is disrupting supply chains and human productivity, and regulatory regimes and public sentiment are starting to adapt and respond; continuing business as usual is a path to redundancy.

As Sanne Nusselder, Global ESG Officer at Fagron, a publicly listed pharmaceuticals and healthcare company, tells us: "Internally I explain that a business is sustainable when we can remain profitable while ensuring that all necessary capital / inputs remain available at the necessary quality and while we keep having a license to operate (legislation, clients, communities)."

Many refer to 'sustainable value creation' (also, long-term or shared value creation) when making the business case for sustainability internally – the language that seems to best resonate with an organisation's decision-makers. Sustainable value creation refers to the positive consequences for the organisation when it has transformed its strategy and business in a way that it prevents negative impacts and achieves positive impacts on the economy, environment, and people. The British Academy puts this as "profitably solving problems for people and planet and avoiding profiting from creating problems for people and planet".[1]

McKinsey[2] argues that sustainability / ESG links to value creation in five ways:

Table 3. The links between sustainability and value creation

	Strong ESG proposition (examples)	Weak ESG proposition (examples)
Top line growth	• Attract B2B and B2C customers with more sustainable products • Achieve better access to resources through stronger community and government relations	• Lose customers through poor sustainability practices (e.g., human rights, supply chain) or a perception of unsustainable / unsafe products • Lose access to resources (including from operational shutdowns) as a result of poor community and labour relations
Cost reductions	• Lower energy consumption • Reduce water intake	• Generate unnecessary waste and pay correspondingly higher waste-disposal costs • Expend more in packaging costs
Regulatory and legal interventions	• Earn subsidies and government support	• Suffer restrictions on advertising and point of sale • Incur fines, penalties, and enforcement actions

Productivity uplift	• Boost employee motivation • Attract talent through greater social credibility	• Deal with 'social stigma' which restricts talent pool • Lose talent as a result of weak purpose
Investment and asset optimisation	• Enhance investment returns by better allocating capital for the long term (e.g., more sustainable plant and equipment) • Avoid investments that may not pay off because of longer-term environmental issues	• Suffer stranded assets as a result of premature write-downs • Fall behind competitors that have invested to be less 'energy hungry'

Top-line growth

Organisations that manage their sustainability impacts build trust with their stakeholders and therefore enjoy greater access to markets, customers and to the capital pool (e.g. via green bonds and sustainability-linked loans). Those who don't, risk losing customers and market share due to negative sustainability impacts and poor ESG practices (e.g., food safety incidents for a grocery retailer, customer data leaks from digital platforms) or customers' dissatisfaction with the organisation's abstaining from the sustainability transition (e.g., public outcry over exploitative sourcing practices for an electronics producer or financing of deforestation projects for a bank).

Cost reductions

The changing input prices of raw materials, energy, water and food commodities can increase operating expenses and costs of production by as much as 60%.[3] Consider a company that invests in a water treatment and re-use facility in a region with water scarcity or an e-commerce company that invests in electrifying its vehicle fleet. By thinking about the long-term, these companies protect themselves against rising costs of water or the risk of water shortages, or from increasing price of greenhouse gas emissions, abrupt and unexpected shifts in energy costs and fossil fuel pricing volatility. In addition, these measures help reduce water consumption and the demand for fossil fuels.

Reduced regulatory risk

The body of sustainability-related regulation continues to grow. The objectives of sustainability policies generally fall into two categories: policies that attempt to constrain actions that contribute to adverse sustainability-related impacts; and policies that seek to promote the 'sustainability transition', e.g., the energy transition and climate change adaptation, sustainable and regenerative agriculture, etc. When organisations fail to act sustainably, they can incur fines and penalties, and increase the risks of litigation. On the other hand, when organisations participate and make bold moves for sustainability, they can access subsidies, government procurement programmes, and other incentives.

Greater productivity and talent retention and attraction

When organisations pay attention to the working conditions and offer fair and adequate remuneration, equal opportunities, and physically and mentally safe workplaces – all fundamentals of the 'S' in ESG – they lift work productivity. Their workforce doesn't need to worry about health and safety, pay or their pensions, and can focus on the job instead.

In addition, the feeling of job satisfaction is complex and builds on many factors, the strongest of which is the sense of purpose and that you're working for an organisation that is making a meaningful contribution in the world. Currently, people from across generations share a degree of solastalgia (a form of existential distress caused by environmental change),[4] climate anxiety, and a strong desire to do something about the state of nature and humanity – either for the world they're living in or for the world they're leaving behind for their loved ones.

Organisations that will not revisit their purpose and develop a genuine response to sustainability challenges will lose talent.

Investment and asset optimisation

Markets are shifting – regulatory responses to emissions, pollution and loss of biodiversity can have an impact on balance sheets of resource-intensive or 'dirty' industries. Consider write-offs and early retirement of assets due to substitution of technologies with lower emissions options, bans on single-use plastics or diesel-fuelled cars in city centres. To the extent that new technology and regulation displace old systems and disrupt parts of the existing economic system, winners and losers will emerge from this disruption process.

Strategy diagnostic

Before you start building action plans and firing ambitions at the organisation, you need to do a reality check with what the organisation can actually support and its needs. Is it in growth phase or crisis? How mature is the sustainability function, is it completely new or is the organisation seeking to achieve sustainability leader status? What are the views of investors on sustainability, how supportive are they? These insights will help you build the strategy that works for the context of this particular organisation, tune it to the amount of change the organisation can effect at this very moment, set realistic expectations, and use everyone's energy, time, and corporate resources effectively and wisely.

You and those around you will burn out quickly if you're running with a 100-point plan that the organisation just can't support at this stage. In contrast, if you find a few areas where the organisation has control and can really commit to improving, you will achieve real, meaningful change and impact. Just like with culture, you first need to understand your starting point.

Organisation's life cycle

One of the considerations when looking at the strategy is where the organisation is in its own life cycle – what are the industry dynamics and how does that shape direction, affect the organisation's capacity, and reflect on your sustainability team?

Growth phase

Common for startups, the growth phase is often characterised by a 'land grab' in a new or innovative area. Capability is nascent and lots of things are figured out on the fly. Decisions are made quickly and without all the available information. This is a hard-working, challenging, and energising time.

This is an unlikely phase to hire a sustainability lead but, for many millennial entrepreneurs and founders, sustainability is non-negotiable, and they want to 'bake it in' from the start. If you're in this context, it's the best time to set guardrails about how business will be done in line with sustainability. In this phase, the emphasis of your job will be about establishing and embedding sustainability principles and practices across the company's operations, culture, and products and services from the outset.

Scaling phase

During the scaling phase, the organisation has found some product / market fit, it's attracting investment, and is developing fast. People are taking a lot of initiative, but they could also be overstretched. It might be challenging to keep leadership's attention on sustainability because of all the other moving pieces on their plate, in which case agree and get sign off on a few priorities you will lead and the teams you will involve.

Many teams are establishing their own processes, infrastructure, and quality standards. On the one hand it might be difficult to reach them but, on the other, this is the moment to build internal partnerships and agree on joint priorities early on. The company is growing its supplier and vendor base, and this provides a perfect window to establish sustainability-based sourcing principles and policies. This is also the time to experiment because you may have a little more budgetary freedom if outside investment can be obtained.

Stability

The stability stage is defined by a period of consolidation when many processes mature, and things get less hectic. This is also when investors get more demanding and request more due process and compliance. If you weren't getting the necessary face time with leadership before, this is the time to move sustainability higher on the agenda and convene leadership for a strategy refresh. Call on the regulatory requirements around sustainability reporting and due diligence as a way to bring attention and resources to the function.

Efficiency and optimisation

If the organisation has over-spent and over-hired, investors are demanding more frugal expenditure, or perhaps revenue is not growing as quickly as it was, then the organisation will enter a phase of efficiency and optimisation. The tech sector has gone through a phase like this since 2023 when many sustainability teams were cut down to the absolute minimum, even at tech giants like Salesforce, Google, and Amazon. In this scenario, you will need to get laser-focused on tangible value creation and key priorities. Nice-to-haves that are not critical to material topics – like philanthropy or awareness programmes – may have to be put on hold.

Be prepared for budget cuts across all functions, including your sustainability team. But don't give up – all storms pass.

Crisis

Every now and again, an established company might be shaken by a crisis. It can be a black swan event like the pandemic, a physical disaster, political upheaval, or a public relations issue where the company's products, values or ways of working are put under the spotlight.

You will need to support leadership to troubleshoot and get the organisation back on its feet. If it wasn't an event entirely out of control of the organisation, like a natural disaster, then take the opportunity to examine the root cause and make conclusions.

Has the company ignored standards of integrity in its supply chain and business conduct? Has it ignored risks that were far out in the future? Has it lost its purpose?

Use the opportunity to reinvigorate ethical values and due diligence processes. Maybe you will introduce greater sustainability controls in your enterprise risk management framework, maybe you have an opening to start a conversation with the people team about labour practices, or maybe it's time to rethink with the leadership team how resilient your strategy is overall and the organisation's purpose.

How does the organisation work?

To embed sustainability deeply in the organisation's strategy, you must understand what your organisation does and how it creates value. The following elements are critical to examine:

- Product / service – Why does the organisation exist, what does it do and how does it add value to society? Does its business model harm society? What is not serving sustainability and needs to be discarded, and what can be enhanced?

- Market – What does the organisation compete on? Price, quality, functionality? How does this contradict or positively connect to sustainability goals? For example, if the organisation is in a race to the bottom for price, it might be difficult to source more environmentally friendly – and more expensive – raw materials.

- Time horizon – What is the time horizon of the strategy? Is there a long-term outlook or is it an all-hands-on-deck situation where the organisation is trying to achieve some immediate goals? If your organisation is not thinking beyond the next year, it will be difficult to offer deep, transformational projects. Does your organisation know what and where it wants to be in 10 years? Then you're in a great position to bring a sustainability vision into this.

- Stakeholder interests – Who are the stakeholders of the organisation? How does it balance stakeholder interests? Whose interests are prioritised? Whose interests are not captured at all?

- Scale – How big is the organisation? How much influence does it have with suppliers and business partners? Is it profitable and how much room exists for sustainability investment? Can it influence its supply chain and market? Amazon and Apple are corporate giants who can set non-negotiable sustainability targets for suppliers who want to continue working with them and set aside greater budgets to support their suppliers with the transition. This might not be accessible for smaller companies, so know your boundaries.

- Historic, systemic issues – How are things done in this industry and what historic, systemic issues exist? An airline company may wish to close down its short haul routes, but these freed up slots will be taken by the competition immediately, eliminating all the benefits of the incentive for the company and for society. Factors such as governmental subsidies of unsustainable sectors and practices, minimum market commodity prices, trade associations and industry lobby groups all need to be understood to create a realistic pathway to change. What needs to change in your industry, and what's the extent to which you can control or influence this process? Can you build coalitions to effect greater change?

- Goals and targets – What goals and targets are set in the strategy? What are the top key performance indicators (KPIs) / objectives and key results (OKRs) the leadership team is tracking weekly, monthly, quarterly? Is this a crowded space, how does sustainability fit in, and are there any contradictions with sustainability goals?

Sustainability maturity

Beyond the organisation's profile itself, you also want to understand how mature its sustainability work and governance is. What has been done before you, what ambitions and gaps exist, who oversees and who is involved in sustainability, and how developed are the various components of the sustainability function such as risk management or reporting? Your organisation might fall under one of the following four profiles.[5]

Starting out

The organisation is just getting started with sustainability. There are different views internally on what this function should do, rarely addressing the full scope of the role. Sustainability efforts are ad-hoc, unstructured, and decentralised, and the organisation needs a framework to determine focus. Materiality assessment has not been done, and data is not collected. The understanding of sustainability is usually synonymous with environmental topics. The role may have originated because of external pressure from investors, regulators, or on the CEO's command because of personal interest. There may be a lot of enthusiasm and momentum, but also a clear need for direction.

This scenario means you'll be going the 'Full Monty' – building, building, building. Expect to spend the first one-to-two years setting foundations, bringing everyone up to speed, setting focus and building muscle, before you can accelerate. If you're under reporting obligations, you will need to move quickly to produce your first 'best effort' report.

This can be a time of frustration, but more than that, it's a time of incredible opportunity to shape direction, think big, and set the bar for the rest of the work ahead. It will feel slow and fast, hot and cold, energizing and draining all at the same time – embrace it, keep calm and move forward.

Judicious minimalist

An organisation that is largely focused on sustainability as a risk management exercise. It has outsourced materiality assessment to consulting firms, who also helped produce its sustainability report. The targets it set are the minimum 'hygiene' levels to manage stakeholder relations and regulatory risks, and the organisation goes 'with the pack'. Sustainability reporting is done by a function not involved in strategy development. Integration with other functions exists only insofar as this supports reporting goals.

This context may exist because of cultural factors, lack of full understanding of the positive impact of sustainability or seeing it as a cost item, or perhaps the organisation's life cycle phase and past events. If the former, you will need to call on all your knowledge, diplomacy, and communication skills to try and flip any negative perceptions or incomplete views.

Emphasise the opportunities that sustainability brings for long-term value creation, invite leaders from peer companies to talk about their experience, and build allies who can help you promote the agenda. Try not to default to reporting as your one and only deliverable that helps the company get through compliance – you will miss out on opportunities and may miss bigger risks too. If the organisation is getting back on its feet, build on the foundations that already exist and enhance them until the internal climate changes.

Confident leader

The organisation has a sustainability management system in place, a clear focus, and a consistent record of progress on material issues.

Sustainability is integrated and working effectively with the rest of the organisation, and material topics are reflected in the strategy. The organisation may have some differentiated products and services and generally has a good grasp of both operational and supply chain impacts. Sustainability has well-established and resourced programmes and is perceived as a partner to other functions.

On the one hand, this might be a great environment to step in as the organisation and sustainability are working as one. On the other, you should ask yourself whether the organisation is really differentiating. It is respected for the quality of its sustainability work and acknowledged as a leader in the field, but it may be missing that vital spark.

In this scenario, you either accept the more operational tilt of the role, e.g., coordinating and directing, managing a big team, troubleshooting, representing the organisation in forums and industry groups, speaking with investors, or you refresh the vision and aim to go from 'good to great' if this is what the organisation needs of you.

Trailblazer

If sustainability is core to a business's purpose, values, culture, operating model, and products and services, the organisation is a trailblazer. These organisations can be the 'new kids on the block' challenging the status quo as well as older organisations that have pivoted to transform their business in line with the sustainability transition. These organisations transform supply chains, pioneer ideas and practices that peers are reluctant to move forward on and that quickly become the norm. The CEO and CSO work closely together, with CEO leading in public advocacy and presence.

This is a high-stakes environment, and it's not for everyone. Be prepared to perform at your best 100% of the time, be on call, and give it your all. Mistakes in this environment can be detrimental to success as all eyes are on you – the eyes of the investors who place their bets on the purpose-driven business; the eyes of the customers, employees and the public who believe in your mission with passion and simply can't be disappointed; and those of competitors who are monitoring your every move in case you take the wrong turn that they can take advantage of.

These profiles will determine where you need to direct your CSO focus. The core objective of sustainability is to reduce negative impacts, yet this function comes with many other components that collectively define how quickly your organisation can move from beginner to leader or trailblazer status. Pay attention to these cues and plan your work programme accordingly. Note also that not every organisation can become a trailblazer – as we said earlier, your purpose can be as basic as producing a good shoe, but if you do that with care and responsibility to your workers, supply chains, and resources (which is hard enough!) you will set yourself as a sustainability leader that others will follow and learn from.

Investor interests

Let's not forget that companies are profit-generating organisations for their shareholders in the first place, so it's important to understand who the company's investors are, what their view is on ESG and sustainability, and their engagement approach.

The EU's Sustainable Finance Disclosure Regulation (SFDR), part of the EU's 2018 Sustainable Finance Action Plan, was introduced to bring transparency in the market for investment products. This has triggered greater investor engagement on sustainability with public and private markets. At the same time, not every investor is prepared to accept a lower rate of return on investment in a company that undertakes activities that address sustainability issues.[6]

As a general rule, institutional investors such as pension funds have a long-term perspective on value creation, while hedge funds, retail investors, and venture capitalists often look for short-term results and may see sustainability practices as a source of cost. Your leadership may recognise the value of sustainability, but your investors may be reluctant to pivot. The inverse is also true where investors can become your greatest allies in pushing leadership forward on sustainability.

Get to know your investors early:

- What is their investment horizon – the length of time over which they hope to achieve their goals from their investment?
- Is the company working towards a particular event (IPO, merger, acquisition, divestment)?
- Do investors have exclusion criteria related to sustainability performance (e.g., some investors will not consider a company with a rating lower than a certain threshold)? What are these?
- What sustainability targets have investors set at portfolio level? With what sustainability topics are they engaging actively? How do they relate to your material topics and are your material topics sufficiently understood by them?
- Are investors prepared to accept trade-offs between financial and sustainability goals?
- Are they prepared to set long-term horizons for achieving sustainability goals?
- Are they prepared to accept qualitative sustainability targets if those lead to desired improvements?

Regional context

If you're a CSO in a global business that spans several regions, you will have to adapt your sustainability strategy, programmes and language to the local context. What may work well in the headquarters where you're stationed might be entirely unfeasible or non-relatable elsewhere.

Consider the following factors when structuring your sustainability programmes and approach:

- Policy landscape – How advanced regulations are to support the sustainability transition, what topics are prioritised, or what limitations can they create.

- Local sustainability reporting regulation – What local reporting requirements exist that may be additional to those that your company is subjected to in the headquarters, what is the overlap and what underlying data are the same; what privacy limitations exist to collecting data points across jurisdictions, e.g., diversity data, and are you using the same definitions of common sustainability terms.
- Emerging versus developed markets – What sustainable finance priorities, incentives and instruments exist? For example, in developed markets, the focus might be on financing green energy solutions, while in emerging markets in Asia, it may be on financing the phase-out of carbon intensive assets such as coal plants.[7]
- Infrastructure availability to support decarbonisation – Conditions like renewable energy availability and accessibility, grid capacity, or battery technology.
- Consumer preferences and sustainability awareness – Willingness and ability to pay a sustainability premium on decarbonised, innovative products and services, sentiments around various sustainability topics and their connection to political views (e.g., the ESG polarisation in the US).

Setting course

With these insights about the organisation in place, you should have a good set of dos and don'ts, sustainability needs, a feeling for how far and how quickly you can go, and how transformational the sustainability agenda can become. You now need to develop your strategy – the document that will set sustainability priorities for the rest of the organisation.

The process to get there boils down to four key steps:

1. Materiality assessment – identify the issues material to your business.
2. Set priorities – define where you have control versus influence on material issues, the level of ambition and the impact the organisation wants to achieve.
3. Develop an execution roadmap – set targets and KPIs.
4. Monetise your strategy – make the business case for your strategy to unlock necessary investments into sustainability initiatives.

At the end of this exercise, you should arrive at a document that is underpinned by the following general structure:

Figure 3. Sustainability strategy template

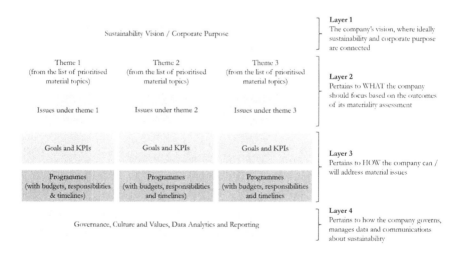

Adapted from BSR, Five Steps to Good Sustainability Reporting, 2020.[8]

Step 1. Materiality assessment

The materiality assessment will help examine the root causes of the impacts the organisation has, the risks to which it's exposed, and the opportunities ahead. It informs all subsequent strategy development work. We cover in detail how to conduct a materiality assessment in chapter 5. Once you've completed this step, you will have a list of material topics – the issues that you will need to understand, track, disclose, and ultimately act upon.

Step 2. Determine influence versus control, and set ambition

Realistically, CSOs, their teams and their organisations have the capacity to address at most three issues from their list of material topics in a way that truly sets them apart. If you attempt to do more than that, you will spread yourself too thin and waste precious time and resources on incremental changes. Your sustainability work won't be distinguishable from that of your peers and customers, and stakeholders won't be able to pin down the issues you really stand for and where you're moving the needle.

The materiality assessment should give you a list of 10-15 material topics, as well as the top 5-6 that are most material to address from an impact, risk, and opportunity perspective (your 'existential' issues). That said, you still need to define the areas your organisation can actually control and where it can act ambitiously, versus areas it can only influence. In other words, you have to determine the limits to your efforts so you can focus and bring about meaningful change on those topics.[9]

This understanding will help you determine how far you can go on those issues and the additional support you will need, such as partnerships, advocacy with political groups and civil society, or external expertise. For example, if you're a tech company that wants to raise the bar on diversity in the industry, you can design the best recruitment programmes to access that diverse pool of talent, but if girls are raised with certain views about their roles in society, that pool of talent will be limited by default. The question then is, are you going to expand your actions to change education systems, cultural norms, behaviours, and traditions – and if so, do you have the bandwidth to handle such ambition, and is it even your remit?

Ask yourself what you want to achieve with how you address these material topics and where you can differentiate, e.g., what inherent synergies between your business model and sustainability exist, what internal and external conditions can serve as tailwinds, and what has never been done before in this industry? Your primary responsibility should be to minimise negative impacts for identified material topics, but how you do it and how transformative you want to be in the process is up to you and the leadership team, so this is the moment to think big.

For example, one of your material topics might be emissions generated by your supply chain. You might address it in a variety of ways: either by procuring green energy credits, or by engaging with your suppliers in setting their own impact reduction targets and offering training and financial resources to decarbonise. One material topic, but two very different approaches to address it.

In the example with green energy credits, the objective can be expressed as meeting basic expectations around impact reduction – this action is mostly compliance-driven, and nobody will recognise the organisation for it. The example with suppliers is truly transformative – the organisation wants to decarbonise the entire supply chain, so it will bring suppliers along who, in turn, will speak for it and raise the organisation's public profile.

Consider the following:

- What is your current baseline performance on material topics? Are you at the point of addressing the basics or are you ready to jump higher? If you have any gaps in assessment, consider taking the time to address those first so you're confident where you stand and won't need to revisit goals and targets as your impact measurement processes mature.
- The future state you would like to achieve and ambition – which topics would you like to take a leadership role in, drive innovation and take truly bold action? Plug in a blue-sky thinking workshop where you throw in ideas with your team, without pre-judgment. Use the 'what if' and 'what else' questions to push the boundaries of your collective thinking.

  Ask yourself and your colleagues what would you like to see changed in the world around you with respect to your material topics, and bring these back to goals and actions that are within your influence.
- Who are the benchmark leaders in your industry – what sets others apart and what sustainability actions are they recognised for? You would have already done some of this during the materiality assessment, but now look deeper at their actions.

  Interface, a carpet and flooring company, adopted biomimicry principles in its carpet design upon recommendation of a group of scientists who worked and studied the company for about a year – something that was entirely unconventional at the time. As a result, this set Interface far ahead of the competition in terms of resource consumption and waste reduction, cost savings and brand value. Study your peers, reach out to them, learn from them. There's enough space and work for everyone.

- Assess the feasibility of your goals – where you have a few options for how to address a material topic, assess your limitations to choose the most effective way forward. You might be constrained by availability of resources, weak culture, or turbulent times inside the company that we discussed before. If that's the case, agree with your leadership team on a set of baseline short-term goals and aspirational long-term goals. In one of the companies at which Anna, co-author of this book, worked, the team knew they just weren't able to support an innovation goal in the ongoing year, but that they would be in a position to revisit it the following year and add it to the sustainability roadmap.

Step 3. Develop a sustainability roadmap, set targets and KPIs

Now cast back from your goals and objectives to understand what needs to happen to achieve them. Start linking activities, resources, funding, targets and KPIs, and deadlines to your goals and putting them all on an execution roadmap / action plan. What projects do you need to start, who should be responsible and who will be involved in other ways? What investment do you need? What immediate actions do you need to take?

For example, if your company is in a high-impact sector and its goal is to reduce emissions, you will need to task the research and development department to research low-carbon innovations, manufacturing sites will need to take the lead on improving energy efficiency, the procurement team will need to revisit its sourcing practices, and so on.

Think through your execution plan carefully – especially the items and activities where success will depend on others' time or financial investment, consult stakeholders across the company to validate their capacity and availability, and have senior leadership sign off on the roadmap. An important consideration is the sponsorship of the CEO so make sure to involve them in the review, sign off and endorse your plan.

Determine KPIs, which are the measures or the proxies that help the organisation understand how it's progressing on its goals and offer a clear reference for everyone in the organisation to align their work to. Break down your long-range ambition to specific, measurable, time-bound, outcome-based KPIs and targets. It will help the strategy to be perceived as realistic and manageable. Use each achievement as an opportunity to celebrate and reinforce the work being done.

Make sure you also have the systems in place to support data collection for your KPIs – you will need to present a record of evidence when reporting progress against goals and targets to your management and to the auditor during sustainability assurance. This is where a lot of the foundational work sits for CSOs and their teams, especially for companies with first-time CSO hires.

In this step, it's also helpful to use the theory of change (TOC), which is about understanding "what needs to happen or what conditions need to exist to achieve XYZ".[10] Many sustainability strategies and initiatives don't reach their full potential because causal relationships between different actors or elements in the organisation and around it are left unexplored. It's often called the 'missing middle' between what a strategy does (activities and interventions) and how that leads to achieving the desired goals.[11] In its essence, TOC is about identifying what conditions need to exist or change to achieve the desired impact, and challenging assumptions or biases about how you think certain actions should play out.

Say you want suppliers to provide better emissions data. To get to a point where data from suppliers flows to you, you first need to create favourable conditions, such as: (1) manage any fear of transparency suppliers may have, and (2) free up their capacity for this work which could mean collaborating with other organisations in the industry who request similar data to create a single data collection system to reduce the burden.

If you simply enforce emission data requirements in supplier contracts without creating these conditions, you may wind up either with suppliers ignoring these requirements or providing you sub-optimal data just to tick the box.

Step 4. Monetise your action plan and show return on investment

Certain sustainability initiatives will require investment and you will need to make a business case to your CFO for capital allocation. If you want sustainability to become a standard line item in the budget, you will have to speak the language of the CFO. This is especially true if you're pitching initiatives which will have a return on investment that isn't evident (or if you're working in a 'judicious minimalist' environment) – the sole backing of the CEO or the argument that sustainability is 'the right thing to do' are not sufficient in a conversation when it comes to budget allocation.

The Return on Sustainability Investment (ROSI) is one such tool that can be used to inform decision-making about investments into sustainability initiatives. ROSI was developed by the NYU Stern Canter for Sustainable Business, and it helps to quantify the benefits from sustainability practices and initiatives and monetise their financial return, where these benefits don't fall under traditional accounting principles.

For example, ROSI offers a methodology to quantify tangible outcomes, such as the net monetary value (USD / EUR saved per kWh of energy) as a result of introducing energy efficiency initiatives at a manufacturing plant or at an office, the cost of avoided fines as the result of introducing safety measures, or the net revenue generated from introducing a sustainability service or product. Importantly, it helps to quantify less tangible outcomes, like employee satisfaction from sustainability initiatives and brand attractiveness, and the resulting reduction of costs related to employee turnover (e.g., avoided cost of advertisement, cost of reviewing job applications, cost of interviewing candidates, recruitment fees, cost of reference checks, etc).[12]

Say you are an e-commerce company and you would like to transition your fleet to be fully electric. A conventional financial analysis might show that it is not economically attractive. With ROSI, you might discover additional benefits like reduced physical and transition risk from climate change (e.g., avoided cost of carbon tax on emissions, reduction in cost of fuel), talent retention because of employee satisfaction with the company's sustainability work (e.g., reduced cost of hiring and onboarding talent), sales and marketing (e.g., avoided cost of advertising thanks to free media coverage, new pool of conscious consumers), and so on.

ROSI helps you to look more broadly when assessing proposed investments in sustainability and equips you to speak the language to which your CFO will be more receptive. The NYU Stern Center for Sustainable Business offers the ROSI tool as a free public good and provides on its website worked examples of how companies from various sectors have used the tool, excel worksheets to adapt to your situation, a practitioner's forum, and a library of case studies.

If you want to go beyond the monetisation of your company's own gains and losses, consider complementing your ROSI assessment with Impact Weighted Accounts (IWA), which is a methodology developed by Harvard Business School to assess the broader positive and negative impacts a company has on society and the environment.

The IWA framework is based on the premise that companies' activities impose external costs upon human, social, and natural resources (externalities). Investors are particularly interested in understanding whether companies are profiting from causing harm, which is why companies should assess their financial profit against these externalities if they want to present a holistic picture of their performance. IWA offers an accounting method that reflects responsible and purposeful management of the company, extending its accounting from legal boundaries to its effective boundaries, i.e., its outcomes and impacts.[13]

The IWA methodology, excel calculation tools and other resources are available free of charge on the Harvard Business School IWA website.[14] These are not elementary calculations and require some knowledge of economic analysis — try to recruit your finance team to work on these tasks. Experience shows that, generally, there's a lot of interest internally in such multidisciplinary work.

Strategy checklist

Getting the strategy as good as it can be from the outset will help your organisation to progress efficiently towards sustainability goals in the coming years and avoid unnecessary course changes along the way. Here's a quick recap of key points for an effective strategy:

1. Study the needs of the organisation and its profile – where are you meeting each other and what's the next step for sustainability in the organisation?

2. Make it focused – avoid the strategy that is all things to all stakeholders. A strong sustainability strategy is based on your unique material topics, with no more than three top-line goals. Don't fall for trends or let the crowd derail your focus. If everyone around is making climate pledges, whilst you're an office company with negligible climate footprint, ignore the noise.

3. Make it specific and clear – big claims like 'purpose over profit' are great aspirational mottos but not enough for execution. Your staff should understand what the organisation is going to do and why that makes sense in relation to its impacts, and how these actions are going to translate back to everyone's daily job.

4. Balance activities that address negative impacts with initiatives that reinforce positive impacts. Minimising harm is perhaps less showy, but it must be prioritised. Also, make sure to address real issues. For example, a social media company that is overly focused on climate change, but is silent on mental health, addiction, and polarisation is a red flag (and a red herring) to your stakeholders.[15]

5. Give yourself time to do the research you need, carry out stakeholder engagement, and validate assumptions and ideas with the leadership team. Push back to buy time if needed.

6. Consult stakeholders and build relationships and trust with the executive team and the board. You will need their commitment during execution.

7. Challenge your leaders – stimulate an unfiltered debate to get to the bottom of things. A sustainability strategy that is just waved through is arguably not strong enough.

8. Be prepared to be challenged – listen just as hard to your leaders. These grizzled executives will likely have years of hard-won experience, knowledge of their business, a list of what not to do, and valuable perspective to help you be effective and to avoid slip-ups.
9. Be realistic about the volume of change that the organisation can handle at once.
10. Communicate, communicate, communicate. Don't keep the strategy to yourself. Give it a visible starting point – launch it at the townhall, give it a few weeks and hold a questions and answers session with staff, post about it, start a Slack channel, highlight good news stories – once the design is done, your role becomes about execution, reinforcement, and support.

Summary

Strategy provides the roadmap for your organisation to succeed. By grounding sustainability in a deep knowledge of what the organisation does and how it adds value, you are creating a unique blueprint for it to survive and thrive in the long term.

It's important to understand the current situation at your organisation; the views of the CEO, leadership team, the history of the organisation, where it is on its journey. You also need to think about where it aspires to get to, and what's possible – from minimum compliance to blazing a trail. Understanding the investor profile and geographic context of the organisation is also key. Materiality underpins everything in sustainability. Your regulatory context will determine the approach to take. Once you have that, select a small number of initiatives where you can really make a difference, and create a budget.

This concludes the foundational section of the book. We've taken you through markers of a strong culture, and how to set an effective sustainability strategy that your organisation needs. It's time now to get to the core of sustainability management: assessing impacts, managing them, and articulating that to stakeholders. Let's get into to the technical areas – the hard skills of the CSO.

SECTION TWO: TECHNICAL AREAS

Chapter 5

Materiality assessment

We have covered how the materiality assessment originated in sustainability reporting but became a strategic tool for companies to understand what they should focus on to operate more sustainably. You can't begin to change if you don't know what to prioritise. This is exactly what the materiality assessment is all about.

Internally, it's a self-diagnostic exercise looking at how the business affects people and the world around it, and how it can be affected itself, since all impacts are interconnected. It takes a broader perspective on financial and operational risk than traditional compliance and finance functions, expanding and completing the organisation's understanding of where it's having impacts and needs to take responsibility for them, where it may have blind spots and be exposed to risks, what can become a source of competitive advantage, and where it is simply expected to fulfil basic legal obligations. Your sustainability strategy, action plan, and subsequent sustainability reporting, should all be a function of the outcomes of the materiality assessment.

The materiality assessment process is the CSO's most important mechanism to 'negotiate' and agree with the organisation what it will absorb in its boundary of focus and direct its resources to. It's very important to get this process right. Most organisations will be new to it, so we will cover how to organise the process effectively in this chapter.

Externally, the materiality assessment helps your stakeholders reconcile why certain topics are being addressed while others are not, and not get distracted when you're being pressured to respond to contentious issues or jump on a new trend.

If you're publishing an ESG / sustainability report with external assurance, the description and evidence of how you conducted a materiality assessment to determine material topics for reporting will be the first thing the auditor will look at with a magnifying glass. Interestingly, the description of the materiality assessment process the organisation followed is as important – if not more – to the auditor than the outcomes.

> Companies that are subject to the EU reporting regime under the Corporate Sustainability Reporting Directive (CSRD), are required to disclose the process of determining material topics with a trail of documentation and evidence supporting key decisions in this process, as well as the material topics themselves.

The materiality assessment follows formal steps that were codified by GRI in 2006 and have since been adopted by thousands of companies around the world. Most recently, these steps have been adopted almost one-to-one in the new European Sustainability Reporting Standards (ESRS) under the EU CSRD. They follow in the next section.

Remember, there is no right or wrong when it comes to the outcomes of the materiality assessment, as every organisation impacts the world in unique ways. However, if you follow these formal steps, you will address the risk of missing any blind spots and create confidence among stakeholders and your leadership team that you are focusing on the right things.

It's important to keep in mind that the materiality assessment is an iterative, analytical and consultative process. It needs information and time to get right. Depending on the size and complexity of your organisation, and maturity of the sustainability function, it can take up to a year to arrive at strong, credible results, which will need to be revisited regularly as the impacts change.

Financial, impact, or double materiality?

To recap from chapter 2, impact materiality helps determine the impacts your organisation has outwards on stakeholders – the environment, society, and economy as the result of its activities. It's expressed through non-financial proxies, like tonnes of CO_2 emissions, cubic metres of water withdrawn, percentage of the gender pay gap, number of data breaches – all of which in turn speak to big issues like climate change, water scarcity, gender equality, or consumer privacy.

Financial materiality is about the financial effect of these impacts and other sustainability issues on your organisation. Double materiality connects both of these 'dimensions' in a comprehensive view of how the impacts of the organisations on the environment, society, and economy affect the company financially.

In sustainability reporting, the materiality approach you must apply will depend on the country or regions in which the organisation operates and the reporting obligations in those jurisdictions. Companies with headquarters or offices in Europe that meet certain thresholds in terms of turnover and employees, are required to adopt a double materiality approach under the EU CSRD. Companies that prepare financial statements in accordance with the IFRS Standards, will use a single, financial materiality approach.

Outside of these legal reporting obligations, the organisation is free to decide which 'dimension' to put at the heart of its materiality assessment. That said, double materiality is the safest path to embedding sustainability into company strategy as it ties together impacts, risks, and opportunities in a way that executives can relate to.

Specifically, it helps to identify:

- Financial, reputational, and operational risks from not managing the actual and potential impacts that your business causes in the real world and on real people, e.g., litigation against human rights violations in supply chain or business disruption because of heat waves on the workforce in the summer.
- Opportunities from managing these impacts and from responding and anticipating market shifts caused by environmental and socio-economic changes, e.g., new product and service offerings or a lower employee attrition rate because of a well-structured employee benefit programme.

Six steps of a materiality assessment

Over the years, the sustainability community has arrived at an agreed materiality assessment framework based on the GRI Standards, complimented by its own collective practical experience. The six-step approach below summarises key steps an organisation should follow not to miss any blind spots and come to results that are comprehensive and credible. These steps are now also adopted in the ESRS Standards.[1]

Step 1. Understand the organisation's operating context

Organisations do not exist in a vacuum, so you need to understand how exactly the organisation converts resources to make and deliver its products and services and realise a return. In this step you need to study what the organisation does, with whom, and where – this will give you critical pointers to potential problematic areas of the business. Important things to look at include:

- The types of activities your company carries out, e.g., sales, marketing, manufacturing, distribution, and the geographic locations of these activities. If your primary activity is manufacturing, what are the labour conditions in factories or processing facilities, how are the factories powered, and how is waste and residue handled?
- The types of products and services it offers. What is your product made of or what raw materials does your service require to operate? Where do these come from, and how are they grown, harvested, processed, and transported?[2] For example, for a company selling food and beverage products or clothes, water impacts are highly likely to be at the top of its material issues because of the large volume of water withdrawal and consumption needed to produce crops and cotton.
- The sectors in which the organisation is active and their characteristics, e.g., whether they involve informal work, whether they are labour or resource intensive. For example, the mining sector is known for creating large-scale influxes of workers which can place pressure on local services and negatively distort social order.

- Who do you employ and how, i.e., full-time and part-time employees, permanent or temporary employees, workers on non-guaranteed hours and zero-hour contracts, and their demographic characteristics (e.g., age, gender, geographic location). Some companies employ workforces the size of countries, so just imagine the impact these companies have on the individual lives of people through their labour practices, i.e., how workers are paid, treated, and developed. If your business model is built on outsourced staff, it may be easy to overlook impacts related to this group because of a lack of formal consultative processes. For example, in 2020, Facebook was sued by offshore workers for mental health issues they developed from reviewing disturbing online content as part of their job.[3]
- The types of business relationships you have (e.g., joint ventures, suppliers, franchisees), the activities they undertake, the nature of business relationships (long-term or short-term contract, project or event-based), and the geographic locations of where activities of the business relationships take place. For instance, a large franchise might not follow the same standards of health and safety as your business, or a supplier might have a poor history of respecting human rights.

Once you map out how your organisation operates, start looking at its sustainability context – what economic, environmental, human rights, or other societal conditions and thresholds exist in the sectors and geographies in which it operates: Are you carrying out physical activities in regions with poor environmental regulations? Are your main business relationships located in areas with a lack of law enforcement? Are you employing people from regions with high poverty? Are you withdrawing water from regions with water stress or where environmental conditions are stretched or degraded? Are you taking advantage of these conditions knowingly (for example by exploiting cheap labour or polluting for free) or are you simply uninformed about these conditions?

Basically, a company is 'slotting in' to an environment with some existing physical and socio-economic characteristics and – depending on how you build upon these characteristics – you can either harm this environment or help it to flourish.

Step 2. Identify the full landscape (long list) of impacts

Now that you understand how the company operates and its context, you need to investigate the problematic areas in more detail to refine the list of impacts. Staying on the water example, if water use is an important activity to enable your business, you want to understand whether there are any associated impacts related to how you use water, such as water depletion or water pollution.

Some impacts may be evident or intuitive because they are the common issues for your sector, type of product, or geography of operations. Are you operating in the agricultural sector? Then how you use the land to manage crops and livestock, and how you treat workers will be your top material issues. Are you a consumer tech company? Then customer privacy and tech development practices are topics to look into.

You can use standards such as the GRI Sector Standards[4] or the SASB Standards,[5] where the experts have already done the work to identify likely material issues for your sector, but remember that an organisation's issues will always be unique. These standards offer a great starting point, but you will need to put in the time to identify all of your impacts, including those that that may be less evident.

Consult a variety of sources for a complete overview — draw on data from any existing impact assessments, legal reviews, anti-corruption compliance management systems, financial audits, occupational health and safety inspections, grievance mechanisms, employee surveys, and external sources such as competitor analysis, civil society organisations, desk research, and news organisations.

Your organisation's risk register will have several impacts covered already and is a good source to validate initial assumptions and bring additional considerations to your list.

Acting upon negative impacts will always take priority based on international instruments, so focus on identifying them first. It's implicit that you will create many positive outcomes as the result of addressing negative impacts if you truly do your work well, but if you rush to talk about community donations before you talk about fair compensation of your own employees, or if you talk about advancing the energy transition while your core business is seabed mining, stakeholders will call you out on being disingenuous with your materiality assessment.

Consider consolidating the long list of impacts into a clear set of no more than 30 issues, and to write a brief description — two sentences maximum — of what each of them means. [6] From personal practice, it's a good test to validate whether its's really clear to you what these issues encompass. This clarity will pay off when cascading issues further across the organisation and to your stakeholders.

Step 3. Consult stakeholders

Ultimately, whatever it does, your organisation will have an impact on human beings in both positive and negative ways. To develop a practical understanding of these impacts, you need to engage your stakeholders. They hold critical views and knowledge about the corners of the company hidden from immediate view, and they can enrich your materiality assessment with critical insights that you might miss otherwise – things going wrong, weaknesses, emerging issues, or expectations.

Engaging with stakeholders is central to assessing material impacts and informing strategy. If you're subject to the CSRD reporting in the EU, your company is required to report on its stakeholder engagement process and obtain external assurance on the process.

We shared some examples of different groups of stakeholders an organisation can have – their relationship with the organisation, interests and dependencies – in chapter 2. You will need to speak to internal and external stakeholders alike.

For internal stakeholders, start with business leaders in key functions. They will help you quickly pinpoint problematic areas, if you manage to create a safe psychological space and trust during the conversation. Later, these people can become your trusted advisors and your allies in execution. Invest time in one-to-one conversations and consider some of the following engagement principles:

- Explain your role and the purpose of engagement – what you are, and are not, there to do.
- Clarify you are not the expert on their topic or business function – this will help establish the right balance of power and confidence that you are not there to judge them.
- Ask open questions about the status quo, rather than closed questions of judgement about performance – you can pick up on any gaps to dive into later.
- Encourage reflection on how their department is connected to the wider sustainability context.

- Ask what room for improvement they see for their department, and their key priorities in the next one to three years.
- Explain how you will use results and any follow up, including allaying their concerns about confidentiality, whistleblowing, and scapegoating.
- Summarise the synergies you see between their work and yours and ask how you can help them.

Next, speak to employees, internal culture carriers, and sustainability ambassadors. If your organisation already has a sustainability community group or taskforce (separate from the sustainability team), consider a group discussion where you can be more direct about risks and impacts, things not working well, and opportunities. Remember though that you may also need to seek out quieter parts of the organisation and draw out their views proactively.

Set expectations that, at this point, you're collecting insight but not committing to specific action yet. You can also run a survey with the entire workforce – just keep the risk of survey-fatigue in mind, particularly if you're planning future consultations for which you will need to canvas staff opinion. Be prepared to get a mixed bag of feedback next to strategic insight – wish lists of nice-to-haves, frustrations for past inaction, and even gaslighting and irony. Finally, if you're seeking to gather input on a particular issue such as diversity, consider focusing the survey on that one issue.

At this stage, speak to investors, suppliers, customers, and regulators. If you don't have capacity to cover them all – or don't have the relationships yet – use proxies such as past customer surveys, customer feedback, feedback from shareholder filings. You will build your engagement process over time.

Throughout your stakeholder engagement, your paramount priority should be to reach affected stakeholders and vulnerable people and groups. These stakeholders can't reach you and yet, they may be the most affected by your organisation's activities. Use the checklist below, adopted from the GRI,[7] to help you validate that your stakeholder engagement is capturing these groups.

Table 4. Checklist to capture affected stakeholders

Factors to consider when engaging with vulnerable groups	Actions	
Are there any stakeholders that do not have a direct relationship to an organisation? Identify all indirect stakeholders.	**Direct** (e.g., employees, business partners, investors)	**Indirect** (e.g., workers in the supply chain or local communities that live at a distance from the organisation's operations, future generations unable to articulate their views)
Is it possible to engage with stakeholders? Direct engagement may not be possible in: (1) cases that involve many stakeholders (e.g., corruption, which collectively harms the population of the jurisdiction in which it takes place); (2) cases that involve impacts resulting in collective harm (e.g., GHG emissions, which contribute to collective transboundary harm); (3) cases when engagement could undermine certain rights or collective interests (e.g., when considering a decision to restructure or shut down a factory, it may be important for an organisation to engage with trade unions. In such a case, engaging with individual workers could undermine the right of workers to form or join trade unions and to bargain collectively); and / or (4) cases where stakeholders are unable to articulate their views (e.g., future generations).	**Yes**	**No** If direct engagement is not possible, engage with credible stakeholder representatives or proxy organisations (e.g., non-governmental organisations, trade unions).

Are stakeholders affected or potentially affected? The degree of impact on stakeholders may inform the degree of engagement. You should prioritise the most severely affected or potentially affected stakeholders for engagement.	**Potentially affected** (e.g., workers who are exposed to the hazard and could be injured)	**Affected** (e.g., workers who are injured from a safety hazard)
Are there any at-risk or vulnerable groups? These are groups of individuals with a specific condition or characteristic (e.g., economic, physical, political, social) that could experience negative impacts as a result of the organisation's activities more severely than the general population. Examples can include children and youth; elderly persons; ex-combatants; HIV / AIDS-affected households; human rights defenders; indigenous peoples; internally displaced persons; migrant workers and their families; national or ethnic, religious and linguistic minorities; persons who might be discriminated against based on their sexual orientation, gender identity, gender expression, or sex characteristics, persons with disabilities; refugees or returning refugees; women.	**Not at risk**	**At-risk and vulnerable groups** If such groups are present, then: (1) use specific approaches for engagement, for example remove social barriers that limit the participation of women in public forums or remove physical barriers that prevent remotely located communities from attending a meeting; and (2) be especially attentive to respecting human rights during engagement (e.g., rights to privacy, freedom of expression, and peaceful assembly and protest) and protect at-risk groups against reprisals (i.e., non-retaliation for raising complaints or concerns).
Are there any barriers to engagement? These can include language and cultural differences, gender and power imbalances, and divisions within the community.	**No**	**Yes** Seek to remove prior to and continue to address during the engagement.
Are there any stakeholders whose human rights are affected or could be affected Human rights have a particular status as an entitlement of all people under international law. The most acute impacts the organisation can have on people are those that negatively affect their human rights.	**No**	**Yes** Prioritise these stakeholders for engagement.

You can draw lists of stakeholders per activity, project, product or service, or using any other classification that is relevant to your company and your operations.

How many stakeholders is a good number for a consultation? There really isn't one answer to this – we've seen engagements that involved hundreds of voices but failed to capture the critical few, and engagements that only concentrated on 'critical friends' and contestants.

Do you need to survey customers to validate that product safety is an important topic? Probably not – it's a compliance 'hygiene' factor that you have the basic responsibility to manage. It will show up on your risk register because of any fines and incidents experienced in the past.

Should you go to length surveying and organising workshops with staff in your production facilities? Absolutely – you may have very limited knowledge of what's going on there, and location managers may be driven by performance incentives to withhold information. Apply a degree of judgement about where insight is needed most and who can provide it and utilise your organisation's knowledge of its critical stakeholders.

Come back to your list of impacts from step 2 – is there anything missing, or did some issues break down into more specific ones? Finalise your longlist with these fresh insights – this is now your compass of topics that your organisation needs to understand, track, disclose on, and ultimately act upon.[8]

Step 4. Assess significance of impacts

At this point, you still won't know which impacts are the most important for strategy. In step 4, you will assess their significance. Best practice is to use a materiality matrix which involves ranking the impacts on stakeholders and plotting them on the y-axis, and separately ranking financial impacts on the organisation and plotting them on the x-axis. This way, you will have a clear view of topics that are marginal, topics to monitor, and topics that are strategic priorities.

Getting there involves some quantitative analysis, and impact materiality and financial materiality are assessed using a separate methodology. This is also where you normally bring in the C-suite and a selected group of stakeholders (again) to rank the impacts. Create an impact scoring sheet based on the criteria below and insist on discussing the results with the group – these are eye-opening conversations that can instantly secure buy-in and bring everyone on the same page about sustainability topics. They can also be challenging if you have a lot of power dynamics or hidden agendas. In this case, you may wish to bring in an external facilitator.

Assessing impacts on stakeholders

First, assess the significance of impacts on stakeholders. You will plot the results on the y-axis of your matrix based on their scoring. Negative actual impacts take priority over negative potential impacts, and both take priority over positive actual and positive potential impacts. Each of these is assessed by a unique combination of criteria, provided below, and adopted from the GRI 3: Material Topics 2021 Standard and the EFRAG Materiality Assessment Draft Implementation Guidance.[9]

Figure 4. Criteria to assess the significance of impacts

	Actual	**Potential**
Negative	**Severity** = Scale (how grave the impact is) + Scope (how widespread the impact is) + Irremediable character (how hard it is to counteract or make good the resulting harm)	**Severity** = Scale + Scope + Irremediable character + Likelihood (chance of the impact happening) (together also know as **risk**) In case of **human rights** impacts, severity takes precedence over likelihood
Positive	Scale (how beneficial the impact is or could be) + Scope (how widespread the impact is or could be)	Scale (how beneficial the impact is or could be) + Scope (how widespread the impact is or could be) + Likelihood (the chance of the impact happening)

- Scale: how grave the impact is – i.e., extent of infringement of access to basic life necessities or freedoms such as education, livelihood, access to fresh water, etc. The scale of a negative impact can also depend on the context in which the impact takes place. For example, if an organisation withdraws water from an area with water stress, the scale of its impact will be greater than if it would have withdrawn water from an area with abundant water resources.

- Scope: how widespread the impact is – i.e., the number of individuals affected or the extent of environmental damage. In case of positive impacts, the number of individuals or extent of environmental resources positively affected.

- Irremediable character: how hard it is to counteract or make good the resulting harm – e.g., through compensation or restitution; whether the people affected can be restored to their exercise of the right in question. In other words, are there any limits on the ability to restore the environment or those affected to a situation at least the same as, or equivalent to, their situation before the negative impact?

Any of the three characteristics (scale, scope, and irremediable character) can make an impact severe, and often, these characteristics are interdependent – the greater the scale or the scope of an impact, the less remediable it is.

In addition, for potential impacts, you need to assess:

- Likelihood: how likely is the impact to occur, measured quantitatively or determined qualitatively. It can be described using general terms (e.g., very likely, likely) or mathematically using probability (e.g., 10 in 100, 10%) or frequency over a given time period (e.g., once every three years).

An over-arching consideration is human rights:

- Human rights impacts: these occur in relation to any human right and are not limited to physical harm. For example, interfering with, damaging, or destroying a sacred space without consultation or agreement with the people for whom the space has spiritual importance can have a severe impact on their cultural rights. It doesn't matter how likely these impacts are to occur – their severity takes precedence.

There's no formal rule in sustainability how to rank or score the impacts, but general practice suggests determining a quantitative (e.g., 1-5) or qualitative (e.g., low-medium-high) scale, and rate impacts with a group of stakeholders. Collate all impacts and their assessment criteria in a table to help sum up the scores for scale, scope, irremediable character, and likelihood, and ultimately filter for negative actual and potential, and positive actual and potential impacts and their weight in relation to each other.

Assessing financial materiality

Now assess the effect that the impacts above may have on the cash flow and financial value creation of the organisation over the short-term, medium-term, or long-term. You will plot these on the x-axis. Financial impacts are generally assessed on four criteria:

- The magnitude of risk – i.e., the cost of inaction to manage the impact, resulting in penalties, litigation, higher cost of capital, higher commodity prices, brand damage and loss of customer trust, as well as the cost of investment the company would be forced to / decide to make to manage the impact.
- The likelihood of the risk materialising (where this is already happening, the likelihood is 100%).
- The magnitude of opportunity from managing the impact – i.e., access to green financial instruments and subsidies, brand value and improved market position and market share, greater customer base.
- The likelihood of the opportunities materialising.

Here too, you can use a quantitative or a qualitative scale as long as the weights are aligned to those used to assess impacts on stakeholders. This will not be a precise science, but you should at least have a discussion with your leaders to align on how you generally see these issues to impact the business.

In some areas, leaders will have strong views because these will be issues under their direct mandate, issues they are familiar with, or issues they may not understand yet but are fearful of, like AI.

In this case, really do prompt reflection using the criteria above, drawing on external expertise if needed – how many customers (scope) will be affected if the product breaches safety norms? What would it take for affected customers to recover their health from the damage (irremediable character)? What are the financial implications from the consequences of product safety incidents and how likely are they to materialise?

These questions should trigger an unfettered discussion. Also be prepared to help with explaining the impacts and how the different criteria apply to them. It's good practice to have a written memo where you describe the topics and their impacts – you would have put one together in step 3.

Step 5. Set thresholds

What's a priority on the matrix and what isn't? In this step you have to determine your cut-off points: the thresholds that will determine where the organisation will act and the material topics it will absorb into its strategic focus; which topics it will monitor, and on which it will merely aim to meet minimum compliance.

If you were to split your matrix into four quadrants, then issues in the top-right would be your highest priorities. These are issues where risks, opportunities, external expectations, impacts and compliance all converge. This is where you need to set real ambition and distinctive action.

After that, it gets more nuanced. The rest of your prioritisation might be based on risk appetite, capacity / maturity, level of exposure to stakeholders, and values. Companies may decide to prioritise some issues that scored high on either dimension separately, for example, because your organisation equally values the issue's importance to stakeholders (top-right quadrant), and / or wants to take advantage of issues that bring commercial opportunities or are high-risk (bottom-right quadrant). The important thing is to decide and to explain the decision.

These decisions are for the organisation to make and to take responsibility. Just be sure that the company is not spreading itself too thin by taking on more issues than it can truly advance and manage well at one time. It's best to be transparent with stakeholders about why you're not addressing certain issues and take the hit, rather than over-promise and under-deliver... and have to take the hit anyway. At least you won't lose precious time and resources trying to fight for something that is out of your control and that has only marginal effect.

Remember that strategy is about choosing what you do – and what you do not – focus on. Prioritising a smaller number of initiatives and really moving them forward is almost always preferable to inching forward on everything. When you reach a target in one area, you can always add a new one, moving down your list over time.

Remember that impacts change over time because businesses start new operating practices, natural effects from activities take time to occur, and new issues emerge. Materiality is dynamic. You should re-visit your list of material topics every one to two years at a minimum.

Step 6. Group material topics into sustainability strategy pillars

Once your company has decided which material impacts it will address, you need to group them into broad pillars that will form your strategy. For example, if you have identified emissions, water pollution and deforestation as your material impacts, you might want to group them under a broad label of environmental protection. Make it short and straightforward – stakeholders will use it as a cue to navigate to the information they are looking for.

Most companies use static formulations ('environment') or dynamic ('protecting', 'taking care', 'ensuring', 'enabling', etc). Most use meta-labels like people / society, planet / environment, and integrity / ethics. Some stick to the three ESG pillars – environmental, social, and governance. Others group impacts by stakeholder group, like colleagues / workforce, communities, customers. You can also bring the UN's Sustainable Development Goals in here and show how the pillars are aligned to them. This is really up to you – just make sure stakeholders can understand and relate to your labels and that the material issues you're addressing are clear.

Working with the C-suite

This is an evident, basic requirement when performing a materiality assessment, but it may be easier said than done in some cases.

If you're the first CSO, or if sustainability governance is poor in the organisation you're joining, you'll have to (re)introduce the materiality assessment to your C-suite. Explain how it is an essential tool to expand the current view on risks, opportunities for innovation and competitive advantage, and cost optimisation. Explain the 'inside-out' and 'outside-in' concepts of materiality.

These are very delicate conversations. You don't want to come across as questioning anyone's expertise, but equally you do need to connect the status quo to the wider sustainability context. You have to come across as strategic and pragmatic but, at the same time, it is impossible to build an argument without talking about impacts of the business on the world and people – a message that may be too sensitive for some.

Some organisations take a day or two for a workshop with an external consultant who serves as a neutral party in these discussions. Finish by creating a steering committee who will be responsible for the materiality assessment process under your guidance, or the consultant's if you're outsourcing.

Insist on investing time to discuss how and why C-suite members chose to prioritise certain topics over others – these are eye-opening conversations that secure buy-in and bring everyone on the same page about how the business relates to sustainability. They can also be challenging if you have a lot of power dynamics. If this is the case, you may again wish to consult an external facilitator for advice on how best to organise a feedback session. With time, you want to get to a point at which leaders understand the connection of their work to sustainability intrinsically, and treat it as the default input to strategic decisions.

Things can be much easier if there's a board member or board committee responsible for ESG. Have them represent the process to the rest of the board, including key milestones, validation of stakeholder groups, topic boundaries, impact prioritisation, and eventual topic discussions and sign off.

Don't make it theoretical – quantify the risks, potential cost reductions, and the financial impacts of opportunities. Your finance team should already forecast risks and returns on a routine basis, layer in the considerations from the materiality analysis in your traditional business analysis. We offer a few methodologies in chapter 12.

Summary

When setting out to conduct a materiality assessment, you should follow these six steps:

1. Understand the operating context of the organisation – what it does, with whom, and where.
2. Identify the full landscape of impacts your organisation may be causing, contributing, or be directly linked to, and consolidate them into a list of no more than 30 topics.
3. Consult your internal and external stakeholders, and importantly – those that are most affected by your organisation's activities and may not be in a position to reach you.
4. Assess the significance of each of your impacts and prioritise them.
5. Set thresholds for what you will, and will not, immediately tackle.
6. Group material topics into sustainability strategy pillars to provide structure to your plan and a language that stakeholders can easily understand.

It's important to cast back to the culture assessment you performed and incorporate the organisation's strategy and future direction. This will ensure your assessment is grounded in the reality of the organisation as it stands today.

Your materiality assessment is the bedrock of your whole sustainability strategy. Whether you have to start from scratch, or re-purpose work done already, this is a fundamental step in ensuring that all the work that follows is the right work. It is also something that you will have to refresh every one to two years, and it will be used in assessments by investors, assurance providers, and anyone who is interested in your organisation's sustainability work.

Now that you know your priorities, it's time to understand how to measure the impacts related to them.

Chapter 6

Measuring impacts

All organisations cause impacts from their day-to-day operations and activities. Think about your infrastructure – the office buildings, manufacturing sites, or stores. You need energy to power, heat, and cool this infrastructure. Depending on whether the source of that energy is renewable or non-renewable, you could be generating CO_2 emissions that cause global warming.

Think about how your employees commute to work, how frequently they travel for business, and which mode of transport they use. Think about the goods you procure to support the business and where those products come from. Think about how you advertise your product or service to customers – the emotional response you stimulate, the norms and values you communicate. Think about the working conditions you provide for employees to execute business activities.

The CSO's ultimate goal is to help the organisation get to a state in which the negative impacts from its operations, products, and services are minimised or prevented entirely. You will have to address a unique set of impacts through your sustainability strategy, depending on your sector, the size of your business, type of value chain, and respective material topics. Largely though, all impacts result from the way the company delivers its products and services, and how it organises operations and activities that support its production and sales.

Operational impacts are related to all activities that your organisation carries out within its physical infrastructure, which require inputs like energy, water, materials, and labour to operate, and which create outputs like pollution, waste, and employee and customer experiences.

Product-level impacts are related to the entire life cycle of the product, from the extraction of raw materials to the end of life. All products that your organisation creates as part of its offering to the economy rely on materials that are extracted by people from nature and put through a complex global supply chain to get delivered to your customers. Think of a laptop that may have hundreds of components, from chips to plastics to circuitry. Organisations that sell services have impacts too – think of entertainment providers, like casinos, who sell the service of gambling, or gaming companies. These services can have severe negative impacts on the people using them, which can manifest in addiction and debt if the use of that service is not managed responsibly.

In this chapter we will cover examples of major groups of impacts your organisation can have, how to measure them via social audits and impact assessments, and tools to manage these impacts.

Impact areas

Any one activity can cause multiple environmental and social impacts. You need to understand all the key ways in which your organisation can impact the world around it and the consequences this can have on the business in return. First, we want to offer a quick snapshot of key impact areas that are agreed on internationally. These impacts descriptions are based on the GRI and SASB Standards.

Environmental impacts and their drivers

These concern key impacts on natural systems – air, land, water, ecosystems, and living organisms – that result from the organisation's use of energy, water, land, and other natural resources.

- Energy – An organisation can consume energy for manufacturing processes, heating, ventilation, and air conditioning (HVAC) systems, refrigeration, lighting, transportation, employee commutes and business travel. Energy can come from fuel, electricity, heating, cooling, or steam. It can be self-generated or purchased from external sources, and it can come from renewable sources (such as wind, hydro or solar) or from non-renewable sources (such as coal, petroleum or natural gas). Major impacts from energy use from non-renewable sources include the release of greenhouse gas ("GHG") emissions, which are a key contributor to global warming and climate change. The seven GHGs covered under the Kyoto Protocol[1] are included within the category – carbon dioxide (CO_2), methane (CH_4), nitrous oxide (N_2O), hydrofluorocarbons (HFCs), perfluorocarbons (PFCs), sulphur hexafluoride (SF_6), and nitrogen trifluoride (NF_3).
- Emissions – We mostly hear about greenhouse gas emissions in the context of climate change impacts; however, air pollution is a much broader impact group. It includes any contamination of the indoor or outdoor environment by chemical, physical, or biological agents, which modifies the natural characteristics of the atmosphere.[2] Major

pollutants include oxides of nitrogen (NOx), oxides of sulphur (SOx), volatile organic compounds (VOCs), heavy metals, particulate matter, and chlorofluorocarbons. These can come from motor vehicles, industrial facilities, and forest fires. Impacts connected to air pollution include respiratory diseases, contamination of soil and waterbody surfaces, and eventual impacts on crop yields, tree growth and health, and plant resilience to pests and diseases.

- Water – Major uses of water include production processes at manufacturing plants (cleaning, rinsing, dyeing, solvent), irrigation in agriculture, as a coolant in power generation and cooling systems, as a component in food and beverage production, in the paper and pulp industry, and in office buildings and facilities (kitchens and bathrooms). Water impacts are related to the amount of water withdrawn and consumed by an organisation and the quality of its discharges. Water-intensive operations and large discharges of polluted water can lead to depletion or deterioration of fresh water, thereby impacting natural ecosystems and local communities' human rights of access to fresh water.

- Materials – These include inputs used to manufacture and package an organisation's products and services, as well as anything else that you procure to run the business, like capital assets (heavy equipment and machinery), office supplies, and food and catering. Materials can be non-renewable, such as minerals or metals; or renewable, such as wood or cotton. Both renewable and non-renewable materials can be composed of virgin or recycled input materials. The type and amount of materials the organisation uses can indicate its dependence on natural resources, and the impacts it has on their availability. The volume and type of materials you buy also has a direct relationship to the waste you generate.

- Waste – Waste can be generated during production and manufacturing processes, in the office from the daily use of 'stuff', from the use of products and services (e.g., packaging), and when products reach their end of life and need to be disposed of. Waste is an interesting material stream. While it's perceived as something unwanted to get rid of, others may see it as a source of income because of the valuable materials that can be valorised from it, like gold and other metals in electronic waste. However, today the waste system operates largely with an 'out of sight-out of mind' principle, where most waste is shipped to countries with low environmental regulation to be dealt with, and only very little of it is actually recycled. This is why the impacts of waste extend far beyond locations where waste is generated and discarded, leading to both human health impacts and environmental pollution. With waste, there really should be no 'throw away' or 'throw out'. In addition, resources and materials contained in waste that is incinerated or landfilled are lost to future use.

- Biodiversity – Biological diversity is the variability among living organisms from all sources, including terrestrial, marine, and other aquatic ecosystems, and the ecological complexes of which they are a part. This includes diversity within species, between species, and of ecosystems. Biodiversity is the foundation of nature which provides us with 'ecosystem services' – the flows of benefits from ecosystems to people, such as clean water and air. In the past 40 years, we have faced an unprecedented loss of biodiversity.

  The Intergovernmental Science-Policy Platform on Biodiversity and Ecosystem Services (IPBES), the leading intergovernmental body on monitoring and advising on biodiversity policies, defines five direct drivers of biodiversity loss, including changing use of sea and land, direct exploitation of organisms, climate change, pollution and invasive non-native species.[3]

Social impacts, including human rights impacts, and their drivers

The International Association of Impact Assessment (IAIA)[4] defines social impacts as impacts to one of the following:

- people's way of life – how they live, work, play and interact with one another on a day-to-day basis;
- their culture – their shared beliefs, customs, values and language or dialect;
- their community – its cohesion, stability, character, services, and facilities;
- their political systems – the extent to which people are able to participate in decisions that affect their lives, the level of democratisation that is taking place, and the resources provided for this purpose;
- their environment – the quality of the air and water people use; the availability and quality of the food they eat; the level of hazard or risk, dust and noise they are exposed to; the adequacy of sanitation, their physical safety, and their access to and control over resources;
- their health and well-being – their state of complete physical, mental, social, and spiritual well-being;
- their personal and property rights – particularly whether people are economically affected, or experience personal disadvantage which may include a violation of their civil liberties; and
- their fears and aspirations – their perceptions about their safety, their fears about the future of their community, and their aspirations for their future and the future of their children.

At first glance, social impacts may look like a very broad definition with some examples being hard to connect to business activity. Let's take agriculture – the sector that is a significant user of land resources. In some cases, whole communities have been displaced so that companies can use their land. Often, the new areas to which communities are resettled are not equivalent in terms of soil quality, suitability for agriculture, access to services, or cultural and social significance.

These communities cannot continue their way of life that may have centred around the land, as they may be a cultural minority in the new area, with the stability of their community disrupted and their aspirations for the future shattered.

Think of companies in consumer finance who decide who to lend to, technology and communications companies that share and sometimes shape opinions, aerospace and defence companies who build weapons, or extractives sectors, or an even simpler example – the invention of the smart phone which has altered many of the above for all of us simultaneously in just a few short years, for better and for worse.

While the impacts described above may sometimes be too broad too measure, there are established proxies to understand how organisations impact people. They are based on how organisations employ people, the working conditions they establish in supply chains, the way they behave on land, and the way they design, produce, and market their products and services to consumers.

- Employment relations – Legal conditions on which organisations employ people, the benefits (or lack thereof) they provide, collective bargaining agreements in place to protect the workforce, length of notice periods, maternity cover, approach to professionally developing staff, as well as assistance with facilitating continued employability, and approach to managing career endings.

- Occupational health and safety – The prevention of physical and mental harm, and promotion of workers' health. This includes the quality of organisation's hazard identification and risk assessment systems, worker training, incident identification and investigation, provision of healthcare services or voluntary health promotion services and programmes, and involvement of workers in developing occupational health and safety policies and management systems.

- Diversity, equal opportunity, and discrimination – Fair and equal treatment of workers, and access to opportunities, as well as non-discrimination of customers, suppliers, business partners with respect to accessibility of the organisation's products and services.

- Customer health and safety – The efforts the organisation takes to maintain the health and safety of the products and services it sells throughout their whole life cycle, and its adherence to customer health and safety regulations and voluntary codes. Some proxies include management of recalls and market withdrawals, product testing, and chemicals / content / ingredient management in products. The very product(s) they sell may have positive or negative impacts on their customers too.

- Marketing and labelling – The organisation's approach to communicating information about the impacts of its products and services as part of product information and labelling and marketing communications. Some proxies include adherence to advertising standards and regulations, incidents of reported misleading or deceptive labelling, and / or discriminatory or predatory selling practices.

- Customer privacy and data security – The organisation's efforts in maintaining the security of personal information of its employees, customers, suppliers, and business partners. It covers collection, retention, and use of sensitive, confidential, and / or proprietary customer or user data. Some proxies include incidents of data breaches in which personally identifiable information (PII) is exposed.

- Procurement practices – Organisation's approach to relationships with suppliers, including lead times and price negotiation behaviour, security, and stability of contracts.

Human rights impacts

Many of these social impacts are encapsulated in internationally agreed human rights, which deserve special attention. These are rights inherent to all human beings and are enshrined in the United Nations Declaration of Human Rights. They are universal legal guarantees protecting individuals and groups against actions which interfere with fundamental freedoms and human dignity.[5] Businesses can impact virtually all human rights – in fact, most of the impacts described in this chapter are human rights even though they are not labelled as such.

To prevent human rights violations and remediate any impacts, businesses set up due diligence processes. According to the UN Guiding Principles, when exercising human rights due diligence, businesses are required to consider, at a minimum, the rights captured in the International Bill of Human Rights (comprising the Universal Declaration of Human Rights, the International Covenant on Civil and Political Rights, and the International Covenant on Economic, Social and Cultural Rights) and the International Labour Organization's eight core conventions outlined in the Declaration of Fundamental Principles and Rights at Work (addressing non-discrimination, bonded and forced labour, child labour, and freedom of association).

Additional human rights standards should be considered as relevant in the particular context (e.g., the rights of indigenous peoples if the business project or activities occur near indigenous lands or international humanitarian law in conflict-affected areas).

Societal impacts and their drivers

The examples above refer largely to impacts on specific individuals. However, certain activities impact whole economic systems at local, national, or even global levels. This inevitably has repercussions on society, though it's sometimes dispersed and hard to see. In ESG vocabulary, these often sit under 'G' as they relate to the overall responsibility of how the organisation governs its integrity and business ethics.

- Anti-corruption and anti-money laundering – Corruption includes practices such as bribery, collusion, extortion, facilitation payments, fraud, and money laundering; the offer or receipt of fees, gifts, loans, rewards, or other advantages as an inducement to do something that is dishonest, illegal, or represents a breach of trust. It can also include practices such as abuse of function, concealment, embezzlement, illicit enrichment, trading in influence, and obstructing justice. Whether it takes the form of petty bribes or large-scale misappropriation of public resources, corruption is a problem for society because it misallocates resources for the benefit of the few and reduces the positive impacts of private sector investment that should serve markets, employment, and healthy economies. It has other negative repercussions like reducing countries' abilities to respond to emergencies, loss of trust in institutions and leaders, and undermining the rule of law.
- Tax – Taxes and other payments to governments are an important source of government revenue and are central

to the fiscal policy and macroeconomic stability of countries. Avoiding or evading tax obligations in countries where the organisation operates, deprives the government of those countries of their source of revenue, which could lead to reduced investment in public infrastructure and services, an increase in government debt, or shifting of the tax obligation onto other taxpayers.

- Public policy – Lobbying and financial or in-kind contributions to political parties, politicians, or causes, which can bring risks to society associated with bribery, corruption, and undue influence.
- Anti-competitive behaviour – Facilitation of monopolistic and anti-competitive practices, including issues related to bargaining power, collusion, price fixing or manipulation, and protection of patents and intellectual property (IP) again undermines trust and leaves individuals worse off.

Industry standards and tools for measuring impacts

Different impacts require unique methodologies and measurement tools. Academics, civil society, and the business community have spent years developing frameworks and tools to help organisations measure their impacts in a standardised way. New frameworks and approaches are coming up too as we continue to learn about sustainability and discover new issues. Below is an overview of most common tools.

Carbon accounting

Carbon accounting, also known as 'carbon footprinting', is a framework of methods to measure the GHG emissions across the organisation's direct operations and its value chain. The methods measure emissions of all seven GHGs, but the term 'carbon accounting' is employed as a proxy, and because CO_2 equivalents for the other six gases are used to simplify the calculation process.

The Greenhouse Gas Protocol,[6] developed in 1994 by the World Resources Institute, is the most widely accepted methodology to measure the organisation's carbon footprint. There is general consensus among policymakers that climate change is the one underlying issue that organisations need to address in their sustainability work – the reporting regimes in Europe and the US have made it mandatory for companies in those jurisdictions to report on GHG emissions, whether material or not, so it is likely that this will be the first impact topic you will address.

According to the GHG Protocol, sources of an organisation's emissions are split into three scopes:[7]

- Scope 1 covers direct emissions from sources that are owned or controlled by the organisation, e.g., from combustion of fuels in gas boilers or company vehicles.
- Scope 2 covers indirect emissions from the generation of purchased energy – the electricity, district heating, or cooling that you buy to power, heat, and cool your facilities. These emissions are called 'indirect' because the emissions were generated outside of your physical boundaries, e.g., at the power plant that produced the electricity that your organisation bought.
- Scope 3 covers indirect emissions that occur in the value chain of the organisation, including both upstream and downstream activities. The latter category can include up to 15 sources of emissions, like emissions associated with producing products and services, processing waste, franchises and investments, employee commute and business travel. Here, too, emissions are generated outside of your physical boundary – on the road when the employee drove their car to work, or at the waste management facility that processed the waste your organisation generated, or the company you own.

The reason we account for Scope 3 emissions is because they wouldn't have happened had your organisation not triggered or facilitated them. And while there's a risk of double counting globally (e.g., the waste management company will report your organisation's Scope 3 emissions from processing waste as their Scope 1 and Scope 2 emissions), this is accepted because the goal of the exercise is to help the organisation identify key drivers of emissions and develop strategies to reduce them.

Organisations are expected to account for 100% of their Scope 1 and Scope 2 emissions because they will have direct access to these through energy bills or their spending on fuel for company cars. They are expected to cover the material categories of their Scope 3 emissions, though this is by far the most contentious area of measurement.

There are several methods in the GHG Protocol to calculate GHG emissions – you will likely require specialist knowledge to do so, either from a consultant or from someone who has a sustainability, physics, engineering, or maths background. You will have to do carbon accounting annually, so weigh the costs of upskilling staff internally versus outsourcing the process to an external party, or build a combination of the two.

Carbon accounting is necessary to set a decarbonisation roadmap and targets, but it is also an input to annual sustainability reporting and submissions to external platforms such as the CDP (formerly known as the Carbon Disclosure Project), so you have to align your processes to these timelines. Buffer at least three months for carbon accounting from the moment you launch the project to final results – and allow more time if your organisation is a complex entity.

The hardest part in carbon accounting is chasing the data. You will want to build the process with recurrence and scalability in mind. To do that, consider the following:

- Work with your tech and IT teams to automate data collection where possible, by creating API connections from primary data sources to your carbon accounting dashboard.
- Embed key dates in annual team's schedules, e.g., every year in January teams have to set aside time for a data collection sprint.
- Create the culture and discipline with your facility managers and suppliers such that data collection becomes part of business-as-usual.

Build internal controls around the process to comply with external assurance if you're pursuing it. Auditors will need to be able to follow the reported information to the source and reconcile it with supporting evidence, calculation methodologies, and assumptions used along the way.

They will want to check the following:

- Is data entered manually, sourced from existing enterprise resource planning (ERP) systems, or routed from third parties?
- Is its manipulation prone to error?
- Is it complete?
- Are definitions aligned with those used in the GHG Protocol?
- Who validates the data, and at what stages of the data chain?
- Is there a risk of material misstatements, such as fewer GHG emissions disclosed than emitted in the reporting year?

You will need to work with an ESG controller, if budget allows, and collaborate with your risk team and internal audit function to help you build these internal controls.

Finally, if you're looking to set credible targets to reduce emissions and develop decarbonisation pathways, consider the Science-Based Targets Initiative (SBTi), a non-profit that has developed wide traction in Europe and offers general as well as sector guidelines for setting targets. The target validation (and renewal) process with SBTi has a cost, however de facto SBTi serves as a seal of approval and proof to your auditor that the organisation has done the work and the thinking to determine its emissions and decarbonisation pathways, and it may save you time and cost during the assurance process. The SBTi methodology has limited application to companies in hyper growth, yet it offers a good framework to get started with decarbonisation pathways.

Water footprint and water risk

Of all the water on the surface of the Earth, only 3% is fresh water that can be used for human consumption, with two-thirds of it locked in frozen glaciers or otherwise unavailable for our use. The Water Footprint tool was developed by Arjen Hoekstra, a professor at the University of Twente, in 2002.[8] It helps measure the water footprint of direct and indirect water use of a process, product, company or sector throughout the full production cycle from the supply chain to the end user.

In 2011, the framework was updated to help place the water footprint results in the wider sustainability context and understand whether the water footprint within a certain geographic area is sustainable from an environmental, social, and economic point of view, in which:

- 'environmental sustainability' assesses whether water quality is within certain limits;
- 'social sustainability' assesses whether a minimum amount of the fresh water available on Earth is allocated to 'basic human needs', e.g., for domestic water supply for drinking, washing, and cooking and a minimum allocation of water to food production to secure a sufficient level of food supply to all; and
- 'economic sustainability' assesses whether water is used in an economically efficient way.

The other two widely used tools among water-intensive businesses are the World Resources Institute's Aqueduct Water Risk Filter[9] and the WWF Risk Filter.[10] They help to understand an organisation's exposure to water risk, by looking at baseline water stress, inter-annual variability, seasonal variability, flood occurrence, drought severity, water quality, basin regulatory risk, basin reputational importance, and conflict, among other factors. These tools don't calculate the volume of water use but they help forecast what impacts an organisation can cause on water resources based on their local characteristics, the implications that can have on business continuity, and help develop a response.

Life cycle assessment (LCA)

Life cycle assessment (LCA), also known as 'life cycle analysis', is a methodology for assessing environmental impacts across the full life cycle of a product, service, or process. All products and services follow five stages along which impacts are assessed in an LCA:

1. Extraction and treatment of raw materials
2. Product manufacturing
3. Transport and distribution
4. Product use
5. End of life

When organisations carry out LCAs, they measure the impacts of a product along more than 90 indicators linked to ecosystem and human health, such as GHG emissions, ozone depletion, depletion of resources, toxicity and radiation, or land use. This helps get a holistic view of how harmful the product is overall and where its impact hotspots are.

The LCA methodology is defined by the ISO 14040 standard and is a very complex technical skill grounded in environmental science that takes years to master. Unlike carbon accounting, which a generalist with good math skills can pick up, LCA is generally something to be outsourced to specialised consultancies or LCA programme graduates.

Biodiversity

As an emerging topic on the organisation's agenda, holistic biodiversity impact measurement tools are relatively new. To understand biodiversity impacts, you will have to look at a number of separate proxies, like the type of ecosystems your operational sites are situated in, the state of biodiversity in and around those sites, threats common to biodiversity in those areas, and so on.

Some current leading tools and frameworks include:

- The Integrated Biodiversity Assessment Tool (IBAT)[11] developed by a consortium of global conservation NGOs. It offers a comprehensive dataset to measure biodiversity at site level based on data from the World Database on Protected Areas, the IUCN Red List of Threatened Species, and the World Database of Key Biodiversity Areas. If your organisation has operations at any of the sites covered in IBAT, you can measure the state of biodiversity at that site and understand how you may be contributing to impacts at that site.

- ENCORE[12] is a tool that helps understand dependencies and impacts on nature and ecosystem services, and determines which negative impacts are most likely for particular areas.
- The Species Threat Abatement and Restoration (STAR) metric[13] measures the contribution that investments can make to reducing species' extinction risk.
- The WWF Biodiversity Risk Filter[14] helps screen for exposure to physical, reputational, and regulatory risk at a company or portfolio level.
- The ICCA registry[15] helps identify areas of importance to indigenous peoples and local communities.
- The IUCN Global Ecosystem Typology tool[16] helps identify the type of ecosystem where the company operates and its state.
- The Biological Diversity Protocol,[17] and the UN System of Economic Accounting[18] offer methodologies to measure biodiversity impacts.
- The IUCN threat classification scheme[19] helps classify the drivers of species' decline.
- The Science-Based Targets for Nature[20] help companies develop targets to reduce their impact on nature, including through freshwater and land use, and biodiversity impacts.

Buildings and facilities

Some businesses are centred around design, construction, and operation of buildings. In 1998,[21] the US Green Building Council developed the Leadership in Energy and Environmental Design ("LEED") standards for 'green' buildings. These have since been used and adopted to various building certification schemes around the world. The principles are updated continually, and their latest iteration includes:

- Sustainable site development – selecting sites that have minimal impact on ecosystems, as well as promoting sustainable transportation and reducing 'heat island' effects (placement of buildings, roads, and other infrastructure in urban areas in a way that absorbs and re-emits sun's heat.[22]
- Water efficiency – efficient water use, water reuse, and the reduction of water waste within buildings.
- Energy efficiency – use of energy-efficient systems, renewable energy sources, and the reduction of energy consumption to minimise the environmental impact.
- Materials and resources – use of sustainable and locally sourced materials, as well as the reduction of waste through recycling and reuse practices.
- Indoor environmental quality – improving indoor air quality, providing adequate ventilation, and enhancing occupant comfort and well-being.
- Innovation in design – innovative strategies and technologies in building design.
- Regional priority – the need to address unique environmental priorities and challenges in different geographic regions.

Human rights impact assessment

The responsibility of business to respect human rights is set forth in national laws and several key international instruments, including:

- The UN Guiding Principles on Business and Human Rights,[23] endorsed by the UN Human Rights Council in 2011.
- The OECD Guidelines for Multinational Enterprises,[24] which are binding on all OECD member states and reaffirm the state duty to protect human rights, including from third parties such as businesses.

- The International Labour Organisation (ILO) Declaration of Fundamental Principles and Rights at Work, which is an expression of commitment by governments, employers, and workers' organisations to uphold basic human values at work.[25]

These instruments set an expectation that businesses conduct human rights due diligence, which includes assessing and responding to any actual and potential human rights impacts that might arise from, or be directly linked to, their activities.

The Danish Institute for Human Rights developed the Human Rights Impact Assessment (HRIA) guidance – the most commonly used toolset to analyse the effects that business activities have on rights-holders, such as workers, local community members, consumers, and others. It recommends that businesses should conduct a human rights assessment in the following instances:[26]

- When a financer or investor requires human rights due diligence as part of a contract;
- When business partners (e.g., joint-venture partners) have been previously involved in human rights abuse;
- When entering a new country context with known human rights issues, e.g., forced labour, restrictions on freedom of expression, or violent behaviour from security forces, and that can be found in human rights risk registers;[27]
- When an NGO, human rights group or other whistleblower raises concerns about human rights impacts arising from the business project or activities;
- When beginning a high-impact, high-risk project (e.g., a new mine, dam, or large construction project);
- When the project or activities are or will be located on protected land or areas occupied by vulnerable populations (e.g., areas near indigenous communities, protected rainforests or refugee camps);

- When internal risk-identification mechanisms flag a site or project for further review and investigation;
- At any point when at risk of complicity in human rights abuses;
- When the project or business activities will affect common property resources used by an entire community (e.g., groundwater, grazing land, or fishing waters); and / or
- When entering a new market or industry that may place consumers at risk (e.g., infant formula).

Further, the guidance identifies 10 criteria[28] for a human rights assessment.

The process should take account of:

1. Participation
2. Non-discrimination
3. Empowerment
4. Transparency
5. Accountability

The content of the assessment should include:

1. Benchmark
2. Scope of impacts
3. Assessing impact severity
4. Impact mitigation measures
5. Access to remedy

Sustainability myths and tricky issues

Alongside the genuine areas for innovation and improvement, there are some approaches to managing impacts that have stuck but are less helpful. At best, they distract well-intentioned people and organisations from the real work that needs to be done. At worst, they are greenwashing – a fig leaf to dress up practices and make them look better than they are.

Below are some examples to watch for – and some ways to improve upon them to get to the bottom of impact management.

Table 5. Sustainability approaches to managing impacts

Practices and terms to avoid	Better approaches
Carbon neutral / net-zero – Used interchangeably in the IPCC Global Warming Glossary,[29] these terms refer to a situation where human-caused emissions of GHGs are 'balanced' by removals of emissions over a specific period, usually into the future. While these terms act as a simple cue for the reader about the organisation's climate action targets, there are two problems with them. First, they mask the fact that emissions are still released and may create a false impression of actual progress. Second, once emissions are released into the atmosphere, they set off natural processes that are impossible to reverse and can't be fixed with removals down the line.	Instead, if climate change is a material issue, focus your strategy on carbon emission reduction and decarbonisation pathways which explain the measures you're taking to release fewer emissions year on year. You can think about absolute reductions, or intensity targets if you're a growing company (CO_2 / EUR or CO_2 / product unit). Work with suppliers to decarbonise value chains. Assess climate risks and develop mitigation and adaptation pathways, e.g., switching energy providers, moving production locations, financing supplier decarbonisation projects, etc.
Carbon offsetting – The practice of compensating for released emissions through buying carbon offset credits. Carbon offset credits are generated by various regulated and unregulated organisations who run carbon sequestration projects (tree planting, soil regeneration) or projects that reduce emissions (renewable energy production). The problem with carbon offsets is that it's a hugely unregulated market, with many suboptimal or even fraudulent projects. Another problem is that carbon offsets shift corporate attention and resources away from reductions, absolving companies from the hard work of changing their operations.	

2050 targets – This has become the standard figure for climate targets across pretty much all industries. However, it is simply too far out in the future – 26 years at the time of publication. Current CEOs, CSOs, and other company management simply won't be around that long. Business strategies are created with shorter timeframes such as three-to-five years. In 26 years, your company might look like an entirely different business, if it exists at all.

Another problem is the lack of transparency of how these targets are set. It's implicit that transitions require time – a lot of equipment and infrastructure in operation today, and the investments that support them, cannot be swapped for more efficient options overnight without significantly harming the company, its workers and the economy, but many climate action plans lack an explanation of what and how will be phased out over the next 26 years and how it will be supported with investments throughout, and in spite of, changing management.

If you are in an industry that does need decades to decarbonise, such Oil & Gas or airline aviation, make your best effort to outline a roadmap with long-term goals, connected to shorter-term milestones. Explain what incentives exist to anchor targets, and any locked-in investments.

In all other cases, focus on more relatable timeframes connected to how long management teams actually function within a company. You can still communicate a long-term transformational vision, but your targets and actions should still be set within an observable future.

Recycling – Another 'false friend' similar to net-zero and carbon offsets but related to waste. Waste management is a very complex global system and unfortunately, most waste does not get successfully re-processed. When you dispose of something, it is highly likely that it will end up somewhere at the other end of the world, polluting the environment and leaking into waterbodies.

Recycling creates a false impression of positive action, perpetuates reductionist thinking about the waste problem, and triggers more consumption by misleading us into the thinking that the waste will be recycled.

Instead, build your waste strategy on the waste management hierarchy. It prioritises actions to reduce and manage waste from most impactful to least impactful: prevention, minimisation, reuse, recycling, recovery, and disposal. Note how recycling is only the fourth option.

Strive to redesign your products and operational services such that waste is prevented entirely. Also, focus on the use of recycled products as inputs, rather than leaving it to others to recycle your waste.

Transition from plastic to paper – A simplification which has won over public opinion. Both paper and plastic have their issues and benefits. Plastic is a lightweight, durable material that has allowed us to optimise production and consumption by enabling to store, preserve, and transport materials and goods. Plastic is a by-product of the oil industry, it doesn't decompose, and certain trace elements in it may cause endocrine diseases if they leak into human bodies.[30] Paper doesn't have these problems, but it causes issues upstream – it is often connected to illegal logging, it is a heavier material, meaning it causes much higher emissions during transportation of goods, and to be sufficiently durable, it often requires adding coatings from chemicals that can reduce its biodegradability. Most importantly, the thinking that paper is an 'environmentally friendly' material shifts the discourse away from addressing the core of the problem – our current level of consumption.	Instead, think about ways to reduce packaging altogether – work with your suppliers to change delivery methods of bulk goods, work with your research and development and creative department to design out unnecessary packaging. Encourage your customers to use less packaging. If you do need to use packaging, hire an expert to do a life cycle assessment on various material options.
Nature positive – New terminology that is evolving in the wake of our attention towards biodiversity. We've seen companies to use it mainly to flag that they engage in ecosystem restoration and regeneration projects. However, just like with 'carbon neutrality', questions remain about whether these regenerative practices outweigh any harm that has been done to nature prior.	Instead, apply the mitigation hierarchy – the central approach in natural resource management. For biodiversity, follow avoidance, minimisation, restoration, and offsetting.[31] Avoidance – measures like advanced spatial planning and timing, e.g., building infrastructure outside species' breeding grounds, or timing seismic operations outside mating season. Minimisation – measures to reduce duration, intensity, and extent of unavoidable impacts, e.g., wildlife crossings. Restoration – measures to restore ecosystems to their original state, or to basic ecological functions and / or ecosystem services, e.g., planting trees and vegetation to stabilise bare soil. Offsetting – measures to compensate for any residual, adverse impacts after the full implementation of the previous three steps.[32]

Impact screening checklist

There are many more standards, guidelines, toolboxes and frameworks in sustainability to identify and measure the impacts of your business activities and processes. You will need to start somewhere, and we believe these tools will cover a large scope of your impacts.

To summarise, below is a checklist of key questions you should ask to understand what's causing impacts and what levers you need to focus on to manage them.

1. Value chain – What is the full value chain of your product – can you draw a process flow and an input-output material flow? What are the political, legal, social, economic, and environmental conditions in the key stages of the value chain that your product moves through?

2. Sourcing and manufacturing – How is your product made? Where do materials come from, how are they extracted and processed, and what are the working conditions there? Do material passports and electronic tagging exist? What manufacturing processes does your product go through? What resources and how much do they require to operate? Are these processes efficient and optimised? Are workers exposed to health risks from production, for example from working with toxic chemicals?

3. Transport and distribution – How is your product transported and delivered to the customer, can you draw a map? What distances does it travel, how many ports and countries does it move through, by what mode, and how much carbon is embedded in distribution? Are your products moving through any evasion ports, or are they being relabelled to take advantage of tax and regulatory loopholes?

4. Use – Is your product active (requires energy and other resources during the use phase) or passive? Jeans require water, detergent, and energy to be kept in use, cars require diesel and electricity, while a table requires no additional resources. How can you design your products to be less resource-hungry (e.g., use natural fibres that don't require as frequent washing)?

5. End of life – How durable and repairable is your product? Does it contain toxic or hazardous components? What are the end-of-life effects? Are there any materials that can't be recovered or hard to process during waste management? If processed in unregulated dumps and recycling facilities, what human health effects can it create? Does your product contain precious materials that can stimulate waste trafficking and human rights violations?

6. Packaging – How is your product packaged? What packaging is necessary to preserve product quality and integrity, and what packaging is secondary and can be reduced? What is the packaging made of? Are there any toxic layers or layers that can limit recycling? If disposed of improperly, what is the effect on the natural environment? Is your packaging optimised for the receiving method, e.g., individually wrapping products that are destined for bulk distribution? There are cost savings to be made here too.

7. Waste management – Who processes your waste, where, and how? What proof do you have about this from the waste management company? For any onsite waste processing, is there a risk of leaks and ground or water contamination? Is waste properly separated, sorted and, where possible, recycled? Are incentives in place to prevent and minimise waste?

8. Supply chain – How far down the supply chain can you trace the products and their components? What impacts is the supply chain generally characterised by, e.g., modern

slavery, poor remuneration, environmental crime? How are suppliers managing the risks? How is your organisation managing those risks?

9. Community – What engagement with (potentially) affected communities exists? At what phase of the project does it happen, what precautionary or corrective measures are taken as a result, and what remedy is provided?

10. Internal controls – As a general rule, you can't be sure about whether or not any harmful practices are occurring until you see them for yourself. Damage is not always a consequence of mal-intent, but more often an oversight in complex business processes without clear owners. This doesn't mean that you have to be suspicious about every business activity and follow it to the source, but you should apply basic sanity checks on the information that is being supplied to you. Visit facilities, check certificates, talk to people on the ground, travel to remote tiers of your supply chain where violations are more likely, check if regular inspections exist, and – if so – what incentives exist to pass them. How are employees trained to recognise and manage critical issues? Don't be afraid to play the uncomfortable role of an internal auditor every now and again – you are ultimately protecting the company's shareholders and reputation and the sooner issues are identified, the sooner they can be addressed.

Summary

You have, by now, helped your organisation to understand its most material impacts and drilled deeper into the actual impacts across factors from energy and water to human rights. There are many industry standards and tools out there that you can use to measure your impacts and make plans on how to manage them.

To bolster and evidence all the efforts underway, and to keep the organisation accountable, you need to consider the policy framework that will support and underpin these efforts. Let's look now at how to develop effective sustainability policies.

Chapter 7

Sustainability policies

Sustainability policies set out principles, rules and expectations to guide the activities and conduct of employees, suppliers, and business partners in their interactions with sustainability issues. Strong sustainability policies protect everyone – external stakeholders affected by the company's activities, such as nature or communities, and the company itself.

At a minimum, sustainability policies help set safeguards to avoid causing harm and offer a set of instructions on how to utilise the organisation's control environment to respond to risk. At their maximum, they anchor the organisation's commitment to sustainability and set principles and rules of business conduct.

Effective sustainability policies:

- are embedded throughout the organisation, and owned by it, rather than tucked away in the sustainability department;
- involve a consultation process with key affected stakeholders during their development;
- are grounded in clearly stated values rather than blanket statements to deflect the regulator;

- are revisited in a timely manner to respond to changing circumstances, objectives, and risks;
- are backed by an executive mandate;
- are clear and accessible to their intended audience; and
- are executed with fairness and rigour, including sanctions for non-compliance.

When do you need a policy?

Developing sustainability policies is very much dependent on the culture, size, and sector of your organisation. We've seen organisations that have built cultures of trust and accountability that empower employees to behave in desired ways. Other organisations resist policies for fear that they will absolve people from using their own judgement, slow down decision-making, and drown valuable time in compliance bureaucracy. Yet other organisations have a workforce and suppliers so vast in numbers and complex that they simply come to a standstill without any clear rules of sustainability conduct.

Some organisations operate in low-sustainability impact sectors with a minimal need for policies; others operate in highly regulated sectors with grave sustainability impacts, prone to litigation, public outcry and damage to nature and stakeholders. Shareholders, banks that provide corporate loans, suppliers, and partners of such companies expect them to have sustainability policies as a default compliance measure.

Our view is that policies are a necessary part of the overall sustainability framework but insufficient on their own. Without a functioning culture, aligned incentives, and fair execution, a policy is but a document on your corporate drive. Consider the following factors when deciding how comprehensive a policy framework your organisation requires:

- Are there material topics or performance areas where you need to stipulate best practices and expectations for everyone within and outside the company to align with?
- What country- and sector-level regulations are you subject to that may mandate you to have a policy on certain sustainability topics? For example, the UK government mandates that any company doing business in the UK with an annual turnover of at least €36 million publishes a modern slavery statement, including its policies on slavery and human trafficking.[1]
- Is misconduct recurring? You will need to look deeper into root causes and the cultural conditions driving misconduct, while at the same time introducing greater clarity on rules of behaviour and sanctions if they are not followed.
- Has there been a change in regulation in response to which you need additional controls? For instance, a new directive on due diligence that will trigger greater focus on human rights issues.
- Has there been a change to your operations or circumstances? For example, you're moving to new markets with weak environmental protection and need to add extra safeguards.

Limitations to policy effectiveness

Even with the best intentions, there are several circumstances that may hinder a policy from having its positive effect, or even work against the company. Before jumping to put in place new rules, hold up a mirror to your leaders and assess how ethical and how strong your cultural foundation is overall. The conclusion might be that you need to focus on some other areas of the business first.

In her book Higher Ground,[2] Alison Taylor suggests the following traits common for unethical cultures:

- Market dominance at any cost where the ends justify the means. In these companies, rules are broken in favour of the company to protect its perceived survival.
- Autocratic leaders who make employees fearful and reluctant to speak up and share concerns. Even if wrongdoings are seen and known, employees choose to keep quiet over fear of being targeted and experiencing repercussions on their career that extend beyond this one company.
- Misaligned incentives where compensation and reward are set with narrow interests in mind and without consideration of broader company goals and the operating environment.
- Cultures of urgency and necessity that undermine stated values and are enabled by powerful in-group dynamics. Everything needs to happen now, there is no time to follow lengthier compliance procedures, commission risk assessments. Red tape is cut, and any attempt to challenge decisions is shut down by groups with authority.
- Addressing these issues is a tall order, and not something you can or should manage on your own. You will need to involve compliance, HR, and trusted C-suite members to address these root causes. Alternatively, your culture might already be strong enough, but employees or certain employee groups may simply lack clarity on grey areas; they may need examples of how to respond to an issue and with whom to raise concerns.
- Defaulting to rules and punishment may actually diminish trust and reduce employees to "blind rule-following at the expense of using ethical judgement".[3] In this scenario, clarify any procedures or rules on your company intranet

or with a target group of employees, and make them very visible and accessible, do periodic refreshers at company meetings, and update trainings.

Contents of a sustainability policy

There is no standard on writing a sustainability policy, but the European Sustainability Reporting Standards (ESRS)[4] offer some best practices and reporting expectations.

To be compliant with the CSRD, companies are obliged to disclose the following minimum information about their sustainability policies:

- A description of the key contents of the policy, including its general objectives and which material impacts, risks, or opportunities the policy relates to, and the process for monitoring.
- A description of the scope of the policy, or of its exclusions, in terms of activities, upstream and downstream value chain, geographies and any affected stakeholder groups.
- The most senior level in the organisation accountable for the policy implementation.
- A reference to the third-party standards or initiatives the organisation commits to respect through the policy implementation.
- A description of consideration given to the interests of key stakeholders in setting the policy.
- Whether and how the organisation makes the policy available to potentially affected stakeholders and to stakeholders who need to help implement it.

What guiding principles can you draw on?

Most guiding principles that you might want to adopt in your policies come from international law instruments stipulating universal rules of behaviour and values around certain topics. These include:

- The 'precautionary principle' and the do no harm principles that come down to preventing environmental damage that business decisions and activities can lead to.
- The 'polluter pays principle' that stipulates that environmental costs of business activities should be internalised.
- Respect for human rights, which means businesses should avoid infringing on others' human rights and address adverse human rights impacts that they are involved with.
- Avoiding any unlawful employment practices.
- Combatting bribery and other forms of corruption.
- Protecting consumers in accordance with fair business, marketing, and advertising practices.

These guiding principles can be broken down to the following clauses you may wish to introduce in your policies or code of conduct:

Table 6. Potential clauses to introduce in a policy or code of conduct

Headline topic	Potential clauses to include
Human rights	
Employment relations	• Unlawful punishment, abuse, harassment, intimidation • Employment termination • Adherences to statutory labour laws
Child labour	• Employment of young persons under 15 • Means to prevent child labour • Working rights of 18 and older
Forced labour	• Bonded labour, serfdom, slavery or slave-like practices, trafficking of human beings
Remuneration and benefits	• Adherence to statutory agreements • Deductions from wages
Working hours	• Adherence to statutory provisions • Description of working hours, breaks and public holidays • Overtime rules
Hiring practices	• All workers to be provided with a written contract in a language they understand • No recruitment fees
Freedom of association and collective bargaining agreements	• Freedom to join trade unions / respect for collective bargaining
DEI	• Equal opportunity • No discrimination based on national and ethnic origin, social background, health status, disability, sexual orientation, age, gender, political opinion, religion, or belief
Health and safety	• Processes in place • Trainings
Environment	
Protection of natural resources and their responsible use	• Dependent on material topics
Ethical business practices and integrity	
Corruption, trade control, money laundering	• Zero tolerance
Political contributions / lobbying	• Rules of engagement
Data protection / confidentiality	• Privacy rights of employees, business partners and customers • Protection of commercial secrets • Insider trading • Respect of intellectual property

Consumer protection	• Product quality and safety • Fair business, marketing, and advertising practices • Attention to children, senior citizens, people with disabilities, vulnerable consumer groups
Gifts and entertainment	• No quid pro quo • Disclosure of gifts received
Speaking up and whistleblowing	• No retaliation • Corrective action • Whistleblowing and contact lines
Conflict management and resolution	• Commitment to mediation / arbitration when a solution cannot be found

At a minimum, we recommend that most organisations have the following:

- An overall sustainability statement, ideally embedded within the vision, mission and values of the organisation.
- A code of conduct, including provisions for human rights, environmental, social and governance requirements; this can be separated into an internal code of conduct / code of ethics for employees and an external code of conduct for suppliers and business partners.
- A sustainability policy unless material clauses are embedded in the code of conduct.
- A set of procedures covering:
    - o the preparation of sustainability reports, including collection and validation of data; and
    - o a link to speak up and whistleblowing procedures, for employees to report misconduct.
- Where the organisation has subsidiaries or franchises, a policy for what is expected of them.
- A human rights statement, unless covered under the code of conduct.

Developing sustainability policies

Once you have identified the need for a policy, you might need to submit a formal proposal to your leadership team outlining why the policy is needed and what it is trying to achieve. Larger organisations will have numerous policies, so you have to review whether new clauses could be added to existing policies or some of them can be consolidated. The rule of quality over quantity prevails here – the more voluminous and prescriptive the policies you introduce are, the greater the complexity and the risk that employees will either obey them slavishly or ignore them. Some issues might be best addressed through better communication, incentive programmes, or performance criteria. Prioritise culture over rules, and substance over form.

Assuming your culture is generally ethical and functional, you can follow these steps to establish your policy framework:

Assess the existing control environment

What policies, procedures, and norms already exist on the topic you're trying to address? Are they complete and up to date? Are the policies effective, and how is effectiveness measured: on outcome (the rate of incidents declining after introduction of the policy), or on activity (training completion rates, incidents registered). Is the system surrounding policy execution effective, or so complex and bureaucratic that it paralyses action and makes the employees want to ignore getting involved at all? Can it be simplified or streamlined?

Consult stakeholders and advisors

These can include stakeholders who will be affected by the policy or whose interests it is trying to protect. For example, if you're writing a policy on forced labour, speak to those who interact with the supply chain in your organisation most closely to understand the local circumstances and behaviours you need to guard against. Identify employees who may be avoiding speaking up.

Consult external parties, such as subject-matter experts, behavioural scientists, legal advisors, or insurance providers who can help you understand best practices, any intricacies, and limitations. For example, flexible paid leave policies have been an attractive employee proposition, but in practice they raise disputes and liabilities around pay outs of accrued vacation days, fairness around granting other types of paid leave, and the equal application of the policy across the company.

Test before you launch

Work through scenarios of policy application, any areas open for interpretation, clauses that may contradict other policies or procedures and confuse employees. Seek clarity at all times. Select a diverse group of employees to help validate the policy. Think through how the organisation will respond to any grey areas in a fair manner.

Sustainability is nuanced and, like it or not, you will have to confront moral dilemmas and make uncomfortable choices that prioritise some situations over others, and potentially even some employee groups over others. This will inevitably lead to disappointment for some, but as long as you create an oversight process that is transparent, unbiased, provides equal opportunities to speak up, treats employees and stakeholders with respect, and leads to resolutions, you have done your best.

Seek approval

If you have an owner of the policy framework, usually someone on the legal, risk or compliance team, work with them early to figure out how to embed sustainability, launch the policy and maintain it over time. Some policies may require approval from the board, so plan in advance.

Roll out

Create a launch and communication plan for the new policy – there needs to be a moment when all current employees are notified about the new policy and take the time to read it. Work with the communications team to develop an effective launch plan. Determine the need for supporting training and guidelines – your policy should be clear and accessible to everyone, but you might want to illustrate certain clauses with examples or give some more context than the text of the policy allows.

One of the best training examples we've seen was on cybersecurity. It was developed by the in-house Information Security team and was built on the actual lived experience of the organisation. It spoke to the actual physical environment of that office, the nature of work and behaviour patterns that employees showed day in-day out, existing cases of spam techniques that everyone could recognise, actual roles, teams, and titles in the company. This doesn't have to cost a fortune and will be all the more effective when fully grounded in the reality of your own organisation.

Review

Post-implementation, monitor adherence to the policy and any consequences. Is it working in the way you have intended or are there any loopholes or misinterpretations? Is it still relevant and accurate? If amendments are needed, repeat the same process, register the changes, and update all supporting materials.

Policy checklist

The Independent Commission Against Corruption[5] offers the following general checklist for developing a strong policy that will serve your organisation and its stakeholders:

1. Use clear, concise language that is easy to understand by native and non-native speakers.
2. Articulate definitions of any unique or technical terms and abbreviations.
3. Try to avoid scope for interpretation or discretion to be applied, e.g., avoid using terms like 'one's discretion', 'usually', or 'where possible' – unless you really intend it to be that way.
4. Include references to relevant legislation and related policies, procedures or supporting documents and ensure they are consistent with one another.
5. Use effective and uniform naming conventions.
6. Include the allocation of responsibilities to specific positions rather than business units.
7. Identify the 'policy owner' – the position responsible for reviewing and updating the policy.
8. Identify who has approved the policy, the date it was approved and the next scheduled review date.
9. Test with internal group of stakeholders before launching.
10. Make it public.

Summary

Policies are a necessary – though not sufficient – element of the sustainability function. They anchor certain expectations and codify them. They link to the existing frameworks and working practices of the organisation, provide guidance to staff, escalation protocols where things are not as they should be, and link to the necessary procedures to implement sustainability initiatives and report on them. Aim for clarity over length and remember that policies are not a replacement for an ethical culture and a well-formed strategy.

Policies are just one aspect in managing sustainability-related risk and in the next chapter, we look at the risk framework more broadly.

Chapter 8

Sustainability risk management

Risk, at its core, is about the "effect of uncertainty on objectives".[1] Sustainability is, we would argue, the over-arching risk that organisations, and indeed humanity, faces. In the commercial world, sustainability risk has the potential to decimate supply chains, income streams and to render whole industries obsolete. It also opens up opportunities – for new ventures, products, and services, for innovation and for growth. Therefore, as CSO, you have a symbiotic relationship with risk management in your organisation. You must learn to speak the language of risk in the context of sustainability and align your efforts with existing risk management initiatives. The CRO should also be a key ally in promulgating the issue of sustainability risk.

According to The Risk Coalition,[2] "…a CRO is one of the few senior executives able to look across the breadth of ESG and sustainability issues and bring together cross-functional teams to address them with an eye to leveraging business opportunities and managing threats."

If your organisation is well-established, it should already have a risk management framework. ISO 31000 is the industry standard for enterprise risk management and covers the activities of planning and designing, implementing and benchmarking, measuring and monitoring, and learning and reporting.[3]

Some key components of the risk management framework include:

- An overall risk management policy, which sets out the responsibilities for risk management in the organisation, between business management (the 'first line' of defence), the risk team (the 'second line') and independent auditors (the 'third line').
- Allocation of responsibilities across the 'three lines of defence', which we will explain in this chapter.
- Risk appetite, set by the organisation's board, e.g., how much (high risk appetite) or how little risk (low risk appetite) the organisation is prepared to take.
- A policy and set of procedures for implementing and managing risk.
- Control and risk libraries, i.e., the complete list of identified risks and the controls to mitigate them.
- A method of assessing risks and control gaps, most commonly the Risk and Control Self-Assessment.
- Action plans, trackers, KPIs – ways of assessing the organisation's progress in managing risk.
- Governance and oversight arrangements.

In one of the other books in this series, *How to be a Chief Risk Officer*,[4] we created a pyramid of risks as a way of organising the thinking around risks. While not intended to say that one risk is more important than another, there is an order to the thinking here – for example, transaction processing risk will be of little importance over time if strategic risk is not addressed.

Figure 5. Pyramid of risks for consideration

Sustainability risk is defined in the EU Sustainable Finance Disclosure Regulation as: "An environmental, social, or governance event, or condition that, if it occurs, could cause an actual or a potential material negative impact on the value of the investment arising from an adverse sustainability impact."[5]

You will notice that sustainability risk is not mentioned in the pyramid above. In How to be a Chief Risk Officer, we argued that it was a fundamental risk underpinning all the others. However, different treatments are possible, and you should discuss with your CRO whether to integrate sustainability within existing risk categories, or to set it up as a standalone item.

Benefits of a standalone sustainability risk function:

- Draws specific attention to the issue;
- Ensures targeted plans; and
- Consolidates the actions to address sustainability into one place.

Benefits of integrating sustainability into all existing risks

- Uses risk definitions with which people are already familiar; and
- Integrates sustainability work with business as usual.

All risk management starts with a statement about the amount of risk an organisation is prepared to take in a particular area. No venture is without risk. Good risk management involves a clear-eyed assessment of the risks being taken, and management of those risks within an appetite, to minimise the chances of the organisation being surprised by adverse consequences (not forgetting there are upside risks too).

In some cases, such as with legal and compliance issues, the organisation may have low to zero tolerance (for example, for money laundering risks, or risks of data privacy leakages). In other cases, they will knowingly take some risks (for example, acknowledging that, if you lend money, some of that money may not be repaid).

When discussing sustainability risk, setting risk appetite is a non-trivial activity. Using your materiality and impact assessment, you need to work with leadership to agree what the appetite is – is it solely about not falling foul of legislation? Or are you trying to change industry, set new standards? Are you a leader or a follower? Will you be active or passive? Will you set goals for 2050 or much sooner? How much financial impact is the organisation willing to take in service to sustainability?

A risk management approach to sustainability

Standard risk management practice takes a three-step process to risk; you identify the risks, assess them and manage them. Below we discuss what that means in the context of sustainability.

Identify sustainability risks

In this stage, you identify risks – what could be the damage to your organisation due to not managing sustainability? Using the layers in the risk pyramid above, below are some of the common risks that link to sustainability:

- Strategic risk – The risk that your product or offering becomes redundant or undesirable with the sustainability transition. Consider how fossil fuels and tobacco companies are seeking to pivot their entire purpose to avoid extinction; look at farmers of agricultural commodities such as cocoa, coffee, olive oil, or rice whose crop yields are severely affected by climate change.
- People risk – Consider here the ability to attract and retain talent if you lack a sustainability strategy and culture. This type of risk also encompasses poor conduct by your people; irresponsible decisions, greenwashing, and failure to engage and act honourably.
- Technical risk – Consider here the need for new systems and solutions to manage and report on sustainability issues, e.g., supply chain monitoring.
- Financial risk – This includes risks of rising insurance costs, losses due to adverse weather events, loss of market share and customers. Consider the risk of claims by communities adversely affected by your organisation's activities or court cases brought by employees for any misconduct. It also includes the risk of reporting misstatements, with associated reputational issues and fines.
- Supplier risk – The EU Corporate Sustainability Due Diligence Directive (CSDDD)[6] requires affected organisations to assess all third parties (and their onward parties) for environmental and human rights issues in their supply chain. Failure to do this adequately brings the

potential of massive fines (up to 6% of turnover) and litigation.

- Buildings and facilities risk – Consider the costs required to bring buildings up to modern environmental standards, mandatory requirements for energy audits, and the risks of failure to do this in a timely manner. Also think about the impact of power and connectivity outages due to adverse climate changes and weather events.
- Change management risk – While the transition costs are less of a risk and more of an issue / cost to be managed, also consider the impact on the organisation's ability to deliver both the sustainability agenda and strategy and product changes simultaneously.
- Regulatory risk – The risk of regulatory changes requiring your organisation to adapt, as well as the reputational risk of being viewed as 'on the wrong side of history' if your lobbying or trade associations' policies are not aligned to your public sustainability agenda. This also includes the risk of fines for non-compliance with regulation, be it 'big' directives like the CSDDD or local environmental pollution laws.
- Legal risk – The risk of changes that will need to be made to contracts due to a changing external environment. The risk of legal cases being brought against the organisation for failure to meet sustainability standards.

How to identify risks

While as CSO you bring a wealth of expertise and knowledge to the organisation, your first months in the role will be consumed with understanding the organisation you have joined. You should place yourself firmly in listening mode. Only by getting under the skin of the organisation can you create a tailored plan, one that is grounded in reality and context, one that the staff will recognise and align to. You can create checklists and prompts to ensure things aren't being missed, but the words in the plan must ultimately feel as though they came from the people who work there.

Below are some of the ways you can surface risks:

- Interviews with the management and board;
- Listening to staff;
- Offering opportunities to surface issues: mailbox, open door policy, regular drop-in sessions; and / or
- Whistleblowing hotlines.

A lot of these will surface when you do your materiality assessment and will sit in existing risk and control libraries.

Assess sustainability risks

Once you have a longlist of risks from your fact-finding, you need a way to make sense of them and prioritise them. This has strong links to the materiality assessment. The classic risk management approach is to plot the risks on an axis of how likely they are to occur, against the significance if they do occur.

Ensure that you consider significance in terms of a multitude of factors including:

- Financial impact;
- Reputation impact; and
- Business disruption – how much of an outage could you accept? How much do you want to mitigate?

Initially, consider the impact if you have no mitigation. Compare this back to the risk appetite. For risks within your appetite, you can continue to monitor the risks, but no further action may be needed. For risks outside of your appetite, you will need to manage.

Manage sustainability risks

In standard risk management, there are five main ways to manage risk:

- Terminate or avoid the activity altogether. Don't sink the well, don't build the building. Stop the line of business.
- Control the risk; implement preventive controls to reduce the likelihood of it occurring. For example, treatment of wastewater to render it safe.
- Transfer or outsource the risk, e.g., via insurance.
- Mitigate or reduce the impact of the risk if it materialises, for example by quickly dealing with a chemical spill
- Tolerate and accept the risk as part of doing business.

We mentioned above the three lines of defence – this is the division of responsibilities recognised by the risk profession to manage risk. The first line is management in the organisation, the 'front line' or 'the business' as it's commonly called; the second is the risk team which provides check and challenge to the first line, and an independent third line who audit the work. In 2020, this model was enhanced to identify three key roles and to incorporate sustainability, as described by the Institute of Internal Auditors:[7]

- The governing body, which establishes and oversees governance mechanisms, including those relating to sustainability.
- Management, which ensures the effective functioning of operations and also oversees the delivery of the materiality assessment, which "establishes the link between the operations of a company, their impact on ESG issues and relevance to key stakeholders"[8].

- Internal audit, which "assures the reliability of internal control processes for ESG data disclosure and reporting"[9].

This begs the question: where does the CSO sit? Does the CSO role hold direct management responsibility or is it more second line, providing check and challenge to the initiatives that are underway throughout the rest of the organisation? We think the CSO role sits most naturally with the second line role of providing "expertise, support, monitoring and challenge on risk-related matters".[10] One bank has even allocated responsibility for sustainability to its CRO, who sees the natural linkage between the two areas.[11]

Embedding sustainability into your risk management framework

Now that you've consumed the theory, you're probably asking how to put this into practice. Chapter 5 discusses how you can integrate risk identification into the materiality process, and chapter 10 covers how you can ensure comprehensive and accurate reporting on risks. Chapter 7 on policies outlines how you can define policies and procedures to protect against identified risks. Chapter 12 on execution discusses how you assign ownership for sustainability strategy, ensuring competence and willingness to act.

As CSO, you should work with management and the risk team to add sustainability into the organisation's risk register. Generally accepted practice within risk management is to identify and manage risks via Risk and Control Self-Assessments (RCSAs). RCSAs are often maligned because, done badly, they can be cumbersome, obtuse, and useless. Done well, they should offer a focused list of the most likely risks to occur and their impact, brought to within the limits of risk tolerance through the use of well-designed controls.

The typical layout of an RCSA includes the following data points:

- Risk name
- Description – outlining what could go wrong
- Impact (across financial, reputational and business disruption)
- Likelihood
- Within appetite (yes / no)
- (If not within appetite) List of the controls to reduce the likelihood of the risk occurring, the detective controls to identify the risk in a timely manner, and the mitigating controls to reduce the impact if it occurs
- Action plan to bring the risk to within tolerance; with ownership, due date, and status (on track, off track, overdue, etc.)

The RCSAs created across the organisation should be tagged with those risks related to sustainability, providing you with a comprehensive list of the key risks, and the actions to manage them. It may not match perfectly with your full sustainability programme, but it should provide a useful completeness check to ensure you haven't missed anything the organisation considers critical.

Summary

As we said at the beginning of this book, the relationship between the CSO and CRO is a key one. The CRO acts as check and challenge to the organisation's risk management agenda, as does the CSO – they should be powerful enough to hold the organisation to account in balancing its risk management against its pursuit of growth and profit. They need to situate sustainability risk appropriately alongside the other risks that the organisation is managing and help management assign the right priority to the important actions that will keep the organisation safe, relevant, and on a sustainable path for the future.

As CSO, you bring a unique and fresh perspective on risk, helping the organisation see around corners and get ahead of the upcoming challenges. Risk processes and reports will help you understand the organisation, and sustainability will enhance risk reporting – a mutually beneficial relationship.

Chapter 9

Investor relations

There are many types of investors, but ultimately, these are people and organisations who are invested in your business and its future, and are paid to support, scrutinise you and provide insight necessary for the investment to succeed.

In the past five years, the market has gone through a steep learning curve. The Sustainable Finance Disclosure Regulation (SFDR) in the EU forced investors to think about sustainability pragmatically – if investors were going to call something an 'impact fund', they needed to be sure it actually was, and that led to a wave of engagement and stricter controls with companies.

In the US, BlackRock CEO Larry Fink's letter to CEOs in 2019 had a turbo-charging effect when suddenly a major investor was telling them to figure out their ESG performance. Then, the announcement of the US Securities and Exchange Commission (SEC) about plans to strengthen its climate disclosure rules acted as a major warning and catalysed companies to start measuring and managing their emissions before the law was finally passed in March 2024.[1]

Angela Jhanji, Managing Director at private equity firm EQT, tells us: "Whenever people have supported sustainability, they have created microcosms of effects that now are inside of the DNA of the middle market, public market, and now the private market too."

Sustainability is a source of value creation. The innovation, new partnerships, resilience in supply chains, and the vision that come with sustainability can open up new markets, increase market share, energise customers, and motivate and retain staff – all sources of value creation. If the company has a strong culture, it can save millions on attrition costs. If large companies are pledging to achieve zero plastic or decarbonisation, companies in the supply chain have no option but to create alternative products and change operating practices, else they will lose customers, their main revenue source. On the upside, they can become first movers in the market, gaining market share.

Ultimately, investors want to see how companies are managing downside risks (avoiding potential losses) and creating upside value potential; they want to see how risk and value creation are reflected in the income statement or balance sheet. When investors assess the company's overall value in order to decide if they will provide capital to the company, they want to understand what impact the organisation's ESG profile will have on this valuation and long-term performance, and how much they would need to invest to get the company to sustainability maturity.

The CSO's role here is to be the strategic visionary and the connector between the worlds of sustainability and business, i.e., explain how topics like climate change, deforestation, pollution, and human rights relate to the operating context of the business, identify risks and opportunities coming from this intersection, and develop a vision for how the company will address them, e.g., via minimum compliance or through differentiation and leadership.

Done well, CSOs can articulate the value of their sustainability agenda, how it acts as the North Star for value creation, recruit more support to their cause, and help raise capital externally. Done wrongly, it can lead to ambivalence, outright resistance, and hefty legal consequences. There's lots of value to bring to the table here, but there are hazards to avoid, and you should work with the rest of the organisation to stay within the lines.

According to IBM[2]: "Incorporating sustainability into the heart of operations can support the design and creation of new products and services, improve the brand and deepen customer loyalty. It can also reduce operating costs, increase the support from financial investors, and encourage company pride and commitment among employees."

A new sustainable finance regime

While the EU was first out of the blocks when it came to sustainable finance, of late, there has been some backlash against sustainability, particularly in the US. Looking at recent climate policy U-turns in the UK[3] or the watering down of EU's main due diligence mechanism, the CSDDD, lobbied by Germany, Italy, Bulgaria, and Austria, it may seem that Europe is not immune to anti-ESG trends either. At the same time, under the surface, most companies remain committed – ESG funds' growth in assets under management in Europe remains positive, with a 4% growth of such assets in 2023.[4]

The shift to sustainability in the market is driven by factors too powerful to be overridden by a few disgruntled voices. With the launch of the EU Green New Deal in 2020,[5] policymakers assigned the finance sector a central role in the transition towards sustainable development and net-zero Europe by 2050. In the end, every euro invested and consumed affects the world around us, and the current regulatory shift reflects a general political direction of travel that says capital allocation needs to work in favour of planetary health and the well-being of people, and that investors have a fiduciary duty to support this.

To enforce its commitment, the EU launched its Sustainable Finance Action Plan in 2018, along with a few other key regulations. They all work together to create alignment in sustainability data flows between investors, companies and regulators, and drive change:

- To create a common baseline for investors about what 'green' investment is and isn't, the EU launched the EU Taxonomy[6] – definitions and classifications of green investments. It includes both environmental and social criteria, though the latter are less developed. Definitions and classifications in the Taxonomy are expanded continuously and are published in the EU Delegated Acts.[7]
- The Sustainable Finance Disclosure Regulation (SFDR)[8] requires capital providers to disclose how their investments consider sustainability performance of investee companies.
- To help investors source these data from companies, the EU launched the Corporate Sustainability Reporting Directive (CSRD)[9] which formalises 20 years of voluntary sustainability reporting into mandatory obligations for companies to disclose sustainability information.
- To standardise reporting metrics for companies and the ways in which they determine materiality, the EU introduced the European Sustainability Reporting Standards (ESRS)[10] – an annex to the CSRD. With the exception of a few standards like E2 Pollution and E5 Resource Use and Circular Economy, these are predominantly derived from

the GRI Standards, which is to say that there has been a significant body of knowledge and practice accumulated in the sustainability community over the years on sustainability reporting and most of these requirements will not be new to experienced reporters.

- To change behavioural norms of how business is 'done' and create a legal enforcement mechanism, the EU is launching the Corporate Sustainability Due Diligence Directive (CSDDD or CS3D)[11]. It sets rules and obligations for companies to manage their environmental and human rights impacts and effectively repositions due diligence to the forefront of business operations. In other words, if CSRD sets transparency expectations for companies, the CSDDD sets behaviour expectations.
- To monitor the overall financial stability in the region, the European Banking Authority (EBA) launched EBA Pillar 3 Disclosure Framework[12] that requires banks to disclose their exposure to ESG risks, % of assets that are 'green', and their pathways towards capital allocation that is aligned with the Paris Agreement.

Together, these regulations create a cohesive system of interdependencies and reinforcement around disclosure and action, evolving the concept of fiduciary duty to include the interests of both shareholders and stakeholders (nature and future generations are legal concepts now). Just imagine the power of this system. This paradigm shift requires that companies reassess their business models, value propositions, supply chain resilience, and how all of that is governed and broadcast to the world.

In the US, investors are seeing important developments in sustainability assessments too. The International Sustainability Standards Board (ISSB) under the IFRS Foundation has released Sustainability Disclosure Standards (single financial materiality approach) which are pending adoption in over 60 jurisdictions globally and are likely to become the main reference for sustainability reporting in the US.

In late 2023, the US state of California passed the California Climate Disclosure Laws that will require companies that do business in California to disclose on their GHG emissions and climate-related financial risks. After almost five years of debate, the US Securities Exchange Commission adopted its new Climate Disclosure Rule in March 2024, mandating publicly listed companies in the US to report on Scope 1 and 2 GHG emissions.

At the time of writing this book, the Shanghai Stock Exchange (SSE), Shenzhen Stock Exchange (SZSE), and Beijing Stock Exchange (BSE) in China have all published sustainability reporting guidelines for listed companies, including a new requirement for hundreds of larger cap and dual-listed issuers to begin mandatory disclosure on a broad range of ESG topics in 2026.[13]

In Canada, the financial regulator, the Office of the Superintendent of Financial Institutions (OSFI), released guidelines on climate risk management in March 2024, setting out requirements for major banks and insurance companies to manage and disclose climate-related risks for fiscal year 2024, followed by smaller institutions the following year.[14]

In Brazil, the Securities and Exchange Commission announced in 2023 that public companies will be required to provide annual sustainability and climate-related disclosures, starting in 2026.[15]

Singapore will implement mandatory climate-related reporting requirements for listed and large non-listed companies, with obligations for some to begin disclosing in line with the IFRS's International ISSB standards starting as early as 2025.[16]

This degree of ambition in capital markets is unprecedented, and sooner or later your CFO and your board won't be able to ignore these developments. As a CSO you have to help them recognise this paradigm shift in capital allocation sooner rather than later.

What investors look for

Investors use varied and complex methods to assess how a company's ESG profile may impact its valuation and long-term performance. Generally, they will look at whether ESG drives a lower cost of capital, higher profitability, and lower exposure to risk.[17]

What this means in practice for the CSO and the CFO is that investors will typically look at the following parameters to determine the ESG profile and maturity of the company, and feed that into their assessment methodologies:

- Your sector – The ESG profile of your product / business model in relation to end markets. This may seem like a black and white area, but it isn't – for example, a company may manufacture weapons, but they can be used in national defence. Investor policies and approaches vary on this topic and it's beyond the scope of this book to discuss. Some investors use exclusion criteria and do not engage with companies involved in manufacturing of controversial weapons, tobacco, coal power plants or coal mining. Others will assign a higher / lower risk factor depending on the sector and its known material sustainability issues. This is not something you can influence as the CSO, but it means you need to give even greater importance to the quality of your materiality assessment and sustainability governance – tobacco, aerospace and defence, and fossil fuel production companies have ESG scores too.

- Your operations – The ESG profile of your operations. What have you done already to improve the ESG performance of your operations and how does that compare to peers in your sector? Here investors will look at your material topics, any glaringly missing issues, selected KPIs and metrics.
- Differentiation – Whether the organisation has been able to unpack what it's really going to stand on and how it's going to get there. This will normally separate trailblazers and leaders from everyone else, so articulate to your investors very clearly where you will truly unlock value, how you will do it and why you think it will work.
- Sustainability report – Its existence and quality, i.e., does it enable the investor to quickly identify your top material issues, how you're managing them, and your performance / progress. It's important to treat your sustainability report as a "barcode for your business"[18], which means providing a concise, focused, and accurate representation of your non-financial metrics.
- Governance and incentives – Who's in charge of sustainability, how are they embedded in the organisation, and how is the organisation incentivised to improve sustainability performance? This includes sustainability representation on the board, the seniority / title of the sustainability leader (if not the CSO), and how they are supported and placed in the organisation vis-à-vis material topics / stated goals. For example, if a plastics manufacturing supplier states that transitioning their assortment to 'green alternatives' is a strategic priority, and their CSO is placed in the marketing department rather than research and development, then this will be a red flag to the investor.
- Risk and due diligence processes and policies – Who is structurally monitoring sustainability risks and what

processes exist to support this? We discussed in chapter 7 how policies are only as good as the culture that they rest on, and investors will look at the full picture including culture. That said, investors want to have the security that the company has at least basic guardrails in place to manage downside risk.

- Consistency – Whether there is consistency in progress updates and delivery. Investors want to see that sustainability is part of business as usual and that resources and attention are allocated to it as allocated to other parts of the business. It's fine if you need time to settle or figure out how you're going to approach a particular sustainability area – it's fine to be transparent with your investors about any hurdles, as long as they see you have a plan of action.
- CSO attitude – Though this may not feed into formal scoring methodologies, when CSOs are pro-active, ask challenging questions, treat investors as partners, and look ahead beyond compliance, this normally gives investors the comfort that these people are truly pushing themselves and their companies in the direction of value creation.

How do investors screen performance?

This is a big and rapidly evolving area with the advance of AI assisted tools. It's important to understand that beyond direct engagement with investors that the CSO can control, a whole world of data scraping and data analytics exists to determine a company's ESG profile. Every interaction with partners, suppliers, customers, every article, panel speech, or social media post leaves a trace – investors don't need to talk to you to get a picture of your sustainability performance, others will say it for you.

Here are just some tools investors will use to assess your performance:

- Direct engagement – conversation between investors and an organisation's representatives about material topics, metrics, targets, incentives, and governance.
- Expert interviews – when investors reach out to subject-matter experts to ask about problematic areas in the sector and what topics should be on the radar of the prospective company.
- Automated analytics – AI data scraping tools that gather and analyse all the data ever posted about the company or by the company in the public domain, e.g., social media, news articles, interviews, videos, references in NGO research, sustainability reports.
- ESG performance benchmarks and ratings (for public companies) – from providers like MSCI, Morningstar / Sustainalytics, S&P Global, or RepRisk.
- Sustainable investment screens – public market insights in investor forums.

Investors look for company data because they need to correlate it to the size of risk or potential investment they will need to make to manage the risk – ultimately, their money. From our conversations with investors, we've learnt that where they can't find the organisational data, they will infer it from analytical procedures. For example, if a company doesn't disclose information about its supply chain, the investor will examine locations to estimate their financial exposure to climate risk. If it doesn't disclose emissions, the investor will extrapolate them based on emissions of companies of similar size / revenue.

Addressing the perception gap and unlocking value

As you can imagine, it's best not to leave your first impression to chance. Many CSOs reading this book will be setting up their company's first sustainability function and may not have a whole lot to present to the world in the first few years as they set the foundations and build up muscle. Even in that context, you can build a credible story about your material topics and your action plan, and feed in portions of information to the market as it becomes available.

For more mature CSOs, don't get caught up in "corporate sustainability theatre"[19] – investors are upskilling too and by now, most firms have strong sustainability leads driving teams of their own who can quickly filter through the thicket of sustainability information. The conversation is getting more mature, so be prepared to show real results, and to be precise in your reporting – words such as 'challenging', 'robust', 'excellent' have specific meanings when working in this space.

Educate your investor relations (IR) colleagues in sustainability, sustainability reporting, ESG ratings and how to communicate the value of the organisation's sustainability mission and be prepared to listen just as hard to them. These executives will have years of hard-won experience, knowledge of their analysts and their idiosyncrasies, an important list of what not to do, and valuable perspective to help you be effective and to avoid slip-ups.

Another consideration is that analysts are always looking for a benchmark, an industry standard to compare your organisation's performance by. This can be hard with sustainability, where perhaps you're innovating and nobody has done something before, or where the commercial payoff for a particular initiative may not be immediately visible. As CSO, and working with IR, you have a challenging role to translate and explain the value of the sustainability agenda in terms the investment community will understand.

Moreover, for the sustainability agenda to be effective, the external message must be consistent with what's happening elsewhere; so, it must mirror what employees are seeing and doing, what your partners are experiencing etc. This can take a huge amount of co-ordination and gravitas, not to mention deep integration, in order to be credible.

Above all else, remember to keep your communications succinct and simple. Sustainability is a complex area, but there usually isn't time to explain all the nuances of a detailed programme to the investor community – your IR team can help you work on the messaging to distil it into what that community will register and understand.

Getting started in investor relations

So, where should you begin as CSO in building disclosure of sustainability practices, in a way that is value-enhancing, makes the connection between sustainability and commercial success, and maintains support for the sustainability agenda, both internal and external?

SRI[20] and the World Business Council for Sustainable Development[21] have a wealth of resources to support the CSO. In 2019, they analysed the IR web pages of 100 organisations and identified the following minimum practices:

- Having a named IR contact with responsibility for sustainability-related disclosures.
- Including a list of the sustainability research firms that rate the organisation, and the latest ratings awarded (if they exist).
- Including detailed sustainability data (report and callouts on the webpage) in a standardised format, allowing sustainability analysts to compare and interrogate them.

But from there, how do you go about turning sustainability into a source of competitive advantage?

Keys to success in IR and Sustainability

- Strive for one strategy – Integrate sustainability into corporate strategy to the greatest extent possible, and avoid referring to sustainability as a separate 'initiative' or 'programme' in the company. Integrate financial and sustainability information in IR materials. Your ESG narrative needs to shine through all materials that investors come across in their engagements with your IR colleagues. Dumping ESG information on investors in a separate slide deck while reference to ESG is completely absent from other corporate materials is a bad idea.

- Educate yourself – Know your industry, know your investor base and their interests, know your customers and community. How well-understood is the sustainability strategy already? Do the agencies rating you have an ESG contact? What do they understand and what is missing in the story? What are peers doing, how do you compare and where can you differentiate?

- Be transparent – Talk about the programmes, the timelines, and the challenges. List the measures you're going to take. If it's going to take time, say so.

- Be brief (and accurate) – You have to learn to use words wisely and deal in short sentences –there is not the time or attention span for long polemics. Don't rant to impress the investor, focus on the material items and topics you need support with. Your ESG strategy should build on a handful of ESG drivers in line with corporate purpose – it should be focused and authentic.

- Be balanced – Give equal consideration to both what you put on the market, as well as how you produce it. If you're producing an electric vehicle on the back of forced labour and resource depletion, it will affect your credibility. Equally, if you've established the best working conditions for staff who develop software but ignore that this software harms mental health, you're sabotaging yourself in the long term.

- Think about your channels – These include your sustainability report, annual report, investor days (both mainstream and ESG specialists) and other online content. Work with your IR team to establish goals and put together an IR communications strategy.
- If you're preparing for an IPO – Approach investors early. It takes time to build ESG maturity that is sufficient to approach more sophisticated investors. You will need to have all the basics of sustainability governance in place, plus factor in time for investor roadshows, 'early look' meetings with analysts, prepare IPO materials, establish a rating strategy, and other preparatory activities – a process that usually takes 9-12 months.
- Ask for help – Above all, investors have an interest to get involved and provide value. If appropriate, reach out to them, ask for help, ask for introductions to CEOs and CSOs of portfolio companies that have done well on sustainability.

Angela Jhanji, Managing Director at private equity firm EQT, explains: "I usually roll out a red carpet [meaning agency and quantified business case buy-in] for CSOs because I want them to succeed."

Activist shareholders

Those who are advocating FOR sustainability or calling out harm

It may be easy to think of these stakeholders as your 'friends' and, indeed, sustained pressure and tough questions at the AGM form a powerful incentive for executives to take an interest in sustainability. However, they can be a fickle ally and quick to turn on you if they perceive you're not making progress quickly enough. There is always a balance to be struck in your delivery, and there will always be those who have a more extreme view than you about what you should (or should not) be doing. Therefore, harness their enthusiasm but exercise caution.

Those advocating AGAINST sustainability

The markets are always fickle. At the time of writing this book, sustainability and ESG have faced some backlash, particularly in the US. It has become fashionable to decry sustainability efforts as 'woke' and non-value adding, and some investors and CEOs have dialled back their narratives accordingly (at least publicly). It was perhaps always going to be the case – after the initial excitement about sustainability, we could have expected some kind of reckoning as the conversation became more mature, increasingly complex, and the cost of the transition began to get clearer.

Activist investors usually act quickly and try to flip governance structures rather than the topic, so the counterpoint to this must be well thought through strategies linked strictly to material topics, real impact (both sustainable and economic), true innovation, and demonstrable progress. Consider (and this is more applicable in the US context) replacing 'sustainability' with less charged language, like 'resilience' or 'operational excellence'.

Summary

Changes in regulation plus an investor focus on sustainability have made Investor Relations a critical area for the CSO. Investors view sustainability as both a source of value creation and a risk management exercise and ESG issues are firmly part of their assessment, complementing the traditional financial drivers.

When assessing your organisation, investors will look at factors like your sector, operations, differentiation, sustainability report, governance and incentives, risk and due diligence, consistency, and the CSO's attitude.

To be successful in this area:

- Strive for a common business and sustainability strategy;
- Educate yourself;
- Be brief, but transparent, accurate, and balanced; and
- Think about your channels.

IR is a specialist area, where individual words have meaning, and a wrong step can have significant consequences. So, above all, ask for help when you need it and remember to stay positive and highlight the upside of all the great work your organisation is doing.

Chapter 10

Reporting

Sustainability reporting is a huge part of the CSO role. At the heart of it is the need to provide business intelligence about how tangible and intangible resources support or detract from value creation for the organisation and its stakeholders.

A common risk with the CSO role is losing sight of the purpose of ESG reporting and letting it turn your function in its complete service, where your work schedule is defined by the start and the end of the reporting season, with any and all ad-hoc reporting requests in between. Remember, reporting exists to help you and your organisation see its non-financial health, manage risks, and leverage opportunities that this information is pointing you towards. Later, external stakeholders will make decisions and form opinions about your organisation based on reported information, but the very first and the main user of this information is your management team.

That said, as an organisation, you owe it to yourself to build a strong foundation for ESG business intelligence, whether this is used for external reports or for ad-hoc management requests. Organisations that are black boxes to themselves and have only anecdotal examples of their performance on key ESG issues are not equipped to make decisions on cost optimisations, strong employee propositions, and risk management.

In addition, sustainability information about your organisation can show up in any number of places – in NGO reports and campaigns, in employee rating sites like Glassdoor, in regulatory non-compliance databases, in media, social media, industry benchmarks and ratings. Not all that information will be accurate and representative of what's really going on inside the organisation, so you have to be proactive in managing the 'source of truth', which should be your sustainability report and company website.

Why a new set of reports?

Sustainability information is often referred to as 'non-financial'. This term was used to distinguish information that was reported outside of financial statements and notes to financial statements and didn't carry monetary value.[1] This view has changed dramatically over the past few years, as our understanding of sustainability risks and what drives value creation has evolved. For example, intangible assets such as strong corporate culture and values, healthy and safe working conditions, and diversity can all contribute to a working environment that motivates employees towards stellar performance. Financial reporting, with its mainstream accounting principles such as GAAP, exclusively captures the monetised end-result of this performance – revenue – which is the ultimate lag indicator.

Non-financial reporting helps capture what might have led to such performance or what is potentially detracting from it and help your organisation act before risks materialise and the value is wasted. It's also an indicator of the ability to add future value. In other words, sustainability reporting exists to provide your management with a broader view on what contributes to value creation beyond assets registered in traditional financial accounting, help it make decisions about capital allocation and respond to risks.

Who's who in the reporting ecosystem

Sustainability reporting starts and ends with capital market regulators and policymakers. Long-term asset managers – like Blackrock, State Street, or Vanguard – and pension funds want to understand what the money they manage is invested in, and the resilience of those returns over time. Policymakers want to take stock of the impacts of individual companies, to understand how they relate to state targets and objectives at national and supra-national levels, and whether any corrective action is needed through new policies. For example, the EU has adopted a long-term strategy to be "climate-neutral" by 2050 under the EU Green Deal.[2] To understand how the EU is progressing on this goal, it needs information from companies operating in its economy about their sustainability performance. A similar mechanism applies to other governments and international entities.

Figure 6. Sustainability reporting ecosystem

Regulators and capital markets	Standard setters	Reporting company / undertaking / issuer	Assurance providers	Data aggregators and rating agencies	Data consumers / report users
	GRI ISSB IASB EFRAG FASB	Your company	The 'Big' 4 Independent assurance service providers	MSCI Bloomberg S&P Global Refinitiv Morningstar Sustainalytics	Capital markets Policy-makers Civil society & NGOs Employees Competitors
Set reporting requirements and transparency rules as the condition to participate in the market, access capital and public goods	Issue standards that companies can use to meet reporting requirements and transparency expectations	Public and private companies that are under obligation to report or who choose to report voluntarily	Proprietary service providers who validate the quality of reported information	Proprietary service providers who aggregate and rank reported information	Stakeholders who use reported information for decision-making

Capital markets and governments set high-level aspirations about the type of sustainability information they're looking for; standard setting organisations such as the Global Reporting Initiative (GRI) or the International Sustainability Standards Board (ISSB) develop standards with specific sustainability metrics, reporting principles and guidance on what and how to report. These organisations do not have regulatory status but some of them may be affiliated with governments or capital markets. For example, the European Financial Advisory Group (EFRAG) has been commissioned by the EU to develop the European Sustainability Reporting Standards as an annex to the Corporate Sustainability Reporting Directive.

These standards are then picked up by the companies (which are also sometimes referred to as 'undertakings' or 'report issuers') that use them to determine what information to report about their sustainability performance and how to measure it.

Before publishing the information, a company may wish, or be required to by law or its investors, to obtain limited or reasonable assurance on its sustainability data – an opinion of an external third-party auditor about the quality and reliability of the information, in exchange for a fee.

Next, data from an individual company needs to be put in market context – how do emissions from one company compare to its peers, are targets ambitious enough, how does it perform on overall sustainability governance? It's impossible for investors and policymakers to assess individual companies other than through active engagement with them, and there's simply not enough capacity in the system for these conversations to take place. This is where data aggregators and rating agencies such as MSCI, S&P Global, and Morningstar Sustainalytics come into play. These are commercial service providers whose business model is built on delivering ratings, rankings, and assessments of companies' performance, including sustainability performance. Arguably, this is an industry not without concerns about conflicts of interest, and how they affect the credibility of scores and opinions. At the time of writing, two major jurisdictions – the EU and the UK – have issued proposals to regulate ESG rating providers.[3]

Report information travels to users – any interested party who may need this information for decision-making purposes. Beyond capital markets and policymakers these can include:

- Consumers who want to know if they can trust the company brand on issues such as how and where the products are made and how people and nature are affected in the process.
- Employees and prospective employees who want to know how the company's modus operandi aligns with their moral compass and value system. For many potential recruits today, alignment between business strategy and sustainability is a critical decisive factor in their choice of workplace.
- Suppliers / business partners that might have their own sustainability performance targets for which they need input from their business ecosystem.
- Civil society / NGOs which assess whether companies are maintaining their licence to operate and social contract.
- Competitors that may use reported information to look for best practice and inspiration, insight into any challenges around common issues, some starting points for their own sustainability roadmap, and – yes – to benchmark their own performance and seek areas of differentiation.

Not every company goes through this exact process – some companies do not participate in ratings, some do not engage in assurance, some report metrics over and above regulatory requirements. However, this gives a general understanding of how disclosure works.

Getting to a baseline

Reporting and transparency have had a wild ride in sustainability. The pressure to 'be transparent' has grown proportionally to society's diminishing trust in corporations' ethical conduct. Sustainability teams organically became responsible for 'fixing' the gap through sustainability reporting, while many business leaders continued to underappreciate the quality of conversation that needed to happen and the accountability they needed to take for material topics. Sustainability teams remained unequipped to hold strategic discussions, with sustainability reporting being an afterthought for the rest of the organisation.

In the meantime, standards setting organisations and the ecosystem around non-financial reporting continued to raise the bar for quality disclosure and the regulation around it. Effectively, for the past 20 years, we have been slowly copying the model of financial reporting across to sustainability reporting. Arguably, companies have struggled to keep up with how quickly this system developed.

This led to a situation where the volume of disclosed data about all the great things companies were doing, wrapped in professional copywriting, and garnished with beautiful images of a perfect world became a mechanism for intentional and unintentional obfuscating in the pursuit of stakeholder trust. The reality is that it is still hard to find answers to the simplest questions in many such reports – which categories has the company included and excluded from its GHG emissions inventory, how were key metrics calculated, why were targets not achieved and what conclusions has the company drawn from this, and what are the most material topics for the company?

As a responsible CSO, you will need to create a reporting framework that genuinely informs, tracks, and explains what your organisation is doing. And you must try to do so without being swamped in the reporting, rather than the doing. Below are some challenges you will confront on the way to building a strong reporting practice, and how to get to a good baseline.

Data availability and quality

The current reality for most companies is that much ESG information is either not tracked, collected, and measured, or the quality of those processes is relatively poor. In financial reporting, data flows into dashboards via mature enterprise software systems. In ESG reporting, data sources are scattered across and outside the organisation. Take GHG emissions – the data for just this one number can easily come from up to 50 sources, including utility bills, procurement records, employee commute surveys, business travel booking systems, suppliers, and so on. Or ask your people team if they can produce gender pay gap data readily and you'll see how complex this is.

You will have to identify which data is available and which isn't even measured, map its primary sources, set up robust data tracking systems, and build data management processes. Some metrics, like the gender pay gap, require complex calculations and multiple data points, like male and female employees, their hourly wage, their functions, age and seniority, the benefits they receive and their monetary value. In a case like that, you will first have to develop a calculation methodology with all raw data inputs, before setting up a collection process.

Not everything that can be measured needs to be

You may often hear the adage that what gets measured gets managed[4] – a beloved phrase in the sustainability reporting community, conferences, and seminars. While it represents a fair argument, the flipside of this is that you can easily lose focus and confuse reporting with action. Come back to your material topics – you shouldn't be collecting data points on issues that are not on your matrix.

Say your employees want to see how many lives were positively affected through the corporate volunteering programme. If you are not an NGO and civic engagement is not the top strategic priority, corporate volunteering is arguably not a priority for you (albeit a motivational data point). You can always ask for volunteers to collect nice-to-haves and share them in a company newsletter, but don't waste time building sophisticated processes around data that tells you nothing of strategic importance. You can have too much data that is still not telling you about meaningful progress on material issues. You must refer back to the materiality and impact conclusions you drew with management and stay rigorous.

Management information and auditable data are not the same

Just like in financial reporting, there is data that supports management decision-making, and auditable external-facing reporting. In some cases, you need absolute precision and traceability, whereas in others, a good-enough metric to support a decision will suffice. If you're spending months finessing measurements and perfecting results to the digit, ask yourself if this is justified.

Let's take the pay gap example again. In this metric, percentage difference between female and male remuneration may be very small, yet it's exactly that difference that will tell you whether you have a problem with your remuneration practices and how big the problem is. On the other hand, if you're obsessing about getting an 80% response rate for an employee commute survey, when the largest share of your emissions comes from energy used in manufacturing facilities, or if you have no intention to provide green commute options to staff, then perhaps you can use a rough estimate or proxy to complete your carbon accounting calculation instead. If you explain the omissions, assumptions, and estimations you used, this can be acceptable.

Make a judgement where it's worth putting time into very precise measurements, because investments, budgets, incentives, and interventions will be attached to the conclusions these measurements give you.

Be prepared to hold fire either way

However much you disclose, stakeholders will always challenge you on that information. Don't expect that disclosure will give you protection against criticism even on issues where you think you're doing well. Some might find your disclosed actions not ambitious enough, some will challenge you on completeness of data, others will use any deficiencies they can find in your management practices to create public campaigns or even file litigation cases.

Indeed, transparency can mean that you're sometimes the 'tall poppy' – ironically, by drawing attention to what you're doing, it leaves you open to criticism. Some of these issues result from unrealistic expectations of companies and lack of understanding of their internal reality, but this doesn't mean that withholding information is the path forward.

If you have taken the effort to understand and measure the impacts, if the company has set challenging but achievable goals, built robust governance and management practices to address them, with FTEs and budget attached to execution, and it's the maximum you can do, then hold the line and be prepared to defend it. If there are material topics you haven't connected the dots on yet, be transparent about this, disclose your plans and timeline to address this, and be prepared to report on progress next year.

Stakeholders may forgive you if you need more time, but they will quickly recognise if you're using this as an excuse for not doing anything at all. On the flipside, robust, honest disclosure on contentious issues can elicit dialogue, give critical insight into how difficult it actually is to 'fix' an issue, lead to powerful coalitions and partnerships, and give peers a reference point for how to deal with similar issues.

Internal controls

We're thankfully past the point when sustainability reports were treated as promotional marketing materials to highlight the good projects companies were doing. The definitions of what makes for material disclosure have become stricter, the review of that disclosure is legally regulated, and the penalties for poor disclosure and greenwashing are real and significant.

Just like a company wouldn't play around with its financial disclosure, the same has become true for sustainability. In France, the government introduced a jail sentence for company directors for non-compliance with the requirements of the Corporate Sustainability Reporting Directive.[5] Most jurisdictions have introduced mandatory assurance of disclosed sustainability information, and this necessitates the need for rigorous internal controls.

When performing assurance, auditors need to be able to follow the reported information to the source and reconcile it with supporting evidence, calculation methodologies, and assumptions used along the way. Is data entered manually, sourced from existing

ERP systems, or third parties? Is its manipulation prone to error? Is it complete? Are definitions aligned with those prescribed by legal reporting requirements? Who validates the data, and at what stages of the data chain? Is there a risk of material misstatement, such as fewer GHG emissions disclosed than emitted in the reporting year?

These questions fall under the ESG Controller's mandate – an emerging function responsible for setting up ESG data lineage and data governance and building on the principles that exist in financial reporting. This function will sit either in your sustainability team or may be an existing professional from finance and internal controls, upskilled on ESG. You will form a close partnership with this role, as you build internal controls.

The Committee of Sponsoring Organizations (COSO) is the leading organisation that develops and updates guidelines on internal controls for business since 1992. In 2023 it published supplemental guidance for Effective Internal Control Over Sustainability Reporting (ICSR), [6] meant to "build trust and confidence in ESG / sustainability reporting, public disclosures, and enterprise decision-making".[7]

ICSR concludes that sustainability information needs to be reliable and prepared with internal control processes and board governance and oversight, similar to the processes used for financial data. We recommend starting by assessing the state of your internal controls using the list below, adopted from the COSO framework.

10 questions to review internal controls

1. How frequently is sustainability data collected? Can it be collected and reported internally in a timely and cost-effective manner?

2. Is there clear ownership and accountability for the collection, maintenance, validation, and reporting / communication of sustainability information, and are appropriate processes in place? For example, if you were to quickly look up numbers on workforce diversity or GHG emissions, would you know who to go to, and what quality of information would you find?

3. Is sustainability information integrated into existing data management and reporting systems? Does the organisation use technology to establish and maintain data lineage, access information, and connect to primary sources, such as API integrations or physical meters onsite? What software providers does it use for data collection and how are those integrated into the organisation's tech stack?

4. Is data lineage (the connection to original sources) maintained throughout information systems and the supply chain? For example, can you trace back the GHG emissions number reported in the last report to the sources of primary data?

5. Are data collection and reporting processes well documented, including controls to prevent or detect misstatements? If an auditor was to run an assurance test on a sample of sustainability information, would they be able to navigate the process with minimum input from your team?

6. Are key definitions, calculation methodologies, assumptions and omissions documented?

7. Are relevant connections and dependencies maintained and preserved between sustainable business information

and other types of information? For example, do supplier tenders and contracts include relevant sustainability questions or criteria, such as disclosure of their GHG emissions?

8. Have internal audit, the compliance team, the CFO team, and relevant third parties such as an assurance provider reviewed the quality of sustainability information, supporting processes, and the system of internal control? Were there findings? Were they actioned?

9. Is there confidence in data quality? Would a CEO or CFO feel enabled to sign a public report with confidence or feature in a TV add, like Apple's Tim Cook in its 'Mother Nature' commercial?[8]

10. Is decision-useful sustainability information integrated into the key analyses supporting management decisions, such as those related to resource allocation, product development, mergers and acquisitions, compliance, and risk management? If sustainability is a parallel, unconnected process to the rest of organisation's activities, it is unlikely that you will find strong internal controls.

What makes for a good report?

There's a certain excitement in writing a sustainability report – you want to highlight the good things your organisation has done throughout the year, the projects and initiatives, and the results. You also need to cover any mandatory requirements, following strict reporting conventions. Together these can make for a very long report with the risk of losing focus on the most important information. Stakeholders will have varying appetites for detail, but generally, they want to be able to quickly navigate the report to see that the organisation has genuinely addressed material topics and met its commitments and targets.

Several established reporting principles[9] exist to guide organisations in writing reports such that they inform stakeholders effectively about the organisation's sustainability performance, and don't subject the organisation to risks around misrepresentation of information. To achieve this, reported information needs to meet the following characteristics:

- Relevance – Containing information that is relevant for the reader's decision-making and assessment of the organisation's performance on material topics, e.g., reporting on targets for Scope 1 and 2 emissions but not on targets for Scope 3 emissions (the largest contributor of emissions for most organisations) if climate change has been identified as a material topic.
- Completeness – Not omitting critical pieces of information, which if left out would skew the reader's understanding of the organisation's impacts and how it is addressing them, e.g., omitting certain entities, targets and actions, changes to strategy, and progress.
- Balance – Fair representation of both positive and negative impacts, without manipulating information and wording in a way that highlights positive impacts and downplays negative impacts or lack of progress. This is important because only an honest discussion of shortcomings and their causes can help move the industry forward.
- Accuracy – Descriptions of how the data has been gathered, measured, calculated, what omissions, assumptions and estimations have been used and on what basis, and the definitions. Accurate data doesn't mean perfect data – it's okay to use estimations where you can't source the data, as long as the assumptions and proxies are appropriate and explained.
- Clarity – Writing and presenting information in a way that is easy to understand. Think about your audience – what

language do they speak, on what devices will they read the report, how much time do they have? Avoid overuse of sustainability jargon and abbreviations, or include a glossary. Help readers navigate the report quickly by providing graphical cues, call outs, and a table of contents with working links. Distinguish between new information and 'standing' information that rolls from one report to the next.

- Conciseness – In spite of executives looking for the 'thud' factor with ESG reporting, nobody has time to read 200-page reports. In fact, we're rapidly moving to a world with automated data-scraping and digital tagging, where all those creative agency fees will be a waste of your budget. It's true that sustainability reports have a lot of educational value, but don't beat around the bush – sure, give some context but then jump into what you need to report. Remember, the more information you give, the less of it sticks.

- Comparability – Reporting information in a way that it can be compared between years / over time, and with other peer companies in the sector. This means using the same measurement units and accepted international metrics year in, year out, maintaining consistency in information presentation and calculation methodologies, or explaining how they have changed and presenting restatements.

- Verifiability – Having internal controls as the backbone of your report. Verifiability implies that if anyone – the auditor, the board, an employee, or an NGO – was to pick a number or a statement from your report, you would be able to offer a trail of how that number was collected.

Planning the reporting process

Two things will define your reporting deadlines, from which all other planning will follow. First are any legal reporting obligations to file sustainability information either separately or as part of annual reporting in the jurisdiction(s) where your organisation operates. Annual reporting is always aligned to annual general meetings of shareholders (AGMs) and securities filings. These events usually fall in March or April for calendar year companies and may fall on other dates for fiscal year companies.

Second is the organisation's choice or commitments to voluntary reporting, many of which have set submission deadlines. Voluntary reporting may apply if your organisation:

- Is a signatory to the United Nations Global Compact (UNGC);[10] reporting cycle between April and July;
- Is a signatory to the United Nations Principles for Responsible Investing (UN PRI);[11] reporting cycle between June and September, with reports released in November / December;
- Is invited to participate or decides to participate in the S&P Global Corporate Sustainability Assessment (CSA), the scores from which inform over 200 indices produced by S&P Global, including the Dow Jones Sustainability Indices (DJSI), S&P ESG Indices and the Paris-Aligned and Climate Transition (PACT);[12] the invitations to participate are sent to companies between February and June;
- Is subject to the Global Real Estate Sustainability Benchmark (GRESB)[13] reporting; submissions are accepted between April and June, with assessments released in September / October;
- Has decided to report to the CDP;[14] in 2024, the response window will be June-September, with potential further

revisions in 2025 due to the consolidation with the IFRS Foundation;

- Falls under other state benchmarks – these are different to the 'big' mandatory ESG reporting requirements (such as the CSRD in Europe, the US SEC, the UK's Companies' Act, or the Singapore Stock Exchange) as they include stand-alone thematic disclosure of ESG-related information to various governmental agencies, such as the gender pay gap, employee commute, or energy consumption. These requirements vary greatly across jurisdictions, so work with your legal and compliance teams to determine what's in scope for your company.

If you're preparing voluntary reporting in addition to statutory, in most cases you will be using the same underlying data (good news!), re-packaging and adjusting it to fit respective submission platforms and forms. Whatever the ultimate report publication or submission dates you're working towards, your yearly planning in the lead up to it should have four phases – (1) gap assessment and process set up, (2) data collection, (3) report production and publication, and (4) reflection and improvement.

Phase 1. Gap assessment and process set up (three months)

Assess what reporting obligations apply to your organisation, what voluntary reporting it would benefit from, or any reporting your organisation committed to in the past. For example, if the organisation signed any charters like the UNGC or the UNPRI. Ensure these are the right commitments to make, and that the organisation isn't either missing some key ones, or over-reporting in areas that are less of a priority.

Based on your material topics, determine standards and metrics that you (have to) use, and the data you need to gather. Identify data owners, take stock of the quality, availability, accessibility of data and the data gaps, and evaluate existing data management systems and tools. Review whether reporting software is needed and, if so, scope out the market, though you shouldn't wait with data collection and will likely only get in time for next year's reporting.

Set up the data collection process. Assemble a team of key topic and data owners and communicate the reporting plan and process. The kick-off is crucial to get right. If your organisation is new to reporting entirely, it follows that most of the internal stakeholders coming to the table will be too, and they may not appreciate the volume of work you're about to introduce. You must ensure buy-in for the project as important, time-sensitive, and value-adding for their own objectives and for the organisation. Take the time to explain the reporting requirements as well as the role reporting plays in the bigger picture of transparency, value creation and transformation.

Think about your report's structure and table of contents, format, the interaction with the company website, and intended report users. For bigger reporting obligations, like the CSRD in Europe, consider holding a workshop with an external consultant to really deep dive into its topics and nuances. Good preparation is essential so that you can hit the ground running with data collection. Bring humour – you'll need some laughter and energy to sustain your team's attention through all those excel sheets.

Discuss with your CFO when to seek management and board approval and work back from the reporting deadlines to the appropriate time of the executive committee and board meetings.

Phase 2. Data collection, checking, and testing (three-to-six months)

If you're reporting for the first time, a lot of the data may not have been tracked before so this process can take three to six months. In year one you're doing your 'best efforts' reporting, i.e., doing what you can and using what's available, setting expectations and processes for fuller reporting in year two. This means you may start with a higher ambition and scope of metrics but realise in the process that you need to scale down until you can source better data.

Register gaps where data collection processes and internal controls are lacking or poor. Have a plan for how you're going to address omissions and assumptions where data is unavailable. For example, energy bills usually come with a three-month delay. In this case, it's okay to make assumptions but you will have to restate the information the following year.

Be prepared that there will be unknowns and choices to make as you assemble the data from across the organisation. Be ready to chase and remind people, and to dig into tricky issues related to measurement methodologies together.

If you already have a sustainability report, data points should be a matter of an update through existing processes, unless you're reporting on new material topics and need to collect new data points. At this level, you should try to fit the data collection process within three months or less. Best practice is for sustainability reports to publish within no more than three months after the close of the financial or calendar year (depending on which you use).

In both scenarios, start populating your report in parallel to data coming in. Don't wait until the data gathering phase is over, but rather try to already set a general template and draft sections that are independent of performance data, like the description of your materiality assessment process or stakeholder engagement process. Have respective topic owners review their sections if your team is in charge of writing or have them complete their sections so you can start looking at the full draft.

Phase 3. Report production and publication (two months)

Finalise the draft text and start the review cycle with the management board, financial reporting team, and your legal office. The board will have to sign off on the report and need ample time to provide feedback.

Prepare the internal and external communication plan with your internal communications and marketing teams. Think of the platforms you're going to publish and promote your report on, the promotion schedule, creative assets, and press releases especially if you're working for a large, publicly listed company. Make any adjustments to your website and any public materials.

Think about which achievements and numbers are truly worth being emphasised and promoted to your stakeholders, and embed them into your communication narratives, company decks, and other corporate materials. Host a launch event with staff – celebrate your achievements and create a platform for discussion. Consider putting the company forward for any relevant awards if appropriate.

Phase 4. Reflect and improve (three-to-four months)

After publication, come back to any gaps parked during data collection, review the overall reporting set up, internal controls, and action changes and improvements. This is also a good time for materiality assessment refreshers which will determine any changes to next year's report topics. If you decided that you need reporting software, now would be the time to procure and set it up.

Assurance

Assurance is an essential component for those organisations who want to give their stakeholders confidence that the reported information is credible, reliable, and free of errors. In simple terms, the process of assurance involves an organisation ('the responsible party', 'preparer' or 'client')[15] asking an assurance provider ('practitioner'[16]) to give an independent opinion on a subject matter, in exchange for a fee. These subjects can include selected sustainability metrics, the full sustainability report, or internal controls and processes. The assurance provider will perform a set of assessment procedures on the subjects agreed with the organisation and issue a written conclusion (assurance report or management letter) that the information is reliable.

Organisations subject to CRSD reporting in the EU or to the SEC Climate Rule in the US are required to obtain assurance of reported sustainability information. In jurisdictions where assurance of sustainability information is not a regulatory or legal requirement, it might be beneficial or requested in the following instances:

- Investors may request assurance of selected sustainability metrics important to them as part of their due diligence before deciding to make, hold or increase investment.
- Boards may request assurance of selected sustainability KPIs to before deciding to introduce or award sustainability-linked executive pay systems.
- Company management may wish to validate sustainability measurements before approving any targets and sustainability strategies.

- Sustainability teams can benefit from testing / validating the quality of their data management systems and internal controls to minimise errors and restatements of information.
- The organisation can benefit from increasing the overall trust in the credibility of sustainability information before it flows further across the organisation's communication channels to stakeholders, e.g., in internal presentations, company website, or social media and marketing. Early detection and remediation of an error is far preferable to having to roll back a previous statement or report.

Essentially, assurance is a process to validate that the sustainability data management foundation you have in place is free of errors and flaws and is future proof. Most assurance providers offer a pre-assurance readiness test, which can be a helpful step for first-time reporters to fortify the sustainability data house and internal controls.

All of this said, assurance does come at a cost, which will depend on the type of assurance (limited or reasonable), size and geographical spread of the organisation, number and extent of selected subjects to assure, and the overall maturity of sustainability governance and internal controls. The bigger, more complex the organisation, and less mature the controls, the higher the fee. Smaller organisations who wish to assure just one metric, like GHG emissions, may start at USD 15,000–20,000 while large multinationals can pay up to USD 1 million for reasonable assurance on a full sustainability report. Keep in mind that currently CSRD requires limited assurance of sustainability statements, but the EU is considering transitioning CSRD provisions to mandatory reasonable assurance in 2028.

Limited vs. reasonable assurance

Broadly, the assurance provider will follow the data trail and governing processes related to the subject in question – a KPI or a narrative claim – to their primary source or starting point to reconcile and validate the quality of these processes. The extent of checks an auditor will perform depends on the type of assurance – reasonable (more extensive) or limited. In limited assurance, the assurance provider will perform fewer or different tests or use a smaller sample dataset.

In limited assurance, the assurance provider may:[17]

- examine the calculation methodologies to understand key assumptions used, limitations and omissions;
- conduct interviews with management, contractors and suppliers, or business partners to understand what processes were in place during the reporting period for which performance is described;
- examine and test the systems and processes in place to generate, aggregate and report the data;
- review primary data used for calculating the metrics and any supporting documentation; and / or
- recalculate the metric using the methods the company has described to use.

In addition to these tests, in reasonable assurance, the assurance provider may:[18]

- test the operating effectiveness of systems and controls;
- assess the significant assumptions and judgments made in the preparation of the metrics;
- assess and test the source information used to generate the metrics;

- in case of narrative claims related to sustainability governance procedures, inspect board meeting minutes, terms of reference of board committees, or job descriptions; and / or
- cover an entire report if that is the subject matter of the assurance engagement, rather than just individual metrics.

Say, a company commissions limited assurance of its pay gap metric. The engagement will likely start with a discussion with employee(s) responsible for preparing the information to identify how the data has been compiled, the calculation methodology, sources of primary data used for the calculation, and any changes to the methodology from last year and the reasons. Then, the assurance provider may review data collection systems to establish how complete and accurate primary input data is, e.g., are all employees' salaries captured, are some groups excluded, how is data manipulated (e.g., any manual currency conversions). They will then issue a conclusion that the metric is indeed plausible and discuss results with management.

How to select an assurance provider and commission a tender

Assurance is a market like any other, with different levels of service quality available. With the increase in regulation and the CSRD in place, the demand for assurance services has increased, and there may not be enough capacity in the short-term to support it. Some teams are stronger, some less so. Everyone is upskilling. Consider the following factors when scoping out providers and options:

- Your needs – Who is the ultimate user of the information intended for assurance and what are your goals with them? Does investment depend on sustainability KPIs, do you want to learn how to improve internal processes, do you need to inform an internal target, or do you need to meet minimum compliance?

- Knowledge and expertise – Do they have specialist knowledge on the subject in question, what's their track record on assurance of this subject, can they demonstrate continuous learning on the subject?
- Reputation and independence – What do others say about them, what are their own governance systems? Do family, friends, or former colleagues work at the assurance services company? Are there any shared financial interests, like holding shares in your company? Does the assurance provider also supply advisory services related to prospective assurance subjects, or audit financial statements, and are these the same teams?
- Cultural fit and availability – Are you confident the assurance provider will be available for you and has the capacity to conduct engagement within your deadlines? If their team needs to fly in for every engagement, this will either drive up the bill or may reduce the frequency of engagement. If their team is too small for the scope of engagement, you risk missing important deadlines.
- Brand name – Are you looking for a 'big name' firm to lend their name to the audit and give credibility? Or looking for experts in a particular field, which may lead you towards a boutique organisation.
- Fee – Generally, the more experienced the assurance provider, the higher the quality of their service and the fee. Equally, the more effective and quicker they may work. Reasonable assurance is always more expensive than limited. Ask if the fee is flat or an indication, what's included (e.g., type of work, number of engagements, travel time and communication). You can manage some of these costs by preparing clear records and process memos and helping the assurer navigate your systems.

- Professional indemnity insurance – As with lawyers and accountants, your provider should hold PII to indemnify them (and you) in the event of a subsequent error or claim.

Summary

Reporting is a huge task for the CSO and there's a challenge in ensuring it doesn't become the only task. Standardisation and automation will be your friends here, as will aligning to existing financial reporting processes and timelines. Think quality over quantity and start small – better to report a smaller amount of factual data than a mountain of dubious assertions which may leave you exposed later. This work, while requiring a lot of up-front effort, should somewhat settle with time, but will never be done – it will continue to evolve in line with the organisation.

Having covered the reporting process, we will now discuss how to communicate about your work externally.

Chapter 11

Communications and marketing

Communicating with the outside world about your organisation's sustainability efforts is an important task – and a double-edged sword. Communicate too little, and you risk not informing your stakeholders about the work you're doing, failing to gain energy and excitement for pioneering new initiatives, or triggering a wider discussion on contentious topics that moves the industry forward. Communicate over-zealously, and you risk being the 'tall poppy', acting as a sitting duck for critics to slaughter your efforts, label you a greenwasher, or even use the information against you legally.

Transparency requires laser sharp focus on internal coherence between what your company does and what it says about itself to the world.

In 2023, a Swedish press bureau led an investigation of retailer H&M's recycling claims[1] – a programme the brand promoted in stores and online. The journalists tagged 10 whole and clean H&M garments with tracking devices, deposited them in the recycling bins in the stores, and then followed the clothes digitally. The result contradicted the claims H&M made about treating clothes in an environmentally friendly and responsible way – together, the 10 garments have travelled one and a half laps around the earth, none remained in Sweden, and three ended up in the regions in the Global South with unregulated waste management systems. H&M responded to say that "the H&M group is categorically against clothes becoming waste and it goes completely against our work to create a more circular fashion industry".[2]

This is not an isolated case – the Climate Change Litigation Database[3] lists 56 cases against corporations for misleading advertisements in the past four years alone. Examples include cases against environmental claims made on companies' Facebook pages, TV ads, posters, and other outlets that violate commercial laws around fair competition and fair advertising and mislead consumers into thinking that products or their behaviours (like travelling on an airline that is 'climate neutral') are more environmentally friendly than they truly are, or claims that are outright false.

At best, these cases are examples of a fragmented approach to sustainability and uncoordinated action internally, where compliance, sustainability, marketing, and operations are not working together. For companies that are genuinely trying to transform and do good, such incidents can be devastating and lose hard-earned stakeholder trust. At worst, some organisations take the cynical view that deceptive communications are a calculated risk, perpetuated by a lax and uncertain regulatory environment,[4] market pressure to 'differentiate' on sustainability, constant pressure from NGOs and activists, and internal culture and incentives. In a hyper-transparent world, these excuses no longer work.

'Green communications' have at times functioned as means to promote 'business as usual' but with a green sticker – a company would promote an environmentally-friendly product line or social project, but for the rest, its business strategy and its decision-making would carry on as normal, disconnected from sustainability. In today's social context, where trust in companies is generally diminished, consumers and other stakeholders are looking for a coherent and consistent narrative about the organisation as a whole – not just the 'green stuff' its sustainability department is doing on the sidelines.

As the CSO, you have two tasks here. The first is to create overall alignment between corporate communications and sustainability – not just inserting bits of sustainability content here and there, but really anchoring the synergy between purpose and sustainability in your strategy and in the core of internal and external communications. If you have done the hard work on materiality assessment with your leadership, and have truly set the organisation on the sustainability transformation pathway, this should be achievable.

The second task is to maintain basic communications hygiene – have your facts and evidence lined up when publishing any numbers and results, ensure traceability of claims, be transparent about shortcomings, stay clear of communicating on issues that are not your material topics, educate the team on basic greenwashing mistakes.

Again, sustainability is really integrated into your company strategy, if:

- you have built proper internal controls and governance processes around managing material topics;
- are very clear about topics outside your control; and
- are not using communications and marketing as means to build a "corporate sustainability theatre"[5] to get stakeholders to like your brand.

If you achieve all three of the above, you should be well positioned to communicate about your sustainability work constructively, and for that to positively serve your brand.

When communications go wrong – greenwashing

When organisations are called out on inconsistencies in sustainability communications, they will usually be accused of greenwashing, the practice of issuing false or misleading claims about sustainability or environmental compliance / performance.

Greenwashing helps no one; it distracts, gaslights attention away from true problems and progress, destroys trust, and drags your organisation down to repair the damage. In time, it will ultimately be value-destroying for organisations that, once exposed, will face legal penalties and struggle to regain credibility from an increasingly informed and unforgiving audience.

Greenwashing claims can pop-up anywhere and travel far – from onboarding materials that employees use as a reference point for individual social media activity, to product packaging, company websites, sustainability reports, public speaking, and all forms of advertising. But in fact, unless a deliberate choice, drivers of greenwashing can have simple origins, and most come down to internal misalignment:

- Loose ends / sloppiness – Rushed communications and drafting, resulting in factual errors and omissions.
- Lack of process – An inadequate review and sign off procedure, e.g., legal team is excluded from review, or the sustainability team 'hands over' the material to non-experts in the marketing department who change the text guided by their own style guide.
- Lack of sustainability communication guidelines – Relevant for large organisations with a high-volume and

variety of product output on the market, where individual category managers write product descriptions.

- Goodwill – The simple desire from employees to celebrate and promote the good work the company is doing, unaware of the definitions and legal repercussions attached to using certain sustainability buzzwords.

Beyond these basic factors, organisations may greenwash because they have no clear focus in their sustainability strategy that helps them distinguish between issues to speak up on and respond to, and those to ignore, especially when they are pressured by civil society and NGOs. Stakeholders may not recognise the extent and limitations of your organisation's influence, assuming that if you are a corporation, you're all powerful. Again, your materiality assessment should lead the way in helping you distinguish between issues that are of relevance and all the others, as well as articulating this position to the outside world.

How organisations greenwash

There's no one greenwashing taxonomy, but we've compiled some common examples of greenwashing on a product level and as general communications tactics.[6, 7] Treat these as a list of things to avoid.

On a product level:

1. Selective disclosure / 'red herring' – Claiming a product is 'green' based on a narrow set of properties and ignoring impacts occurring at other life cycle stages of a product. For example, a claim boasting paper made from sustainably harvested wood, but omitting impacts related to its highly polluting manufacturing process.
2. Lack of definition / vagueness – Claims too broad and ambiguous, e.g., something being 'green', 'eco', 'clean',

'fair'. These terms have earned a positive association, but they can mean a universe of things, and without a definition, they are meaningless.

3. Unproven claims – Making claims that are not backed up by easily accessible supporting evidence, like third-party certification, privately commissioned or public studies.

4. Outright lying – For example, claiming something is 'good' for the environment, when it is just a little 'less bad' than it was before.

5. The non-sequitur – Building on one valid claim to make another, unproven, claim. For example, a company claiming that a product has 'less sugar', and then claiming that therefore this product improves health.

As a general 'green communications' tactic:

6. Rallying behind a lower standard – Setting the bar really low and then celebrating when you hit it.

7. Deceptive imagery – Windmills, solar panels, nature landscapes... honestly, consumers deserve better, unless you're showing a photo of an actual solar PV installation on the roof of your facility.

8. Bait and switch – Offering a sustainable product as a niche offering, more expensive than all other non-sustainable offerings.

9. Greenlighting – Directing all attention to a sustainability initiative or green features of a product, while diverting attention from other poor sustainability practices.

10. Greenhushing – Underplaying, under-reporting, and obfuscating sustainability data.

11. Greenrinsing – Changing targets right before communicating on progress, therefore avoiding accountability.

12. Greenshifting – Shifting the blame and the work on the consumer, e.g., flying less, changing behaviours.

13. Greencrowding – Joining alliances, pledges, coalitions to boast collective action and hide behind it.

'Sustainable', 'biodegradable', 'recyclable', 'eco-friendly', 'environmentally friendly'.

We've grown to use these terms to suggest that a product is good for the environment. They were great at marketing and positioning products towards the 'conscious consumer' segment, yet they are very misleading about the true impacts of the product. For example, something can be biodegradable or recyclable, but this doesn't mean the product will be recycled nor be disposed of correctly so it can decompose. It also doesn't say anything about how the product was produced and the full scope of impacts along its life cycle. For example, sugarcane is a source of biodegradable plastic packaging, but its production is sometimes associated with grave environmental and human rights issues.

Claims like 'eco-friendly' or 'sustainable' are examples of lazy marketing: they are too vague and non-descriptive and open themselves up to legal challenges.

Instead of using these terms without appropriate consideration, carry out a full life cycle assessment of your product and determine its impact. Be clear about what the actual sustainability benefit is and provide contextual information. Support your claims with evidence, like results of the life cycle impact assessments, and check your communication with the legal team.

Regulatory developments

Predictably, we knew that some of the early hype around sustainability could encourage people to overstate their green credentials for marketing purposes. We're now in a 'second wave' where regulation is catching up to this fact and, in some jurisdictions, imposing penalties for over-stating or mis-stating its sustainability achievements.

For example, the EU has acknowledged that claiming to be green and sustainable has become a competitive factor, with green products registering greater growth than standard products in the EU in recent years.[8] In response, the European Commission published a proposal in 2023 for the EU Green Claims Directive that would: (1) outline the first set of detailed EU rules on the substantiation of voluntary green claims, and (2) target instances of alleged 'greenwashing'.[9] The directive is expected to enter into force between 2024-2027, and to be enforced via penalties, confiscation of revenue and temporary exclusion from public procurement.

To give some colour, the proposed directive includes the following requirements for claiming sustainability benefits of a product and general provisions:

- A ban on displaying a sustainability label that is not based on a certification scheme or established by public authorities;
- A ban on generic environmental claims used in marketing where performance cannot be demonstrated in accordance with EU Ecolabel or officially recognised ecolabelling schemes in the Member States;
- A ban on making environmental claims about an entire product, when the supporting evidence for such a claim only concerns a certain aspect of the product;
- Specification if the claim relates to the whole product or part of the product, or all activities of the company or part of the activities;
- Reliance on widely recognised scientific evidence;
- Proof that environmental impacts, aspects, or performance are significant from a life cycle perspective;
- Consideration of all environmental aspects of impacts that are significant to identify environmental performance;
- proof that the claim is not equivalent to requirements imposed by law, e.g., labelling a product with a claim that it doesn't contain chemicals that are banned by law anyway;
- Evidence of comparisons to other products or companies in the relevant sector;
- Clarification of impact trade-offs;
- Clarification if offsets are used with further detail;
- Time-bound commitment for improvements inside own operations and value chains for any claims about future performance;
- Clarification of the role of the consumer in using the product that is necessary for the accuracy of the claim (e.g., water-friendly dry detergents);
- Availability of any supporting information about the claim alongside it, via weblink, QR code, or other means;
- Prohibition of comparative claims made against products no longer in sale;
- Prohibition of aggregated scores (i.e., a total 'environmental' score across a number of metrics); and
- Regular review of, and updates to, environmental claims no later than five years from the date of the underlying studies or calculations.

There are many other regulatory developments around the globe at the moment. CMS, a global advisory service, offers a comprehensive overview of those for organisations to monitor.[10]

Designing your communications strategy

We started the chapter with the argument that sustainability communications should keep you out of trouble. Being transparent and balanced about achievements and misses and providing accurate and clear evidence of your sustainability claims should provide you with some ammunition against the critics. However, there's so much more that a thoughtful approach to communications can do for your organisation. It can invite discussion on contentious topics and create a tailwind for norms and behaviours you're trying to shift. It can help you find partners and allies from unexpected places, and it can help drive engagement with your cause.

In general, corporate sustainability communications:

- are tools to inform your customers about the harms and benefits of your product, and balanced progress on sustainability responsibilities;
- should be grounded in accountability for how you fuel consumption, e.g., on human insecurities and vulnerabilities;
- can be catalysts to trigger reflection on norms and behaviours, and support change;
- should treat all recipients with respect, and not take advantage of opportunities arising from information asymmetries or lack of expertise among recipients; and
- are a means to articulate your sustainability profile to investors and other stakeholders.

Salesforce turned its sustainability communications into a thought leadership tool. The company didn't spare any effort in sharing insights and learnings about its sustainability journey, from articles about how to start carbon accounting, to white papers on decarbonising the IT infrastructure and organising a low-carbon work from home environment – something its people had to go through themselves.

Oatly turned the discussion on plant-based milk on its head with its daring, brilliant, and consistent communications including its "Wow, no cow" ads.

Patagonia is always one step ahead in challenging the industry to do better, but also reflect on the real challenges of changing the status quo.

What these companies have in common is that sustainability is part of their purpose and is fully integrated into strategy. But beyond this, their communication stands out because it has clear goals and focus, substance, consistency, an authentic tone, and content that is relevant to the chosen audience. In the end, these efforts probably converted into sales and new customers, but we believe their true value is much greater and it's about raising the bar in the industry, shifting norms, and supporting the sustainability transition.

Consider the following aspects when building your sustainability communications strategy.

Define objectives

What are you trying to achieve? Is there an issue you need to draw attention to because the status quo is not sustainable, and the industry norms are limiting change? Is there something you're doing particularly well in how you're addressing your material topics that you want to use as a reference point to help others in the industry and position yourself as the leader? Is there trust to repair based on how you have communicated sustainability efforts previously? Do you need to create basic awareness that your organisation has a sustainability strategy? All of these goals will require unique approaches and can change over time as your sustainability function and strategy evolve. Note that we're taking a broader view on communications where it's not just the vehicle to target the conscious consumer segment.

Assess status quo

If you're coming to an existing sustainability function, assess the sustainability communication processes, assets and effectiveness in relation to defined goals. At a very minimum, the organisation should have an internal sustainability page with assets for staff for public use, and an external sustainability webpage that acts a single source of truth for stakeholders.

Look at the ownership, cadence, and format of past sustainability communications: What has been effective, and what can be parked / revisited? Are assets up to date and do they reflect your material topics? Who's in charge of creative and how does the process work? Does the company have any policies or guidelines on how to engage on social media and respond to various triggers? What partner websites is the organisation referenced / listed on and are those serving your communication objectives? Is the organisation working with a creative agency and are their services worth the money?

Plan and set KPIs

If you're the first CSO in the organisation, you'll need some time to settle and set the overall sustainability course. Communications may not be your immediate priority and that's fine – whatever you communicate outside will create a reaction, so best to speak up when you're ready.

That said, any piece of communication needs planning and lead time, from big marketing campaigns about a new product or initiative, to a blog article or social media post. Your creative team needs time to design visuals and they will likely have their own system for managing asset creation requests. Your comms team will have a publishing calendar that needs to have space for your announcements. If you're planning a bigger campaign, such as the release of an ESG report, you may wish to create a press release, engage media, create social media assets, and adjust the webpage. Think through these key dates and milestones in advance and create a plan with your Communications team. Think of the media channels, events and platforms where you need to be present to achieve your goals.

Set KPIs that are activity-based (e.g., number of customers / stakeholders reached, number of media campaigns), outcome-based (e.g., number of new followers on social media channels, # of leads converted into customers), and impact-based (e.g., percentage reduction in negative publicity from NGOs).

Create process / set responsibilities

Regardless of big ambitions, it's your responsibility to maintain basic communication hygiene. Is your organisation ready for transparency? You wouldn't want a minor mistake to tear down the hard work in setting up internal controls and sustainability governance. As we discussed, greenwashing is often unintentional, caused simply by a lack of understanding / attention to sustainability communications as a legal domain. People might have thought that they were just promoting the good work of the company.

Think about your organisation – how does sustainability information originate and travel to stakeholders? What path does it go through, and what checks are built along the way from capture to aggregation to presentation? You don't need to become the sustainability communication police or take away the freedom from others to do their jobs, but by installing some basic internal controls and procedures from the beginning, you can eliminate bigger problems later on.

It's a good idea to run a workshop / training with your communications and sustainability team on sustainability enablement or bring expertise from outside. For example, media and events company GreenBiz runs an annual Comms Summit,[11] a recent addition to its conference menu in response to growing demands from the sustainability community for guidance on how to communicate well and in compliance with emerging greenwashing laws. Train your teams on the basics of accurate sustainability communications, leveraging existing experience in financial reporting. There are many guides out there, and we have added a checklist below.

Experiment

Unless you're coming to an organisation with a strong, existing brand and a well-working communications machine, you will need time to feel out your audience. It's fine to experiment. Try new formats and channels, tease out thought provoking messages via A/B testing, try unconventional collaborations. If you're doing meaningful work that is connected to material topics, you can take the time to find your formula. Just remember, there will always be a digital trace for whatever you publish, so make sure evidence and numbers are always backing up any claims.

A communications checklist

Below, we outline a summary of how to try to avoid greenwashing in your communications.[12] These tips will act as a guide when scrutinising and inputting to your organisation's comms strategy:

1. Be honest and accountable.
2. Do not communicate on topics unless and until your own organisation is making a meaningful effort in the area.
3. Do not under-communicate the harm that your organisation is currently causing – better to admit being part of the problem and to be transparent about your efforts to improve.
4. Do not over-communicate about a small, non-material project – re-cycling your coffee cups is not much use if you are still mass-burning carbon and destroying communities.
5. Be clear about the sustainability benefit your product offers, substantiate claims with facts, and keep them up to date. Review any claims with the legal team.
6. Use established labels for your industry (e.g. Fairtrade) – do not subscribe to inferior or unproven badges and baubles.
7. Beware of claiming that something is 'better' for the environment – most products have a negative impact in some way. If you can't substantiate it, don't claim it.
8. By all means, donate to and sponsor good causes, but don't use these as a fig-leaf for your own practices – the bulk of your efforts must go on improving your own performance.

Summary

Your role as CSO is to keep an eye on substance over form. If it feels wrong to you, it probably is. Your fundamental goal in your organisation is to change the culture, so people understand what true sustainability means in their context, they sign up to what it's going to take to get there, and they don't fall for quick wins, gimmicks or short-term publicity stunts along the way. If you're having to act as the gatekeeper, stopping comms going out the door at the last minute, know that you need to move your focus further up in the organisation, building true understanding and buy-in from your stakeholders.

This concludes our section covering the technical aspects of the CSO role. We've looked at materiality, impact, policies, risk management, investor relations, reporting, communications and marketing.

The next section is about pulling it all together. We will look at some over-arching aspects of the role, like how to build the right team, how to leverage and procure technology that meets your needs, and we'll look at what's coming next.

SECTION THREE: PULLING IT ALL TOGETHER

Chapter 12

Setting up for execution

For many first-time CSOs, the really hard work comes after the strategy is agreed. You will still need to figure out how to hold the organisation accountable and how to set up sustainability oversight, evaluate and agree how much budget you need, and set up programme office. This intermediate step before taking off is where you set yourself and your team (if you have one in place) up for success.

Setting high-level oversight with the board

To be successful, CSOs need to manage up to the board as much as they need to manage down to the business. Depending on sustainability maturity, the CSO might be the only subject matter advisor to the board on sustainability issues. Your formal responsibility to the board might be effective execution of the sustainability strategy to support value creation, but an equally important one is to upskill the board and create better models for sustainability oversight.

Sustainability knowledge on boards is often critically lacking and, without it, boards will struggle to understand the linkages between what the company does and how that affects the world around it, and vice versa. Boards need to have the vision and courage to challenge today's business models, so these models remain fit for purpose in years to come and are serving society constructively. Board members can't do that adequately if their entire professional expertise is built on what 'was' – professional worlds where sustainability didn't even feature.

One of the root causes of the lack of sustainability expertise on the board is simply that enough time simply hasn't passed for sustainability talent to reach the type of track record commonly found among board appointments. This may appear unfair to sustainability and the brilliant talent out there, but your job is to educate the board to diversify and look differently at how they source sustainability expertise.

Where sustainability knowledge is weak or lacking, CSOs can help boards by bringing outside expertise from their own sustainability networks to complement in-house updates on particular topics and to maximise sustainability learning. Boards need to have a regular inflow of outside views and data.

This can be done in a variety of ways:

- Inviting external subject matter experts for ad-hoc advice, for example, if the board is deliberating on a particular matter and needs additional insight.
- Introducing a learning plan on ESG topics using external course providers, with regular drop-ins with external subject-matter experts and practitioners to add colour and relevance to those topics – get creative here, invite your investors, peer CSOs and CEOs, and NGO voices.
- Creating touchpoints to sustainability by bringing board members onto industry groups, independent external sustainability councils, membership organisations, and key conferences.

Beyond this, CSOs should work with the legal counsel to define governance models that fit the current governance structure, level of directors' sustainability knowledge, sustainability management structure, corporate culture, and the needs of stakeholders / shareholders. Ideally, you want to work towards a model in which sustainability is present as a regular topic on the board agenda to anticipate any issues and ensure top performance, rather than being a periodic plug-in when the board needs to sign off on the materiality matrix or address incidents.

INSEAD[1] defines six models for corporate governance that have varying degrees of effectiveness for sustainability performance:

1. Sustainability is fully integrated into board operations and decision-making – this is the ideal model for effective sustainability governance.
2. A dedicated ESG / sustainability committee reporting to the board.
3. ESG responsibilities added to an existing committee, such as the Risk Committee.
4. Multiple committees having ESG responsibilities.
5. One director assigned the role of ESG champion.
6. ESG not formally embedded except for signing off on material topics and the annual sustainability report.

Checklist for periodic sustainability reporting to the board

Once you establish ESG oversight with the board, you will get into a cadence of reporting / progress updates to them. Below are some items to include in your report:

• Reminder of materiality definitions.
• Reminder of key impacts and associated goals, both in-year and multi-year.

- Progress in the past quarter; milestones hit, missed and why.
- Highlights and key contributors (could be people, departments, divisions).
- Horizon scanning of key relevant sustainability events; in your sector, affecting competitors, globally.
- Regulatory developments; upcoming key dates.
- Update on reporting deadlines, expected involvement / sign off.
- Budget update – spend, whether on track or not, any new cost items; savings identified and other wins.
- Staff events and staff feedback.

Designing incentives

How can you activate the organisation for change and set accountabilities? Integrating sustainability performance into executive incentive plans and employee reward systems could be an effective way to hold internal stakeholders accountable for progress on sustainability strategy. However, there are a few things to consider for this mechanism to really work in service of your goals.

Traditionally, incentive plans are based on achieving quantitative financial goals like revenue, cash flow, EBIT / EBITDA, earnings per share, or total shareholder return. Sustainability metrics are an entirely new cog wheel in this mechanism. Progress is not as straightforward to measure as financial performance, accountabilities can cross multiple areas, sustainability metrics can contradict some financial metrics in the short-term, and they often require much longer measurement periods than are set for traditional incentive plan periods. When designing incentives via sustainability-linked executive pay or other mechanisms, you want to make sure that they are moving the needle on sustainability forward and that performance targets are[2]:

- Incentivising meaningful behaviour and outcomes – As an example of what could go wrong, a short-term 'net-zero' target can lead to a surge in low-quality offsets purchase rather than a more desirable investment in supply chain decarbonisation. Or a short-term target to have more women in the workplace can affect hiring practices but not behaviours and policies around re-integration after maternity leave.

- Ambitious yet realistic – Don't set performance targets that are too easy to achieve, such that they create an almost guaranteed bonus or that they reinforce something that needs to change anyway. Equally, try not to set unreasonable targets that will require adjustments if it becomes clear at some point that performance will not be met.

- Grounded in data and your company's capability to support execution – You need to know the current performance baseline and have the systems and processes that will support measurements and assurance along the way. For example, if your company wants to set an emissions reduction target but you don't have the data warehouse and processes to even measure emissions fully and accurately to begin with, then you might want to wait until you address those items first.

- Aligned across the business – If you're a global business, how are you cascading global goals and targets to the regions? Clearly communicate any reasons for differences between regional targets and the expectations you're setting for different teams and regions.

- Measurable – Help your compensation committee minimise subjective judgment when deciding executive pay. Offer a clear framework for measurable sustainability targets against which they will have to assess performance.

> ## An example of how sustainability-linked pay can go wrong
>
> In 2018, an oil and gas company awarded an annual bonus to the CEO for meeting environmental goals, while the same year the company had a major oil spill incident. The reason was that executives' performance review didn't account for the volume of spilled oil, but for the number of significant spills, and that number wasn't significant.[3]

Consider the items below when deciding how to choose and design the right incentives mechanism:

- Sustainability programme maturity – What is the organisation's overall sustainability maturity? If sustainability targets and goals are written in the company strategy, have been signed off by the board, and there is some history of execution, this might be an appropriate moment to consider executive-linked pay. If you are starting sustainability work for the first time in your company, assess if your culture and systems are ready to support executive-linked pay.
- The purpose of incentives – What are you trying to achieve that you need incentives to support with? If you are evolving the company culture and behaviour and need to involve a broad group of employees, consider setting targets for team leads who can 'model down' sustainability norms and practices. If you are targeting a narrow set of material topics, you might want to set stretch targets for respective owners. If you need to manage sustainability risks across the company, consider setting targets for the C-suite and key executives to keep key stakeholders laser-focused on these risks.
- Shareholders' views on sustainability – Regulatory regimes in Europe and in the US are introducing mandatory disclosure on whether and how executive pay is linked to sustainability

objectives. At a minimum, sustainability-linked executive pay is a topic for boardroom discussion. Get familiar with your shareholder's positions and policies on sustainability and where your organisation's size and relationships allow, discuss the approach to incentives together, for example:

o Are shareholders prepared to accept trade-offs between financial and sustainability goals?
o Are they prepared to set long-term horizons for achieving sustainability goals?
o Are they prepared to accept qualitative sustainability targets if those lead to desired improvements?
o Are they comfortable with the level of sustainability knowledge of the board so that the board remuneration committee can exercise good judgement when awarding executive pay?

Such a discussion is likely going to be one of the hardest you will face, but it is also one that will set the tone for the rest of your sustainability work with the organisation.

How to design compensation plans

If you have decided to introduce sustainability-linked compensation, consider the following:

- Align with the existing compensation system – Some companies do not work with a bonus system or are not mature enough to have a remuneration committee in the board. Work with your people team and the general counsel to align on how executives are incentivised to achieve superior results and tailor them to the organisation and its values.
- Screen for contradictions with other targets – Do your executives' targets contradict or reinforce each other? If the CRO has a revenue increase target through product sales, and you have an emissions reduction target, then

it is either an opening for a conversation about a robust decarbonisation plan or it is a ready-made conflict.

- Balance annual improvements with long-term value creation – Normally, there are two types of incentive pay next to base salary: (1) a long-term incentive plan (LTIP) – options and restricted stock that are paid out over a three-to-four-year period and which is usually 60%-70% of total executive pay; and (2) the annual bonus or short-term incentive plan (STIP) – typically cash and which is generally 15%-20% of total executive pay.[4]

Progress on most sustainability goals is best measured over the long term. Consider many companies' claims to achieve net zero, all of which require a long-term transition plan. Even the most ambitious deadlines of 2030 stretch beyond most LTIP time-horizons. One way to address this is to set milestones that are rewarded through short-term incentives but that maintain the foundation for long-term value creation and serve the purpose and mission of the company even when the business model and strategy change.

An example of how sustainability-linked pay can work well

One of the experts interviewed for this book told us they use long-term targets over a three-year period for executive management, which have worked very well to encourage executives to think beyond quick wins. Managers of business units have no more than five very specific measures they need to implement, e.g., transitioning to a renewable energy service provider, replacing an old piece of equipment with a more energy-efficient solution, making a proposal for three sustainable packaging consumer solutions and introduce one to the market by year X. This expert maintains that such incentive design has significantly increased middle management's understanding of the challenges to transition to sustainability and their contribution towards them.

Table 7. Types of sustainability and ESG incentive metrics[5]

Metric	Considerations
Scorecard	• Sustainability metrics do not have specific individual weighting but are part of a broad mix of sustainability or non-financial business metrics. • Gives the compensation committee flexibility to judge achievement subjectively. • Currently the most common structure, used by 36% of S&P Global 500 companies[6] with ESG metrics.
Individual components	• Sustainability metrics are not used on their own but as part of a discretionary individual assessment (e.g., as part of a 'leadership' category). • Second most common structure, used by 28% of S&P Global 500 companies[7]. • Allows for individuals to have different goals and relative weighting.
Weighted components	• Metrics are broken out with specific weightings and goals within a composite performance target. • Requires sustainability metrics that are clearly measurable.
Underpin or global modifier	• Sustainability metrics are used to adjust the entire pay-out up or down. Some companies use a negative modifier only; achievement does not increase the pay-out, but a missed target results in a negative adjustment even if the financial performance target is achieved. • Can be viewed as punitive and encourage gaming of the system.
Stand-alone plan	• Allows the company to design an additional plan in a way most compatible with the types of goals it would like to achieve. • Because the existing incentive plans remain in place, there is a risk that the new plan is hard to explain or viewed as duplicative by investors.

Other incentive mechanisms

Where sustainability-linked executive pay may not be an effective option for your organisation, work with your people team to understand your company's reward approach and how you can include sustainability within it. We touched on this in chapter 3, but it's worth remembering that employee rewards outside of executive pay can offer much more flexibility in recognising qualitative and harder-to-measure contributions to driving the sustainability agenda.

Together, these small steps add up and help create company-wide behaviour shifts and encourage innovation – just be careful to balance recognition for what's right to do or needs to happen anyway with recognition for where a stretch is really necessary or where employees clearly excel in their contributions. Examples include monetary rewards (such as cash bonuses), public recognition, employee benefits or awards, and professional development.

Bear in mind that no incentive is as strong as a sense that you are doing the right thing, that your work is important, and that it is valuable and impactful. Compensation is but one of a set of tools to reinforce the right behaviours, so don't over-index on it, and ensure to balance it with appealing to people's own motivations. These are stronger and more enduring influencers of behaviour.

Structuring reporting lines

There is no one-size-fits-all to structure the sustainability function and it very much depends on the size of your organisation, its maturity and ambition, organisational structure, the personalities involved, and the specific responsibilities required from the CSO. In some cases, reporting lines fall into place naturally, and in others, you need to give time to find the optimal operating model for your team.

To report or not to report to the CEO? Not all CSOs do – nor do they need to. CEOs are helpful in creating tailwinds for CSOs at the beginning and are pivotal to aligning the sustainability strategy with the strategy of the organisation. However, after setting up the sustainability foundations, CSOs might delegate ownership for respective sustainability activities across the organisation. They continue to hold unique responsibilities of their own, but after the initial 'take off' of the agenda, they don't need to be so closely involved with the CEO anymore.

In another scenario, an organisation might appoint the CSO to focus on a specific task initially, so it is more effective for the CSO to work directly with the respective C-suite leader. If you're being hired into a new role and have the freedom to structure reporting lines, try to find answers to the following questions:

- What were the drivers to create the CSO role? What specific responsibilities does the organisation want you to focus on?
- Who is the primary champion for the sustainability agenda? Who advocated for the creation of your role?
- How involved is the CEO in the different aspects of the business? How do they balance their role as organisational figurehead with their position as a day-to-day decision maker?
- Does the CEO have the time and inclination for you and your work?

Depending on the answers, you might decide on a reporting line to someone who is more accessible, closer to day-to-day operations or to the key topics of your sustainability strategy with a monthly or quarterly cadence of alignment meetings with the CEO.

Whatever the reporting lines, the CEO is a key figure in the sustainability transformation. The level of employee support and senior leadership buy-in will be much greater when the CEO clearly communicates that sustainability is a priority for the company. This can be via plug-ins during company townhalls, quarterly performance updates, CEO messages to the organisation in company newsletters and across internal communication tools, and external marketing activity involving the CEO.

If you're just setting up the function, work with the CEO and your internal communications lead on a communication plan and don't be afraid to over-communicate in the first year of the function – you need to send a clear signal to the organisation that this is now a strategic priority and you're on a path to adapt the organisation to it accordingly.

Developing the budget

Just as with any other C-suite role, you will need an adequate budget to run your function and deliver on strategic objectives. Sustainability expenses are a new line item for organisations and their scope may not be fully understood yet. You will have to develop the budget and explain to your CFO what it will help deliver. There are two major budget categories for sustainability: (1) operational costs to run the function, and (2) investments in business transformation and sustainability initiatives.

Operational costs

These costs can be grouped in various ways depending on your organisation's format for submitting the budget to the CFO. The costs will vary for every company and depend on the size of your team, the needs as per your sustainability strategy and what's already available in the organisation (such as a company-wide data management tool).

Here are some universal line items to consider.

1. People – Remuneration for your sustainability team, plus fully loaded costs such as investment in their professional development through courses, training and conference

visits, offsite workshops and team retreats, bonuses and promotion.

2. Consulting, research, and services – You may need to involve external expertise on a whole range of issues where you don't have in-house expertise or capacity, for example helping you conduct a materiality assessment, calculating GHG emissions, performing a life cycle assessment on a product, research into a specific emerging area, and so on. If this is a service you foresee you will need regularly, consider at what point it will become more economical to hire an in-house expert instead.

3. Marketing and brand – This includes branding content production and everything that's concerned with communicating about your work to the outside world like social media campaigns, video production and digital advertising. Consider the overlap with the Marketing and Public Relations team as well, and if the budget will be held by them, secure an allocation to the Sustainability function.

4. Learning and development – How do you want to raise the collective knowledge of the organisation on sustainability? Consider buying a license to a sustainability learning platform for employees, the costs of awareness campaigns, guest speakers' fees, training and planning events for the board and the executive leadership.

5. Sustainability reporting – Unless they are leaders with a long reporting history, few organisations are able to manage the reporting process on their own. They usually recruit consultants to guide them through the process, especially if it's their first time. Costs can range anywhere from USD 30,000 to USD 300,000 and up. Also factor in mandatory assurance / auditing costs, starting at USD 40,000 for SMEs and upwards for large enterprises. Often, reporting costs will be owned by the Finance team,

in which case ensure to bring in sustainability reporting into their scope.

6. Stakeholder relations and advocacy – You will normally want to attend selected industry events and conferences, join industry membership organisations and sustainability leadership groups for which membership fees can vary from USD 1,000 to USD 80,000 a year.

7. Tools and software – This is highly dependent on the systems your organisation already has, but you might want to purchase licenses to bespoke sustainability software platforms that enable donations and grant-making, or to bespoke sustainability reporting tools.

Depending on how you structure the role in the organisation and how you set accountabilities, you might include some of these line items in other team's budgets. For example, expenses related to sustainability learning might sit with your learning and development team usually nested under the people team. Or the marketing team will have a line item 'Sustainability' in their budget. Work closely with these owners to get your items included.

Budget for sustainability initiatives and business transformation

Are you an e-commerce organisation that has committed to electrifying its fleet of delivery trucks? Are you a manufacturing business that wants to make its operations resilient to climate change? Are you a construction company that is investing into new building materials?

This is where you need to do a cost-benefit analysis with a cross-functional team to understand the level and type of investment – in terms of capital expenditures (CapEx) and operating expenditures (OpEx) – that these initiatives will require and where to source funding for them.

CapEx and OpEx are an established way to categorise an organisation's spending – the costs and expenses it needs to pay to continue running the business. In short, CapEx includes major purchases that a company makes, and which are used over the long term. Normally, these include physical assets, such as buildings, equipment, machinery, and vehicles. OpEx, on the other hand, includes the day-to-day expenses that a company incurs to keep its business running, like employee salaries, rent, utilities, and property taxes.[8]

In the context of your sustainability budget, 'green' CapEx could mean investment into retrofitting facilities to become more energy efficient, upgrades to low-carbon technology, electrification of physical assets like fleet or diesel-based machinery and equipment, or renewable energy generation. These activities will vary depending on your sector. For example, for companies in the energy services sector who are actively transitioning their business models away from servicing fossil fuels extraction, storing, transportation and refinement, 'green' CapEx will represent the majority of their capital expenditures as they are upgrading and re-orienting their whole infrastructures towards renewable energy generation and transmission. These investments can usually be depreciated over a period of years.

Green OpEx usually covers direct non-capitalised costs relating to research and development into new technologies, short-term lease, maintenance and other direct expenditures relating to the day-to-day servicing of assets of property, plant and equipment that are necessary to ensure the continued and effective use of such assets.[9]

CapEx and OpEx to finance the sustainability transition of your organisation can run into the tens and the hundreds of millions. If the general costs to run the function (like people salaries or assurance costs) are relatively straightforward to understand and to fund, the green CapEx and OpEx expenditures, you will need to involve the executive leadership and the board to commit to, and to help source funding. If internal funding isn't available, financial instruments such as green bonds or sustainability-linked loans may be an option. They are also an important measure for your investors to understand whether the company has a credible plan to transform business activities towards sustainability. Investors will be using your disclosed CapEx and OpEx values to measure how much of their own portfolio is supporting the sustainability transition, climate change mitigation and adaptation.

Consider these two examples to understand the difference between the application of CapEx and OpEx to qualify sustainability investments and their magnitude:

- A cement company has performed a climate risk assessment of its facilities which indicated that they are vulnerable to flooding. The company has decided to increase the capacity of the drainage systems to make them more resilient to flooding. The costs of these measures for all facilities amounts to EUR€500 million, which represents 80% of the company's capital expenditures.[10]
- A company decides to invest into rooftop solar energy generation to meet its emission reduction targets under the climate transition plan. They can structure this as CapEx in which case they would own the assets and full project costs – the solar PV panels and any additional infrastructure and services required for installation; or they could structure this as OpEx in which case they would outsource the installation and maintenance of solar PV panels to a service provider, and would treat renewable energy generation as their utility costs. There are various factors to consider in both scenarios, including lifetime of assets, payback periods, maintenance costs, in-house expertise to manage a project like this and capacity.

A good reality test for a company's ambition is looking at carbon reduction budgets for companies that have made public net-zero or carbon neutral claims. Today, quality offsets range from USD 80-200 per tonne of CO_2, so the costs for large companies can quickly run into the millions. Irrespective of whether offsets are a good strategy or not, make a quick back of the envelope calculation of what the company would need to invest into offsets based on its publicly reported annual emissions and ask whether this budget is available.

Setting up a programme office

While sustainability projects may be run by people in different parts of the organisation, you will likely want to keep a central record of those projects and how they're progressing. This is the function of your programme office.

Some key elements of this central function should include:

- The list of key projects that are agreed upon, costed, and approved, as well as their signed-off rationale and definition of what success looks like.
- Roles and responsibilities, including key accountabilities for each project.
- The budgets for each of those projects and where they are held.
- Actions, dates, milestones; when actions are due and how progress is tracking against those.
- Measures, KPIs; the analytics that will show improvement and movement towards the key goal.
- Reporting mechanisms, e.g., weekly update summaries, issues and risk registers. How they're communicated, e.g., emailed into a central place, weekly stand up, etc.

- Reporting cadence – when you need to get updates from others, and how frequently you update management and the board on progress.

Again, your organisation's culture, maturity and way of working, and your own capacity, may amend or reduce this list naturally – what 'good looks like' will be different for every CSO.

Building a network

Your role requires you to keep up with an enormous amount of regulatory change, new scientific findings, revised best practices across sustainability topics, new players in the industry and trends. You will have to be able to filter through those quickly and understand how they apply to your organisation and any changes they may require to strategy or processes. Some of you will be setting up the sustainability function from scratch or encountering new challenges. In all of these instances, it's important to have someone to consult; someone you can go to and ask, 'what do you think' or 'how did you do it'?

Arguably, your best source of information and inspiration will be other CSOs, the people who are in the same shoes as you are and have dealt with similar experiences. Don't underestimate this resource. You'd be surprised just how many informal networks and regular coffee check-ins CSOs and their teams have. Together, we can skip the pains of trial and error, learn useful tips and examples, and get to the point in our organisations much faster.

Consider these options to look for peer support.

Direct outreach to peers

On LinkedIn, via shared contacts, or via an introduction by someone from your company. This is the most straightforward route, avoiding any overhead and costs. Unless very heavily constrained by non-compete rules, most CSOs will be willing to talk to you. Be specific and respect their time – explain your pain point and what advice you're exactly looking for. Offer topics you can help with in exchange. Keep your door open if others contact you. Your personal brand and your attitude can go a long way to service you.

Professional networks

These vary from industry groups and include paid membership networks convened by sustainability-dedicated organisations, like the World Business Council for Sustainable Development, as well as free CSO networks. All have their unique characteristics:

- Industry groups – these will address topics unique to the nature of your sector, e.g., the effect of sector-specific regulation on the business or its branch or sector decarbonisation pathways. These groups often bring competitors in one room and operate under Chatham house rules. Sometimes, this results in a rich, unfiltered discussion, and sometimes, peers may still be reluctant to share.
- Sustainability membership networks – these can vary in the maturity of CSOs they convene. Some will set entry requirements at the higher ranges of characteristics such as company turnover and look at years of experience in the CSO role. Others will be keen to convene more diverse groups.
- Free CSO networks – these are often created out of an initiative of a service provider or an individual. For example, a software company that launches a forum for customers, a consulting company that starts a CSO network, or a professional who creates a peer discussion forum. If they are managed and curated well, often these

can bring a good debate and intimacy that more formal settings may lack.

Conferences and workshops

These are plentiful and you have to be vigilant in filtering their quality. If a conference, screen the speaker's list and agenda, if a workshop, ask for a participants list. These events are a great place to get high-level input on a range of questions quickly if you're proactive during scheduled networking moments.

Working groups

This is a unique environment in sustainability. Many non-profit organisations create knowledge resources based on input from practitioners. Consider the Science Based Target Initiative, the Global Reporting Initiative, or the European Financial Reporting Advisory Group. All of these organisations develop their standards and frameworks by convening working groups where experts and practitioners contribute their expertise pro-bono over a year or two. These are unique environments where, together with others, you can learn an incredible level of detail about a certain topic, foster deep professional connections, and contribute to common sustainability knowledge. Entry criteria mainly look at level of expertise on the topic, commitment and capacity and availability to contribute long-term.

Summary

Execution is about connecting high-level strategy with action. It is about setting up governance and oversight, structuring incentives that will work, optimising reporting lines and setting budgets. You may need a programme office to oversee all the different streams of work. And you'll want to invest in a range of support structures for yourself, including formal and informal industry groups and networks. Rigorous execution is what will make your strategy a reality and delivering operational excellence is what will lead to success. You will want to build a team of complementary skills around you, and that is what we cover next.

Chapter 13

Getting a team together

As the previous sections show, the sustainability function requires a broad range of expertise and skillsets. Some of these may sit in your team and others across the organisation. To the extent your budget allows, you should aim to invest in bringing in and developing strong sustainability talent to set up the function for long-term success.

In most organisations, sustainability is still formalising, so management may not yet be used to the idea of a sustainability department akin to more traditional disciplines like human resources or finance. Organisations are hiring climate scientists, ESG controllers, ESG data analysts, decarbonisation managers, reporting managers, and many more. You will need to map out sustainability needs and assess skills gaps and make the case to your CEO or the CFO why you may need some of these roles.

If you're coming to an organisation that has an existing sustainability team, you will want to review whether it is fit for purpose and, if needed, make the necessary changes to upskill, repurpose, and bolster existing talent.

Often, you may find that staff hold sustainability responsibilities alongside their primary roles on a voluntary basis – if they bring tangible value, and they have the appetite, review if you can transition some of these people to your team full-time; if not, seek to make more formal commitments with their managers about sharing this resource.

Review which hires are foundational and therefore urgent – such as an ESG data analyst or reporting manager – so you can kick off the hiring process early and fill roles quickly. Other roles will require time to determine based on future strategy and how you decide to embed the function in the organisation. Further, you should conduct a thorough review of available internal talent that may wish to transition to the sustainability department and staff who are motivated to upskill. The benefit of internal mobility is that staff know the business and its internal and external ecosystem, can hit the ground running, and are motivated to make an impact.

In addition to forming the team, you're also responsible for creating its soft landing within the organisation. You need to create the conditions for success when the organisation may not yet be familiar with what people in sustainability roles generally do and work to embed it effectively in the organisation's structures. If you have restructured an existing team, you will need to manage any disappointment and build trust. Once things get rolling, you will need to grow and professionally develop your team, as well as manage routine people administration and any people dynamics.

Remember as well, the need for integration with the organisation. Nothing will grate so much with an organisation as a new, raw, idealistic team of rookies coming in, thinking they have all the answers, when they have zero corporate knowledge and experience. Yes, your new team has skills to bring, but everyone on the team (including you) must take significant time to listen, to learn, to visit sites, and to talk to as many people as possible, before even beginning to embark on the road to transition. This is an easy trap to fall into, and a perilous one. If goodwill and trust are not fostered from the outset, they are difficult to win back later. Serve all of your pronouncements with a big side of humility and a desire to learn, if you want to win hearts and minds. Consider secondments into and out of your team. Have your staff work on the front line and see things for themselves. Sit in the canteen, listen to conversations.

Forming the right team

Ultimately, the size, composition and the structure of your team will depend on the company's material issues and sustainability strategy. This in turn is determined by the size of your organisation, the complexity of its business and operating activities, the degree to which it is regulated and geographic presence.

Traits, competencies, and expertise

When setting up your team, you want to bring the breadth of expertise required, and build out the skillsets that you don't possess yourself. Key competencies that you will need to have, or have access to, include:

- Data analysis – Skills ranging from data gathering and analysis to synthesis and effective presentation.
- Research – Where you need to commission specific pieces of work to investigate elements of the organisation's operations, or external impacts. Skills such as conducting surveys, building research proposals, engaging other actors such as academia.
- Communications – As with you, your team need to possess good communication skills, to convey the sustainability

mission and to explain concepts, at times to a sceptical audience.

- Programme management – You will need to set up a programme office overseeing the various pieces of work underway, and having a skilled programme manager will facilitate this.
- Subject-matter expertise – Skills across the board, from emissions to decarbonising, waste management to packaging, human rights to due diligence, ESG reporting to regulation, choose the expertise you need to help you.

However, beyond just looking for the skills you need, you also want to hire people with the right character traits, and ones that will sit well within the organisation's culture. You will need to adapt this to your situation, but some common traits to look for include:

- Resilience – As we've shown, this is not always an easy path. There will be obstacles and setbacks. Of course, you will support your staff when this happens, but hiring for resilience will hopefully mean you don't have to pick people up off the floor every day.
- Diplomacy – As you've learned in getting to the CSO role, you need to forge alliances across the organisation; with active supporters, neutral actors and outright opponents. Your staff need to possess the judgement in what to say, and how, to get the best results.
- Listening skills – Caring about the organisation and its mission. Nobody wants a foghorn, just transmitting messages and dictating outwards. Success in this role requires a willingness to listen and understand, and not just to trot out what someone did at their previous organisation.
- Adaptability – For sustainability to become a competitive advantage, it will require the organisation to come up with

creative solutions, to innovate. To get the best out of your efforts, you want people who are curious, who can think creatively, who genuinely grapple with issues and seek ways forward. Someone who is inflexible will likely not find those innovative paths forward.

There are some characteristics when hiring that you need to watch out for, as they may cause you issues in the future and lead to regretted hires:

- Overly strident views – It's normal for sustainability experts to feel passionately about their cause. They know more than most about the issues we face, and the mountain we have to climb in a short and vanishing window of time. It's normal to get frustrated and anxious, and for that to spill out at times, but this can jeopardise your mission. A voice that is too strong, too soon, that is misjudged, or that doesn't understand the organisation can have an adverse effect, solidifying opposition to your cause and making your role ever harder.

- 'Opposition in disguise' – Someone seeking to undermine the organisation. Some organisations know that they must actively divest, stop or re-orient some of their service lines. They are genuinely working on transition scenarios, doing their best in current market and regulatory environment (for example, former tobacco company Philip Morris's pivot to smoke-free products, or the fossil fuel companies transitioning to alternative energy provision, like Danish company Orsted). Every employee of the company signs up to work for the good of that company long-term no matter its background – bad faith has no place here.

Roles and responsibilities

Who you need on your team is highly dependent on the breadth of your sustainability strategy and goals. In chapter 1, we covered the key relationships of the CSO and the synergies to other business functions. For sustainability to have a truly transformative effect and to avoid any duplicative work and overhead, it should be embedded within those functions to an extent possible.

At the same time, you need a foundation for your department, which can be composed of the following fundamental roles:

Table 8. Roles and responsibilities in the sustainability team

General function	Role	Programme of work
Strategy	Chief sustainability officer	• Sustainability strategy • C-suite relationships • Board reporting and relationships • Culture and engagement • External relations with industry and government groups, NGOs and media • Business transformation / change management
	ESG business analyst	• Quantitative data analysis, modelling, and scenario development
Reporting	ESG controller	• Develops internal controls and processes • Prepares assurance process • Systems integration
	Reporting manager	• Reporting life cycle management • Monitoring reporting developments • Submissions to rating agencies • Participation in public comments
Legal and compliance	ESG compliance manager	• Monitoring and advising on ESG regulation. • Advising on new ventures and projects and whether they adhere to new and upcoming regulation.

Engagement	Community manager	• Liaison with affected communities and stakeholders. • May conduct surveys, interviews, and other analysis to support decision-making.
Programmes and initiatives	Project managers and coordinators	• Roles that lead specific sustainability topics as per sustainability strategy, such as supply chain / sourcing, decarbonisation / net zero, packaging, product circularity, human rights, civic engagement, etc.

Not every organisation needs all of these roles, and the boundaries between the roles are not always as clear cut as shown above. You may need to bootstrap the resources you need – especially in the early days. For example, a reporting manager and an ESG controller could be combined into one role.

Hiring talent

Where do you find the talent for these roles? Your talent acquisition team will already have a good process lined up for sourcing and attracting roles, but you can throw in these additional avenues for consideration:

- Sustainability programmes offered at universities – join their career days or share job openings with programme coordinators.
- Top sustainability voices / influencers on LinkedIn – these leaders often have a great pool of followers, and you can try to ask them to re-share your vacancy.
- Direct candidate approach through competitors, LinkedIn search, and sustainability conferences speakers.

Also, it's important to get the employee value proposition (EVP) for your department right. You want to make your team is an attractive place for the best people. Much of the EVP will stem from the vision, mission and values of the organisation.

The possibility of making a real impact will be the most important element for many people. Doing good, challenging work, and continuing to learn from others, both on the job and via training matter too. Organisations get the staff they deserve; the more valuable, motivating, and important the work, the higher the calibre of talent you can attract.

Bear all these elements in mind, above and beyond the hygiene factors of salary and working conditions.

Embedding the team

Having identified the skills for which you need to hire, there are various ways to set up and integrate your sustainability team into the company structure. Generally, the sustainability team acts as a centre of excellence and a catalyst of change on specific sustainability issues. It has its own unique responsibilities and also works with respective teams to help them push beyond business as usual in their areas of responsibility and expertise.

We cover three models below, with pros and cons for each:[1]

Model 1. Small sustainability team with responsibilities spread across business functions

The sustainability team sets company-wide sustainability goals, but execution is delegated to respective business units. Business functions co-develop implementation roadmaps and initiatives in consultation with the sustainability team and have the autonomy to execute on those using their own resources and budget.

In this structure, business functions have the accountability for achieving sustainability targets and therefore it is in their interest to embed sustainability in the day-to-day operations and culture of their team. It enables and sparks innovation across the business as it pushes teams to think of solutions to unconventional problems, and it empowers business units to use their expertise to solve for unique challenges autonomously and own the success.

For this structure to work, sustainability needs to be a visible and non-negotiable commitment of the board and the executive team, written into the company strategy, otherwise it risks sliding down the agenda. The CSO then acts as an advisor to business units, offers guidance and troubleshoots, holds the rest of the organisation accountable, maintains the view of corporate-wide performance on the topic, and generally oversees that the company is steadily moving forward towards its strategic objectives. The sustainability team would still own unique subject-matter responsibilities, such as reporting or carbon accounting, but would rely on the rest of the business to execute the strategy.

This structure can be replicated in small and large companies alike that deal with a broad range of sustainability issues. For example, if the organisation has committed to addressing the gender pay gap as part of its sustainability strategy, the sustainability team may work closely with the people team to offer best practice and advice on reporting expectations or requirements, agree on goals and timelines, and co-develop a roadmap. Once signed off by the CPO, the people team would execute the plan.

Another example is if the sustainability team may have incubated a new business idea to set up reverse logistics – the type of supply management that takes returned goods back from customers to the company to further re-use materials – to support circular economy goals. They would work closely with supply management teams to develop the business case and once validated and approved, the responsibility to execute on the project would move to the supply chain management team.

- Advantages: high degree of ownership by the organisation. Sustainability is embedded in operations. The most co-operative of the frameworks.
- Disadvantages: this setup may not work when the function is entirely new without any prior history of sustainability projects and low awareness, as the CSO first needs to get buy in and show the way forward, before teams can work autonomously.

Model 2. Larger central team

This set-up works for large, mature organisations with a long record and volume of sustainability work, and where it needs to be coordinated across subsidiaries, regions, and committees. The sustainability team might have several sub-units responsible for aspects of the strategy – research and development, investor relations, reporting, carbon accounting, stakeholder engagement, marketing and communications, learning and development, and some people topics like DEI and community engagement.

In this setup, the sustainability team owns the sustainability budget fully. The decision-making power and incubation of initiatives is centralised with the team, and its topic leaders have a direct relationship with heads of business units.

For example, the marketing team convenes a regular meeting comprising marketing heads from all units, where the head of sustainability marketing represents the schedule of activities and plans of the sustainability team.

- Advantages: affords a high degree of budget, autonomy, and power to the CSO. Keeps control of the sustainability initiatives in a central place.
- Disadvantages: may cause conflict and duplication with other departments. Plus, the rest of the organisation may

feel that sustainability is imposed on them, rather than something of which they are a part.

Model 3. Stand-alone CSO with a cross-functional committee

This structure might apply when the function is new and the CSO's first priority is to establish sustainability within the company, understand the business and status quo, and define boundaries and scopes of responsibility with functional leads.

The CSO will assemble a committee of leaders representing key functions relevant to the sustainability goals and co-create the strategy with them before approving it at the board level. Through this approach, the full organisation is involved in strategy creation, ensuring buy-in from the outset.

Once the strategy is approved and the sustainability team starts to grow, the set up might shift to model 1 with the committee maintaining an oversight role.

- Advantages: cost-effective, low-risk and non-intimidating for an organisation starting on its sustainability journey.
- Disadvantages: without proper backing and execution, may not reach full potential or can risk becoming a window-dressing exercise.

No matter the structure you set, make sure that sustainability has a clear 'home' and topic owners in your organisation. Staff at all levels need to know who to approach for expertise, idea proposals, and escalations. Make sure your sustainability team is clearly profiled in your company's org structure, with owners for respective topics and guidance on how to approach your team.

Smaller companies will simply use direct email to contact the sustainability lead, others will set a team email, yet others will have an issue tracker system through company IT tools where the sustainability team can monitor and prioritise issues before addressing with the CSO in weekly meetings.

Leading the team

As the leader, you need to consider the motivation levels and wellbeing of your team. This can be a challenging space to work in; your team will face apathy, gaslighting, delay tactics and at times, outright negativity and resistance. How can you create a supportive space for them to come back to, to share and vent, to ask for help, to support, re-gather one's reserves and go back out into the fray again? What does that look like in your team?

It's not solely up to you as the team leader to fix every problem, and you don't want to create that kind of reliance on you – but you should aim to create a coalition of willing and supportive people, who know it's OK to ask for help, and who will help each other 'crowdfund' solutions.

Remember as well that it's a useful and disarming technique to ask your most difficult and resistant stakeholders for help: 'What would you do if you were me?', 'How would you tackle this issue?', 'Where are we going wrong?', or 'How can we make this better?'.

You may at times get tumbleweeds, but you may also be pleasantly surprised at the alternative solutions that get put forward when you stop, take a breath, and ask for help.

Don't neglect the need to continue to develop your team – sustainability is a rapidly-evolving area, with new learning and new regulation dropping weekly. Build in time and budget for ongoing learning and development, conferences, and webinars. Your team will be re-charged, and you will be confident that collective knowledge is up to date.

Summary

For some working in sustainability, you may be a lonely team of one. In this case, you will need to draw on all your reserves of creativity and persuasion to get others to work with you. Your budget may only allow for some outsourced work to begin with. You may have a modest team that you can build over time, or you may inherit a team that you need to evaluate. Whatever the scenario, have a vision of the skills and personality traits to which you're going to need access in order to bring sustainability to life in your organisation, and work to bring that into being. Consider the options to structure sustainability in the organisation, from a centralised model to playing more of a co-ordination role. Remember your role as leader is to support and motivate your people and to protect them.

Besides the requisite skills, you're going to need technology systems to support your work. Given the vast and growing market of sustainability software, it's crucial not to lose sight of your objectives.

Next, we cover the considerations you need to keep in mind when investing in technology for the sustainability function.

Chapter 14

Investing in technology

The main objective of enterprise software systems is to help the organisation streamline its business processes in a way that brings efficiency, reduces errors, frees up time, and helps extract analytics. Your day-to-day work will cover a multitude of operational tasks that can be supported through technology – from measuring carbon footprints and forecasting emissions to managing corporate donations and volunteering. Automation, emerging technologies and business intelligence systems can all reduce the amount of time and effort spent on operational tasks.

However, software systems come at a cost, so you want to make sure your investment is working for you. There are strategic choices to be made about what technologies to choose, whether to outsource technology and how to set up your sustainability technology architecture, with pros and cons for each.

Fundamentally, IT systems should support you with the following:

- Automating data collection, either by sourcing it from existing software and hardware systems, or by plugging into public or proprietary databases such that, ideally, you don't need to collect these data manually via surveys or excel sheets from your colleagues, suppliers, partners, or third parties.

- Scanning and alerting you to relevant regulatory and compliance developments so that you don't need to follow updates manually and mapping these requirements to your existing processes and operations.
- ESG performance analytics, measuring performance against set criteria and flagging discrepancies
- Monitoring your supply chain and their compliance with relevant regulation such as CSDDD.
- Synthesising many sources of data, bringing them together in a way you can work with and visualise, tracking trends over time. Ideally, helping with causation analysis and linkages.
- Automating the extensive work required in producing regular reports, consistently and without errors.

Sustainability technology landscape

It is easy to get overwhelmed and lose sight of your objectives when you start scoping out the market for sustainability software technology solutions.

To give just a couple of figures, the market for ESG reporting software alone is predicted to be worth USD 4.35 billion by 2027[1] representing a 30% increase from its value in 2021, while global carbon accounting software is projected to be worth USD 64.39 billion by 2030[2] from its current value of USD 15 billion.

Even if there's some overlap between these figures, it gives an idea of the growth the sustainability technology sector is going through as it is trying to fill the gap between sustainability regulation and companies' internal capabilities to meet it. But, as PWC summarises, "the bonanza of the ESG software market has started, though the best is yet to come".[3] To put this thesis in context, as a young corporate function compared to, say, finance, sustainability has not had a 100-year head start for a software service providers system to develop – just imagine, SAP released its first accounting software product in 1973!

Tech entrepreneurs and software giants alike are racing into the sustainability software market. Most likely, you will have received or will receive a prospecting call or email the moment you update your LinkedIn profile with your new CSO title. Many of these solutions are just starting out on their journey and trying to grab customers to help iterate their products.

To protect your time and navigate the IT procurement process effectively, it's important that you identify your needs before reaching out to any providers and have a list of technical requirements, functional criteria, and business questions on hand during scoping conversations. We will discuss these areas in turn below.

Categories of sustainability software

The sustainability software market is huge, but there are broadly seven types of operational sustainability tasks that are addressed by vendors:

1. Carbon accounting

Software tools to measure, monitor, and manage the organisation's greenhouse gas emissions. Most advanced tools generally include libraries of emission factors and country electricity factors. These are applied automatically to any energy consumption or procurement data that you upload or that they source from your other systems. They also include a text-reading engine to scrape data from your utility bills and a commute survey engine.

Many of these tools also offer emissions forecasting, reduction pathways and target-setting engines, as well as integration with carbon offsetting and removal providers.

Keep in mind that this may require you to make physical upgrades, like installing meters in factories, vehicles, and other assets around the world, particularly if you want to measure GHG emissions accurately across your whole infrastructure. This may be a significant investment, in both the software and the accompanying hardware.

2. Product stewardship

Mostly used by research and development teams in product manufacturing organisations, these software tools help your organisation design more environmentally friendly products. They can include product design, chemicals management, product compliance and life cycle assessment engines. Generally, they enable you to cross-check your current or potential product attributes with global product regulations and run sustainability impact assessments on various design options.

3. Supply chain management

Tools that help you map your supply chain for exposure to environmental and social risks and manage compliance and resilience related to supplier due diligence, human rights, deforestation, and climate change regulation. These tools can track and trace the impact of products across every step of the supply chain, from the origin of raw materials well down the tiers of the supply chain upstream to their final destination at your warehouses. They often also offer a business intelligence pack to keep you informed about regulatory updates, industry standards, and compliance requirements – an important element in this evolving area.

Keep in mind that these tools won't absolve you from the task of supplier engagement completely – the reality is that many suppliers simply do not track sustainability data. For some impacts such as de-forestation, vendors often rely on geospatial data where impacts are physically visible. For others, like emissions, these tools will use proxies or benchmarks of data from other customers with similar suppliers. Most likely though, you will have to engage with your suppliers to train and support them with data collection, especially if you're a bigger player.

4. Smart infrastructure and resource management

A broad set of tools that help you improve physical asset utilisation: energy, water, waste management and procurement. Functionality can cover real-time resource use monitoring, resource losses and inefficiencies mapping, demand management, and renewable energy integration. Your facilities manager should be in the lead to use these tools and act on results, but you will be using a lot of the output data for your sustainability reporting.

5. ESG performance management and reporting

These comprise tools that offer libraries of ESG reporting frameworks and standards, automate the collection and organisation of ESG data and ultimately help organisations track performance and produce reports in accordance with those frameworks and standards. Some more advanced tools may include built-in benchmarks to compare performance with peers, and compliance plug-ins to monitor ESG regulation, a task manager to coordinate the reporting process with internal stakeholders and record all activity and data compilation methodologies for auditing later on, and a report generation and design engine.

The benefit of these tools is that they cut out the work for you to synthesise hundreds of disclosure requirements and individual data points across different standards and frameworks and offer one place out of which to manage the reporting life cycle. That said, the bigger challenge with ESG reporting for many first-time reporters will be to identify and source data that has never been collected before or may not even exist, and this is not something a tool will do for you – you will need the raw data first.

6. Employee engagement and donations

These include tools that help you manage corporate giving activity, volunteering, and awareness campaigns. These platforms often work with aggregators of vetted charities around the world and enable you to set up a Donor Advised Fund and manage employee donations with charities available on the platform. They also offer menus of pre-built awareness campaigns on sustainability topics, often with some gamification and rewards. The limitation of these tools is often that you can't choose charities outside of what is offered on the platform, plus the high transfer fee on donations.

Building your sustainability IT ecosystem

Progress towards sustainability requires that your organisation engages with sustainability data in an entirely new way (or perhaps for the first time) and that will lead to a change in how people, processes, and data work together. The sustainability technology market is growing rapidly but don't be misled – no end-to-end solution exists to address all your needs and any automation comes at a cost, so you will need to choose judiciously. Sustainability is a very broad field so think through your IT strategy carefully to make sure that your decisions and investments pay off.

Questions to start with

- Identify needs – What do you need from your technology stack? Do you need to calculate carbon emissions, model climate risk, or plan a decarbonisation pathway? Do you need a tool that consolidates reporting requirements across frameworks and regulatory standards, and stores the underlying data for you to generate CSRD, GRI, TCFD, TNFD reports? Do you need to manage employee donations?

- Identify pain points – What are the unique pain points the software solution will help you solve? Look again at your list: are there any false expectations? For example, at present, no software can reliably measure biodiversity impacts. These are so complex in nature that no quick fix solutions exist. Equally, few carbon accounting software solutions exist that completely cut out manual data collection entirely, even if the pitch claims to.

- Determine levels of sophistication that match your company maturity – What's the size, age, and geographical footprint of your organisation? Generally, the bigger, more mature, and globally spread out, the greater the volumes of sustainability-related data to manage and the benefits of automation, but also the more scope for existing systems to help. On the contrary, if you're a small company looking for a quick ballpark estimate on your GHG emissions to know where to focus efforts, you may fare better by seconding an engineer to your team, hiring a working student or a consultant to do the calculations for you, rather than locking yourself into expensive software with an annual renewal before you're ready for it.

- Survey existing systems – How does the organisation currently process the data you seek and what pre-existing systems and processes might already be capturing some of the data? Some enterprise software systems that your organisation is using currently might already have the functionality or modules that you're looking for. Ask your IT team about contract conditions with these providers – can you add modules free of cost, or at a reduced cost? Can you activate functionality that was idle because there was no demand for it before? For example, some employee travel and booking software providers automatically calculate GHG emissions but finance teams and office managers who are the primary users of these systems don't use these features. If you're a big user of data centres, Google Cloud Provider, Amazon Web Services and Microsoft Azure all provide GHG emissions data in the billing centre. Ask your IT team and they will download a report for you. Workday allows to scrape much of the data on social metrics like gender diversity, parental leave adoption, pay gap, etc.

Procurement process

With these initial questions answered, and assuming you need a new system, you will need to establish a technology project group to coordinate scoping, procurement, set-up, running, and maintenance of the system. The main steps in a general IT project are outlined below.

- Get approval – Having mapped the pain points above and established that there isn't an internal system that can help, you'll need to explain this and get approval for investment in a new system, to be either built or bought.
- Outline the scope – Key to the success of any project is to clearly outline the scope and benefits, and to stay focused on this as the project progresses. If new requirements surface, you should either get formal approval to change

the scope or hold off on meeting those requirements until a later stage.

- Define roles and responsibilities – Who will the users of the system be and are they represented in the project group? Who will implement and run the system? Who will troubleshoot? Who's responsible for the accuracy of the data? It's critical to establish these responsibilities early in the process.

- Chalk out your budget – You will have lots of cost items to manage and especially in smaller organisations, your initial budget might be limited. Software solutions can start as low as USD 5,000, with limits varying wildly depending on organisation size, with the upper ranges quoted to us during the interviews of up to USD 1 million. Building something in-house costs the time of your team too; however, it's a one-time investment without a renewal fee. Your IT department can work with you on a total cost of ownership model. Modern SAAS solutions have greatly simplified these calculations.

- Decide whether to build or to buy – Now that you know what solutions exist internally and your pain points, sketch out the envisioned data flow, inputs, and desired outputs. For example, your desired output might be a map of suppliers in water-stressed areas. The Water Risk Filter from WWF offers a map of areas with water stress – brainstorm with your IT team to see whether they can connect supplier data to the Water Risk Filter basin data. Creating an early prototype may pay off as you discover that some solutions may be within reach to build internally.

- Choose solution – Assuming you decide to buy externally and have the list of requirements on hand, the next step is to perform market analysis to identify a list of potential vendors. Work with your IT and procurement teams to create a Request for Information (RFI) / Request for

Proposal (RFP) where you list your functional needs, digital security and compliance requirements and questions. Engage with the security team before you reach out to vendors because they may have non-negotiable go / no-go security requirements, and you don't want to discover those later down the road.

As well as the software requirements, you'll want a set of questions to feel out the maturity of the solution and the company – does the team have actual expertise on the topic they're selling a solution to, what's their funding model, how big is their customer base, what's on their technology roadmap, how are they monitoring regulatory updates, what is included in customer support, how big is the support team, what has gone wrong in the past? With the latter, it's unlikely that the vendor will give you direct answers, but their responses might drop some clues. Ask if you could access a sandbox dummy account to try things out yourself – it's often hard to get a good feel for the quality of the solution through a 30-minute demo in a controlled environment.

Implement solution

- Test, test, test – Prior to any rollout, you will need to test the system, both in terms of its reliability and accuracy, and from an end user standpoint to ensure it's working as expected and users understand how to use it.
- Implement solution, run, and review – Here is where you and your technology partners set up the solution, embed it in the IT environment and introduce it to the organisation. Do you need to migrate data from elsewhere? What user access levels do you need to set up? What is the role division between your company's IT team and the vendor's IT team – what falls in each other's scope? Do

you need a roll-out and communication plan to onboard and alert key stakeholders?

- Monitor, feedback, and maintain – Monitor how the solution is working out for the organisation and whether it's solving the pain points. Submit requests for missing functionality. Maintain an ongoing dialogue with the vendor to ensure you benefit from technology upgrades and new or scheduled feature launches.
- Realise the benefits – Circle back to your initial requirements to ensure that the system delivered the benefits you originally sought. If yes, mark and celebrate that with the team. If not, establish why and see what learnings can be gleaned from the process and whether you can make it better.

Warning signs

You will be compelled to jump to technology solutions to free up time, but be careful with false promises and check for these red flags:

- The tool is buggy during the demo – the solution might still be very new, consider if you want to be an early adopter.
- The vendor can't share a tech roadmap with you – this might signal that the company doesn't understand its customer profile very well yet or is short of funds.
- The company has no subject-matter experts on the topic the tool is addressing.
- Post launch and set up, the time you spend managing the tool outweighs the benefits – this can include time spent with account managers to fix bugs or the complex administration of the tool.

Summary

The sustainability and ESG software arena is huge. You can spend months just scoping out the market. Once you've done your due diligence and have a short list, don't tie yourself up in knots or delay moving forward. Ultimately, no software is going to be an immediate plug-and-play and you will need to invest time and involve stakeholders in set up, regardless of the solution. The key is to choose with care, decide firmly and move forward.

Consider what your business needs are and stay disciplined. Follow a process to choose whether to build or buy solutions and, if applicable to adopt the best solution fit for your needs. And don't forget to check back in to ensure it's doing what you need and has been worth the investment.

Having come this far, taking you through sustainability culture, strategy and execution, technical aspects of the CSO role, and the setup of your team and supporting technology, it's now time to turn to the emerging issues in the sustainability space that you will want to maintain a watching brief on.

Chapter 15

What's next

Sustainability is an evolving area and, as CSO, you have a responsibility to keep yourself abreast of regulatory and environmental changes, as well as supporting your team and the wider organisation in keeping informed. Below are some of the current topics that are worth tracking for the impacts on your organisation and your role.

The evolution of the UN SDGs and new sustainability narratives

We are six years away from needing to reach the 17 United Nations Sustainable Development Goals (SDGs) with their 169 targets, that were adopted by 191 governments in 2015. Yet, as UN itself warns, "the world is woefully off track to achieve the SDGs by the 2030 deadline."[1]

Assuming we're going to fail miserably, we still need to sustain the desire to work towards positive outcomes – what will that look like?

The SDGs have succeeded in bringing an all-encompassing view of sustainable development and engaging a wider group of stakeholders in the discussion than ever before, including the corporate sector, industry, and civil society. Where the Millenium Development Goals (the predecessor of the SDGs) primarily focused on poverty alleviation in the Global South and were somewhat concealed within the corridors of the UN, the SDGs offered a very practical – not perfect and not complete – but practical compass of the 17 issues to address, from protecting nature to providing decent quality of work.

At the same time, the SDGs still predominantly spoke to the same paradigm – doing better but not doing anything radically different. Placing too many hopes on technology to be the answer but ignoring the role of culture, arts, humanities and social science in advancing our ways of thinking and being. Promoting sustained economic growth that benefits all and reduces inequality, but not challenging how we measure growth to begin with and what does a meaningful life defined by mental rather material abundance mean.

The SDGs gave us the comfort that we can achieve sustainable development by deconstructing it into 17 buckets; we also need to look complexity in the eye and acknowledge that there will be uncertainties, that we don't have all the answers, and that improvements come only when we approach problems as the systemic issues they are. While not taking our eye off the 17 goals, we need to advance our systems thinking to find holistic ways of safeguarding our collective future.

CSOs have a role to play in terms of the level of ambition they set for the organisation to transform and how they reflect these new narratives in strategy and operations.

As Vera Moll, Director of Sustainability Reporting and Strategy at global consulting firm KPMG, tells us: "CSOs need to ask themselves what they are in the job for. Do they 'just' want to manage the topic, or do they want to lead the organisation on it? This difference in approaches will impact how one can execute in this role, with very different outcomes."

Staying on course despite adversities

We have now crossed six out of the nine planetary boundaries – the environmental conditions within which humanity can continue to develop and thrive for generations to come.[2] At the time of writing in March 2024, air and ocean surface temperatures have remained the highest for 10 consecutive months in a row compared to their temperature in the respective month in a previous year.[3] Our ecological, social and geopolitical situation is tenuous as it is, yet we are pushing the boundaries of a safe operating space even further. We don't know how the world will look like over the next few years, but it is very likely that we can expect deeper cracks in the system and new – unfamiliar and uncomfortable – challenges. Temperature anomalies, localised resource scarcity and changing landscapes will have real physical impacts on global commerce, supply chains, agriculture, migration, social unrest and inequality.

Is our focus on getting to the desired outcomes resilient enough? If at any point politicians take a U-turn, scrap regulation or block much needed developments, how will companies respond and what will become of the CSO role? While we're mostly enjoying the growth of the profession, we have to remember that change is the only constant and that to continue to do good, we must create deep commitments and understanding of sustainability within our organisations.

Sustainability offers a cross-section to everything a company does, from strategy development to risk management, sourcing, innovation and change management.

As Markus Pretzl, Director of ESG at TIP Group, a privately-owned transportation and logistics services company, vividly notes: "A simple way to test just how deeply the sustainability commitment runs in an organisation is to ask a CSO whether they think they have the possibility of becoming a CEO. Can they imagine a situation where a CEO of a company is someone who used to run a sustainability function. If not, then you are not positioning yourself correctly in the organisation".

What comes after transparency?

We started this book with the argument that we live in a world of hyper transparency which is what has elevated the CSO role in the organisation to begin with. Regulatory mandates around corporate transparency will push more disclosure and more data on the market. Technological developments like geospatial imaging of environmental impacts, distributed ledger technology and AI enablement of sustainability data measurement and collection, will help validate the quality of that data and get to conclusions faster. Already today you don't need an emissions report to locate emission hotspots – software like Climate Trace[4] uses satellites, remote sensing techniques and artificial intelligence to do that much more quickly. In the next three-to-four years, we'll get to an entirely different level of data availability, accessibility and credibility.

At that point, some of us will realise that 'the emperor is naked' and has been naked all along; some will realise that their sector does not have a viable path for transitioning and securing a spot in the future. If the one number, the level of CO_2 in the atmosphere, keeps rising year-on-year despite all of our reported efforts and numbers, what truth does that speak about our corporate sustainability efforts and the sustainability 'industry'?

As with everything, we have come through a learning path. We needed to have the awareness that there is a problem, and the sustainability movement has succeeded in that between the 1960's and 2000's. We then needed the tools to measure how big the problem is. We have succeeded in that too between 2000 and today with the global movement on corporate sustainability reporting, with a thick line in the sand drawn with the latest regulatory changes that make non-financial reporting the law in major capital markets of the world. We are now at a point to really start doing the hard work and thinking holistically.

Reaching for impact

We hope that this book has provided you with a framework to think about the CSO role and with practical, actionable advice to put into practice. Bear in mind that this is a rapidly evolving area, and that every organisation is on its own pathway. Supported with the tools in this book, you will still need to bring a great deal of ingenuity and flexibility to your role – and have to figure things out on the go. However, while challenging, this also has the potential to be one of the more exhilarating aspects of the role.

Remember to step back and look at the big picture of where you're working. A word to the wise – don't let form overshadow substance. What your organisation is doing, really doing, in its day-to-day activities and whether it is adding to the problems or solving some is the only thing that ultimately matters. It is very easy to get drawn into the world of reporting and regulation, and even to get enthusiastic about the 'doing good' projects that the organisation contributes to. Ultimately, minimising harm and doing more good than harm must be the goal.

CSO can, and should, be a positive role, one that acknowledges the enormous challenges that humanity faces, but also bridges that gap between where we are today and where we need to get to. One that identifies the path and makes it look achievable. One that celebrates each success, builds motivation and momentum. One that fosters partnerships, reaching beyond the lines of the department and organisation and identifies improvements that can come from up and down the value chain.

That said, the CSO role is one that should be prepared to speak truth to power, to call out the harm that's being done, to shine a light on areas that some might prefer are not highlighted. To speak uncomfortable truths and to be persistent in voicing them; to be a conscience; to hold up a mirror. You will at times face disagreement from colleagues, disappointment from those who wish you to go faster, and resistance from those who think you are pushing too hard.

A longtime corporate sustainability practitioner tells us: "The interesting thing about the CSO is that they have to understand the minutiae but speak as a futurist. Have to voice uncomfortable truths but maintain the ear of influencers. Push boundaries but keep trust. Pragmatic and visionary. A disruptor but in a way that doesn't alienate. Have to understand the devastating environmental and social issues of our day while maintaining a sense of optimism, curiosity. Be a listener and have a clear point of view. This is a fascinating role."

The sustainability transition may well render some products, services, organisations and even industries less relevant in the future. You are not there to apologise for our evolution, but you can perhaps help to orient the less willing and to point towards the innovation and genuine improvement that can come from those organisations that are willing to adapt, to innovate, to think about new possibilities.

Finally, look after yourself.

As a CSO, you have chosen a calling, and you have a deeper insight than most, into just how precarious a state the world is in. Once you see it, you can't unsee it, and you carry that knowledge as a burden every day, as you try to drag others into that state of understanding. There's so much further that this issue needs to go, in order to bed itself into our general consciousness. The gap in understanding, in truly understanding at a visceral level, the damage we're doing to our world is still far too large.

Remember to take a break from it and to remember that no single person, or even movement, can shoulder this entire responsibility. You will not be an effective influencer if you are brittle, frustrated or tense. If you want to gather a movement of motivated people around you, you need to feel open and empowered. You need to believe that you, and your organisation, can truly make a difference and feel the benefit of the coalition of others, all around the world, who are doing the same as you.

The human race is resilient and ingenious and has dealt with many setbacks before – maybe, just maybe, with the right dedication, motivations and co-operation, maybe we can solve this too.

We wish you well on your journey.

Acknowledgements

This book was born out of a place of trust and curiosity. Anna met Jenny at an online work event in late 2022 and learnt about her 'How to be a …' book series. She read the 'How to be a Chief Operating Officer', Jenny's first book, over the weekend thinking "I wish there was a book like this for sustainability professionals". A few months later, an opportune moment came along – Anna was laid off from her sustainability job. The fintech sector where she worked at the time was going through a turmoil and the company shrank in size. With some time on her hands, Anna reached out to Jenny to pitch the book idea. We've never met in-person, nor worked together before, but we both embraced the idea with excitement and commitment to make it work and have built a relationship of trust and reciprocity in the process. A year later, we had the book. Jenny – I am grateful to you for your support, gentle guidance, integrity throughout this process, and all the work we've put in.

This book was also born out of the need to reflect on a decade-long work in sustainability, where the profession is headed, and how can we all support each other to continue doing meaningful work and reaching for impact. Many people helped shape the experiences, expertise, and perspectives that served as the foundation of this book and inspired to write it. Anna owes her particular thanks to Bastian Buck, Patrick Willems and Katerina

Levitanskaya, Svetlana Golubeva, Eva Gladek and their brilliant teams at GRI, IFC and Metabolic. Thank you for your trust, your mentorship, and the many opportunities you have given me over the years. I also owe huge thanks to all the sustainability practitioners I've met over the years, many of whom became good friends. Our global sustainability network is a constant source of inspiration, emotional support and professional advice on all things sustainability. Thank you to all the dear friends at MIND, the EGN network, Margarita Lysenkova, Oscar Sabag and Gibran Vita.

We owe huge thanks to everyone we interviewed, on and off the record, and the experts who gave generously of their time to review the early drafts of the book. Rossa White, Nadine Smith, Angela Jhanji, Alyson Genovese, Eszter Vitorino Fuleky, Hero Boonstra, Markus Pretzl, Sanne Nusselder and Vera Moll – you have all helped so much, thank you.

Thank you to our wonderful editors, David Woods-Hale and Kriti Toshniwal, whose expertise and thorough but light touch made the process very enjoyable. Thank you to Brett Hilker and the Self-Publishing school team for their support through the publishing process.

Thank you to the following organisations for their highly relevant content and for allowing us to reference their material where permission was required: GRI, BSR and McKinsey. Every effort has been made to trace the owners of copyright material. If there are any omissions, please contact Jenny at jennifer@coo-author.com.

Writing a book is demanding and isolating and we wouldn't have managed without the support of our families. Thank you to our parents for believing in us and for teaching us that hard work is the only way to move forward. It made the year fly by.

From Anna - Sam, you have equally invested your time and effort in this project by taking on my parental duties for evenings and weekends months on end while juggling your own high-pressure career and our many family projects. My greatest thanks go to you. And Aleksey, thank you for your patience every time I had to decline your loving invitations to play. I hope this won't set the wrong precedent.

With gratitude,

Anna and Jennifer

Appendices

Appendix 1

First 90 days checklist

In your first 90 days, you need to inventorise the organisation's sustainability maturity and get a bird's eye view on the status quo – what has been done before you, existing commitments, governance structures, and more. Do this before or in parallel with strategy development, and ideally before you take on the role to understand the fit.

Aspect	Questions to ask	How is this relevant?
Strategy and roadmaps	1. Does a sustainability strategy exist and are there roadmaps to support its execution? 2. Does sustainability feature in the organisation's overall strategy? If so, how – is it a separate objective; does it underpin the business purpose; is it referenced across other strategic objectives; how do other values support or contradict sustainability? 3. Are company KPIs connected to sustainability? Are senior executives' goals and remuneration connected to achieving sustainability outcomes?	Strategy sets direction for the organisation's priorities, activities, and spending for the coming years. If sustainability doesn't feature in it, it doesn't exist, and you will not be getting the level of resources (time and money) you need to pivot the organisation to sustainability. You also have to screen for any major competing objectives as well as how any synergies between CXO and CSO functions are reflected in the strategy and playing out in practice. For example, the product team might have an objective to allocate X% of time to research and development to innovate and develop new product offerings, but in reality, the team is not consulting with the sustainability function to explore innovation opportunities. Or the procurement team is not interested in where its materials are sourced from, or they have a cost reduction mandate, which is not compliant with sustainability targets for their supply chain.
Policies	4. What sustainability policies exist? 5. How do principles in the existing policies support sustainability? Where do they contradict sustainability objectives?	If you lump all company policies together and do a quick scan, you will likely find contradictions in what different clauses are driving forward. For example, a clause in the travel policy might stipulate that employees must choose the cheapest mode of transport for business travel. This may result in the most polluting modes of air travel and will contradict your sustainability goals. Your job is to get an overview of these contradictions and define which are most material to address and to challenge because they will continue to act as blockers to the company's sustainability objectives.

Public commitments and statements	6. Has the organisation made any sustainability-related claims on its website, on its products, sustainability / ESG or financial reports, press-releases, blog posts, or other marketing and communication materials? 7. How are these claims supported by internal research or consulting advice, stakeholder consultations, board or senior executives' approval? 8. If claims about targets exist, then what plans exist to support their achievement?	A claim on the website to achieve carbon-neutrality by 2030 without any supporting internal discussion and plan will lock you in a position to validate it or worse –lose time on achieving a target that might not even be material to your impacts. If you're coming to an organisation without any – or with very little – sustainability history, scrutinise every public claim and don't be afraid to retract it if needed. You will save yourself a litigation case and you will help the organisation and its teams focus on the right things.
Projects and programmes	9. What sustainability-related activities, projects, and programmes exist? Who owns them, who executes on them?	This information will help you understand how sustainability is embedded in the organisation and whether there are set accountabilities for certain aspects of sustainability. If so and if it makes sense to you, your focus in the first six months will be to build a strong partnership with these owners so that you reinforce each other's work. In other cases, you might want to move ownership to your team who has the subject-matter expertise. It's also the time to ask how well any existing programmes fit with the sustainability strategy –are they a nice-to-have but offer only incremental changes, were they launched perhaps too early and are taking time away from other important initiatives?

Systems and processes	10. What data collection systems and processes exist across departments? 11. What is the schedule for reporting (financial, ESG, integrated)? 12. What is the state of ESG reporting? 13. Who is the organisation's auditor and who is the ESG assurance provider? What conflicts of interest exist? 14. What sustainability vendors and suppliers does the organisation work with?	Data is the lifeblood of the organisation, and you will need a lot of it from across the company for all sorts of purposes –impact assessment and management, regulatory reporting, strategy development and KPI setting. Critically, it's not just about the data points you track directly, but it's about the ability for you to derive information from data points that are not related to your department at all. You are dependent on the maturity and quality of other departments' data management systems so inspect early the status quo and the plans that exist to improve data management.
Budget	15. What is the organisation's annual cycle and approval process / when are budgets submitted to the board for review? 16. What budget exists for sustainability? If the function is new, what is the funding the company is prepared to set aside? Is there sustainability funding "hidden" in other areas?	Obviously, you will be proposing a budget based on the strategy you develop but feel out early whether the organisation is prepared to invest real dollars in sustainability and what ranges are you talking. See what budgets exist in other teams and what they are spent on. The people team usually runs a large budget for culture and employer branding –can some of that be allocated or shared with sustainability, e.g., for awareness campaigns and volunteering?

Knowledge and awareness	17. What is the organisation's collective sustainability knowledge, i.e., what sustainability expertise exists on the board and in the C-suite; what training programmes exist and what percentage of employees do they cover; what awareness activities exist; what sustainability community groups and forums exist and what is the level of activity on those forums? 18. How is sustainability work communicated to employees, i.e., channels, frequency, level of detail?	Sustainability will require involvement from just about all functions in the organisation one way or the other. You want to make sure everyone has a basic understanding of what sustainability is – and isn't – so you don't get dragged into discussions where you have to defend your professional practice and explain that sustainability is not just about recycling. You will also need to create visibility into the activities of the sustainability department to get everyone motivated and supportive, so understand what level of attention is currently given to communicating sustainability internally.
Investors	19. What were the drivers to establish the CSO role? 20. What is the board composition? Which investors are sustainability-driven, and which are focused on conflicting goals such as short-term profit maximisation? 21. What is the history of activist investor voting during the annual general meeting?	Your role might have been created for many reasons –meet ESG compliance, motivate employees, create a competitive advantage through sustainability, manage ESG reporting. They will give your role unique focus and colour, and they will come with their limitations. Root out these factors to find common ground.

Appendix 2

Ten books to read on Sustainability

1. Alison Taylor, Higher Ground (Harvard, MA: Harvard Business Review Press, 2024).
2. Kim Stanley Robinson, Ministry for the Future (London: Orbit, 2021).
3. Kate Raworth, Doughnut Economics (London: Random House Business, 2028).
4. Marianna Mazzucatto, The Value of Everything (London: Penguin, 2019).
5. Tony Juniper, What Has Nature Ever Done to Us? (London: Profile Books, 2013).
6. Bill Gates, How to Avoid a Climate Disaster (London: Penguin, 2022).
7. Paul Polman and Andrew Winston, Net Positive (Harvard, MA: Harvard Business Review Press, 2022).
8. David Attenborough, A Life on our Planet: My Witness Statement and a Vision for the Future (London: Ebury Press, 2022).
9. Ed Conway, Material World: A Substantial Story of Our Past and Future (London: HW Allen, 2023).
10. Paul Hawken, Regeneration (London: Penguin, 2021).

References

Chapter 1

1   Acaroglu, Leyla. *Swivel to Sustainability: A Full Systems Business Transformation Guidebook*. New York, NY: Disrupt Design LLC, 2022.

2   Purpose Disruptors, "How does the advertising industry take full responsibility for its climate impact?" Accessed May 14, 2024, https://www.purpose-disruptors.org/advertised-emissions.

3   International Chamber of Commerce. "ICC Advertising and Marketing Communications Code (2018 Edition)." Accessed May 14, 2024, https://iccwbo.org/news-publications/policies-reports/icc-advertising-and-marketing-communications-code/.

4   Mendelow, A. "Proceedings of the second international conference on information systems." Cambridge, MA (1991).

Chapter 2

1   Brundtland, G.H. *Our Common Future: Report of The World Commission on Environment and Development*. Geneva: UN, 1987.

2   Ibid.

3   Freshfields Bruckhaus Deringer. *A Legal Framework For Impact: Sustainability Impact In Investor Decision-Making*. London: Freshfields Bruckhaus Deringer, 2021.

4   Interestingly, there were several iterations of the term before UNEP FI arrived at 'ESG' in 2004 – 'Social, Environmental, Governance' (SEG) was an option but was dismissed because it was unclear what comprised 'social issues'

as well as the risk of having a "whiff of socialism" about it, and 'Governance, Environmental, Social' (GES) was an option to emphasise corporate governance as the most important of the three factors but was also dismissed for being "not so catchy". Beyond this anecdotal example, ESG does not offer an opinion of what a company should focus on as part of its sustainability strategy, nor the vision of transformation it should set out for itself.

5   UN Global Compact. *Who Cares Wins: Connecting Financial Markets To A Changing World*. New York: United Nations, 2004.

6   UN Environment Programme Finance Initiative. *The Materiality of Social, Environmental, and Corporate Governance Issues to Equity Pricing*. New York: United Nations, 2004.

7   Ibid.

8   UN Environment Programme Finance Initiative. *A Legal Framework for the Integration of ESG Issues into Institutional Investment*. London: Freshfields Bruckhaus Deringer, 2005.

9   Deloitte. "EC launches initiative to update the NFRD." Accessed May 14, 2024, https://www.iasplus.com/en/news/2020/02/nfrd.

10   The International Organization of Securities Commissions. *Sustainable Finance and the Role of Securities Regulators and IOSCO*. Madrid: IOSCO, 2020.

11   International Financial reporting Standards. "IFRS Foundation Trustees consult on global approach to sustainability reporting and on possible Foundation role." Accessed May 14, 2024, https://www.ifrs.org/news-and-events/news/2020/09/ifrs-foundation-trustees-consult-on-global-approach-to-sustainability-reporting/.

12   Herron Lee, Alison. "Modernizing' Regulation S-K: Ignoring the Elephant in the Room." Accessed May 14, 2024, https://www.sec.gov/news/public-statement/lee-mda-2020-01-30.

13   Henisz, W., Koller, T., and Nuttall, R. "Five ways that ESG creates value." *McKinsey Quarterly*, November 2019.

14   Bowen H.R. *The Social Responsibilities of the Businessman*. Iowa City, IA: University of Iowa Press, 1953.

15   Caroll, A.B. "A Three-Dimensional Conceptual Model of Corporate Performance." *The Academy of Management Review*, Vol. 4, No. 4 (October 1979):

497-505.

16   Committee For Economic Development. *Social Responsibilities of Business Corporations*. New York: Committee for Economic Development, 1971.

17   Caroll, A.B. "The pyramid of corporate social responsibility: Toward the moral management of organizational stakeholders" *Business Horizons*, Vol. 34, Issue 4 (July–August 1991): 39-48.

18   Global Reporting Initiative. *GRI 1: Foundation 2021*. Boston, MA: Global Reporting Initiative, 2023.

19   Impact Management Platform. "Key Terms and Concepts." Accessed May 14, 2024, https://impactmanagementplatform.org/terms-and-concepts/.

20   Ibid.

21   United Nations Resolution. *Transforming our world: The 2030 Agenda for Sustainable Development*. New York: United nations, 2015.

22   Global Reporting Initiative. *GRI 207: Tax 2019*. Boston, MA: Global Reporting Initiative, 2021.

23   The Tax Justice Network. "The State of Tax Justice 2023." Accessed May 14, 2024, https://taxjustice.net/reports/the-state-of-tax-justice-2023/.

24   Global Reporting Initiative. *GRI 1: Foundation 2021*. Boston, MA: Global Reporting Initiative, 2023.

25   Ibid.

26   Cambridge Dictionary. "Materiality." Accessed May 14, 2024, https://dictionary.cambridge.org/dictionary/english/materiality.

27   Global Reporting Initiative. *RG 3.1 Sustainability Reporting Guidelines, 2006*. Accessed May 17, 2024, https://www.mas-business.com/docs/G3.1-Guidelines-Incl-Technical-Protocol.pdf.

28   Beinhocker, Eric D. *The Origin of Wealth: the Radical Remaking of Economics and What it Means for Business*. Boston, MA: Harvard Business Review Press, 2007.

29   Stakeholder Theory. "About." Accessed May 14, 2024, http://stakeholdertheory.org/about/.

30   Avlonas, N., Nassos, G. *Practical Sustainability Strategies: How to Gain a Competitive Advantage*. London: Wiley-Blackwell, 2014.

31   Note that future generations are also considered a stakeholder even though and precisely because they can't articulate their views. For example, The Maastricht Principles on the Human Rights of Future Generations consolidate existing human rights standards to enhance the protection and fulfilment of the human rights of future generations.

32   Avlonas, N., Nassos, G. *Practical Sustainability Strategies: How to Gain a Competitive Advantage*. London: Wiley-Blackwell, 2014.

33   Collins Dictionary. "Purpose." Accessed May 14, 2024, https://www.collinsdictionary.com/dictionary/english/purpose.

34   NASA. "Atmospheric Carbon Dioxide Tagged by Source." Accessed May 14, 2024, https://svs.gsfc.nasa.gov/5110.

35   Corporate Governance Code. "Dutch Corporate Governance Code 2022 (English translation)." Accessed May 14, 2024, https://www.mccg.nl/publicaties/codes/2022/12/20/dutch-corporate-governance-code-2022.

Chapter 3

1   Schein, Edgar, H. *Organisational Culture and Leadership: 5ᵗʰ ed.* London: Wiley, 2016.

2   Ibid.

3   Tenney, Matt. "What is Sustainable Business Culture." *Business Leadership Today*. Accessed May 14, 2024, https://businessleadershiptoday.com/what-is-sustainable-business-culture.

4   Taylor, Alison. *The Five Levels of an Ethical Culture: How to Build and Sustain Organizations with Integrity*. San Francisco, CA: Business for Social Responsibility (BSR), 2017.

5   The Conference Board. *Building a Sustainability Culture*. New York, NY: The Conference Board, 2023.

6   Meyer, Erin. *The Culture Map: Breaking Through the Invisible Boundaries of Global Business*. New York, NY: PublicAffairs, 2014.

7   Acaroglu, Leyla. *Swivel to Sustainability: A Full Systems Business Transformation Guidebook*. New York, NY: Disrupt Design LLC, 2022.

8   Stanford Encyclopedia of Philosophy. "Social Norms." Accessed May 14, 2024, https://plato.stanford.edu/entries/social-norms/.

9   Wikipedia. "List of cognitive biases." Accessed May 15, 2024, https://en.wikipedia.org/wiki/List_of_cognitive_biases.

10   Dewar, C. and Keller, S. "The Irrational Side of Change Management," *McKinsey Quarterly*, April 1, 2009.

11   Beinhocker, Eric D. *The Origin of Wealth: the Radical Remaking of Economics and What it Means for Business*. Boston, MA: Harvard Business Review Press, 2007.

Chapter 4

1   The British Academy. "What is the Future of the Corporation?". Accessed May 15, 2024, https://www.thebritishacademy.ac.uk/programmes/future-of-the-corporation/about/#:~:text=Profitably%20solving%20the%20problems%20of,not%20profiting%20from%20creating%20problems.

2   Henisz, W., Koller, T., and Nuttall, R. "Five ways that ESG creates value." *McKinsey Quarterly*, November 2019.

3   Ibid.

4   Albrecht, G., Connor, L., Freeman, S., Higginbottom, N., Kelly, B., Pollard, G., Sartore, G., Stain, H., Tonna, A. "Solastalgia: the distress caused by environmental change," *Australas Psychiatry*, Vol. 15, Suppl. 1 (2007): 95-98.

5   PwC. "The Four Profiles of ESG Maturity." Accessed May 15, 2024, https://www.pwc.com/sk/en/environmental-social-and-corporate-governance-esg/four-profiles-of-esg-maturity.html.

6   In 2022, PWC ran a survey among 227 investment professionals across 43 territories and a range of industries, with assets under management ranging from USD 500 million USD 1 trillion or more. They found that only 29% of respondents said they "would be willing to accept a lower rate of return on investment in a company that undertakes activities that address sustainability issues relevant to its business' performance and prospects". PWC. "Global Investor Survey, 2022." Accessed May 15, 2024, https://www.pwc.com/gx/en/global-investor-survey/PwC-Global-Investor-Survey-2022.pdf.

7   Eco-Business. "What are Chief Sustainability Officers Prioritising in 2024?" Accessed May 15, 2024, https://www.eco-business.com/news/what-are-chief-sustainability-officers-prioritising-in-2024/.

8   BSR. "Five Steps to Good Sustainability Reporting, 2020." Accessed May 15, 2024, https://www.bsr.org/en/reports/five-steps-to-good-sustainability-reporting

9   Taylor, Alison. *Higher Ground: How Businesses Can Do the Right Thing in a Turbulent World*. Harvard, MA: Harvard Business Review Press, 2024.

10   Center for Theory of Change "What is Theory of Change?" Accessed May 15, 2024, https://www.theoryofchange.org/what-is-theory-of-change/.

11   Ibid.

12   NYU Stern, Center for Sustainable Business. "ROSI™ Methodology." Accessed May 15, 2024, https://www.stern.nyu.edu/sites/default/files/assets/documents/NYUSternCSB_ROSI_Labor.xlsx.

13   Barby, C., et al. "Measuring Purpose –An Integrated Framework", Accessed May 15, 2024, https://dx.doi.org/10.2139/ssrn.3771892.

14   Harvard Business School. "Impact Weighted Accounts." Accessed May 15, 2024, https://www.hbs.edu/impact-weighted-accounts/Pages/explore-our-data.aspx.

15   Taylor, Alison. *Higher Ground: How Businesses Can Do the Right Thing in a Turbulent World*. Harvard, MA: Harvard Business Review Press, 2024.

Chapter 5

1   The European Commission. "Commission Delegated Regulation (EU) 2023/2772 of 31 July 2023 supplementing Directive 2013/34/EU of the European Parliament and of the Council as regards sustainability reporting standards," *Official Journal of the European Union*. December 22, 2023. Accessed May 15, 2024, https://eur-lex.europa.eu/legal-content/EN/TXT/PDF/?uri=OJ:L_202302772.

2   Acaroglu, Leyla. *Swivel to Sustainability: A Full Systems Business Transformation Guidebook*. New York: Disrupt Design LLC, 2022.

3   Newton, Casey. "Facebook will pay $52 million in settlement with moderators who developed PTSD on the job.," *The Verge*, May 12, 2020. Accessed May 15, 2024, https://www.theverge.com/2020/5/12/21255870/facebook-content-moderator-settlement-scola-ptsd-mental-health.

4   Global Reporting Initiative. "Sector Program." Accessed May 15, 2024, https://www.globalreporting.org/standards/sector-program/.

5   SASB Standards. "SASB Standards Overview." Accessed May 15, 2024, https://sasb.ifrs.org/standards/.

6   Taylor, Alison. *Higher Ground: How Businesses Can Do the Right Thing in a Turbulent World*. Harvard, MA: Harvard Business Review Press, 2024.

7   Global Reporting Initiative. *GRI 3: Material Topics 2021*. Accessed May 17, 2024, https://www.globalreporting.org/publications/documents/english/gri-3-material-topics-2021/.

8   Taylor, Alison. *Higher Ground: How Businesses Can Do the Right Thing in a Turbulent World*. Harvard, MA: Harvard Business Review Press, 2024.

9   European Financial Reporting Advisory Group. *Draft EFRG IG 1 Materiality Assessment*. Brussels: European Financial Reporting Advisory Group, 2023.

Chapter 6

1   United Nations Framework Convention on Climate Change (UNFCC). "Kyoto Protocol to the United Nations Framework Convention on Climate Change." December 1997. Accessed May 13, 2024. https://unfccc.int/resource/docs/convkp/kpeng.html.

2   World Health Organisation. "Air Pollution." Accessed May 15, 2024, https://www.who.int/health-topics/air-pollution#tab=tab_1.

3   Intergovernmental Science-Policy Platform on Biodiversity and Ecosystem Services. "Models of drivers of biodiversity and ecosystem change." Accessed May 15, 2024, https://www.ipbes.net/models-drivers-biodiversity-ecosystem-change.

4   Vanclay, F. "International Principles For Social Impact Assessment." *Impact Assessment and Project Appraisal*, 21(1) (February 2012):5–12.

5   The Danish Institute for Human Rights. *Human Rights Impact Assessment Guidance and Toolbox*. Copenhagen: The Danish Institute for Human Rights, 2020.

6   Greenhouse Gas Protocol. Accessed May 15, 2024, https://ghgprotocol.org/.

7   Greenhouse Gas Protocol. *A Corporate Accounting and Reporting Standard*. Washington: World Resources Institute and World Business Council for Sustainable Development, 2024.

8   Aldaya, M., Chapagain, A., Hoekstra, A., Mekonnen, M. *The Water Footprint Assessment Manual: Setting the Standard.* London: Earthscan, 2011.

9   CEO Water Mandate. *Aqueduct Water Risk Atlas (2013).* Washington: World Resources Institute, 2013.

10   WWF Risk Filter Suite. "Physical Risk." Accessed May 15, 2024, https://riskfilter.org/water/explore/map.

11   Integrated Biodiversity Assessment Tool. Accessed May 15, 2024, https://www.ibat-alliance.org/.

12   Encore. "Exploring Natural Capital Opportunities, Risks and Exposure." Accessed May 15, 2024, https://www.encorenature.org/en.

13   International Union for the Conservation of Nature. "Species Threat Abatement and Restoration (STAR) metric." Accessed May 15, 2024, https://www.iucn.org/resources/conservation-tool/species-threat-abatement-and-restoration-star-metric.

14   WWF Risk Filter Suite. "Biodiversity Risk Filter." Accessed May 15, 2024, https://riskfilter.org/biodiversity/home.

15   Global ICCA Registry. Accessed May 15, 2024, https://www.iccaregistry.org/.

16   Global Ecosystem Typology. "A Global Typology for Earth's Ecosystems." Accessed May 15, 2024, https://global-ecosystems.org/.

17   Biodiversity Disclosure Project, Endangered Wildlife Trust. *Biological Diversity Protocol.* Johannesburg: National Biodiversity and Business Network, 2020.

18   United Nations et al. *System of Environmental-Economic Accounting— Ecosystem Accounting (SEEA EA). White cover publication, pre-edited text subject to official editing.* New York, NY: United Nations, 2021.

19   IUCN Red List. "Threats Classification Scheme (Version 3.3)." Accessed May 15, 2024, https://www.iucnredlist.org/resources/threat-classification-scheme.

20   Science-based Targets Network, Global Commons Alliance. "The first science-based targets for nature." Accessed May 15, 2024, https://sciencebasedtargetsnetwork.org/how-it-works/the-first-science-based-targets-for-nature/.

21   Wikipedia. "LEED." Accessed May 15, 2024, https://en.wikipedia.org/wiki/LEED.

22   United States Environmental Protection Agency. "Heat Island Effect." Accessed May 15, 2024, https://www.epa.gov/heatislands.

23   United Nations. *Guiding Principles on Business and Human Rights: Implementing the United Nations "Protect, Respect and Remedy" Framework.* Geneva: United Nations, 2011.

24   OECD. *OECD Guidelines for Multinational Enterprises 2011 Edition.* Paris: OECD Publishing, 2011.

25   International Labour Organization. "ILO Declaration on Fundamental Principles and Rights at Work." Accessed May 15, 2024, https://www.ilo.org/declaration/lang--en/index.htm.

26   The Danish Institute for Human Rights. *Human Rights Impact Assessment Guidance and Toolbox.* Copenhagen: The Danish Institute for Human Rights, 2020.

27   Principles for Responsible Investment. "How to identify human rights risks: A practical guide in due diligence." Accessed May 15, 2024, https://www.unpri.org/human-rights/how-to-identify-human-rights-risks-a-practical-guide-in-due-diligence/11457.article.

28   The Danish Institute for Human Rights. *Human Rights Impact Assessment Guidance and Toolbox.* Copenhagen: The Danish Institute for Human Rights, 2020.

29   Intergovernmental Panel on Climate Change. "Glossary." Accessed May 15, 2024, https://www.ipcc.ch/sr15/chapter/glossary/.

30   Munck, Jane, et al. "Impacts of food contact chemicals on human health: a consensus statement," *Environ Health*, 3:19(1) (March 2020):25.

31   Stevenson, M. and Weber, C. "First Things First: Avoid, Reduce… and only after that – Compensate." WWF, 2020. Accessed May 15, 2024, https://wwf.panda.org/wwf_news/?362819/First-Things-First-Avoid-Reduce--and-only-after-thatCompensate.

32   The Biodiversity Consultancy. "Mitigation Hierarchy.: Accessed May 15, 2024, https://www.thebiodiversityconsultancy.com/our-work/our-expertise/strategy/mitigation-hierarchy/.

Chapter 7

1   Gov.uk. "Publish an annual modern slavery statement." Accessed May 15, 2024, https://www.gov.uk/guidance/publish-an-annual-modern-slavery-statement#who-needs-to-publish-a-statement.

2   Taylor, Alison. *Higher Ground: How Businesses Can Do the Right Thing in a Turbulent World*. Harvard, MA: Harvard Business Review Press, 2024.

3   Ibid.

4   The European Commission. "Commission Delegated Regulation (EU) 2023/2772 of 31 July 2023 supplementing Directive 2013/34/EU of the European Parliament and of the Council as regards sustainability reporting standards," *Official Journal of the European Union*. December 22, 2023. Accessed May 15, 2024, https://eur-lex.europa.eu/legal-content/EN/TXT/PDF/?uri=OJ:L_202302772.

5   Independent Commission Against Corruption. *Integrity Spotlight*, January 2022.

Chapter 8

1   Tranchard, Sandrine. "Damage to reputation or brand, cyber crime, political risk and terrorism are some of the risks that private and public organizations of all types and sizes around the world must face with increasing frequency. The latest version of ISO 31000 has just been unveiled to help manage the uncertainty." ICO, February 15, 2008, Accessed May 15, 2024, https://www.iso.org/news/ref2263.html#:~:text=Risk%20is%20now%20defined%20as,on%20an%20organization's%20decision%20making.

2   Hindson, Alex. "What is the relevance of the rise of ESG to Chief Risk Officers?" The Risk Coalition, March 2, 2021. Accessed May 15, 2024, https://www.riskcoalition.org.uk/blog-posts/what-is-the-relevance-of-the-rise-of-esg-to-chief-risk-officers-x765a.

3   ISO. "ISO 31000." Accessed May 15, 2024, https://www.iso.org/iso-31000-risk-management.html.

4   Geary, Jennifer. *How to be a Chief Risk Officer: A Handbook for the Modern CRO*. London: Neilsen, 2022.

5   The European Commission. "Commission Delegated Regulation (EU) 2021/1256 of 21 April 2021 amending Delegated Regulation (EU) 2015/35 as regards the integration of sustainability risks in the governance of insurance and reinsurance undertakings," *Official Journal of the European Union.* August 8, 2021. Accessed May 15, 2024, https://eur-lex.europa.eu/legal-content/EN/TXT/HTML/?uri=CELEX%3A32021R1256.

6   European Commission. "Corporate sustainability due diligence." Accessed May 15, 2024, https://commission.europa.eu/business-economy-euro/doing-business-eu/corporate-sustainability-due-diligence_en.

7   World Business Council for Sustainable Development. *Embedding ESG and sustainability considerations into the Three Lines Model.* Geneva: WBCSD, 2022.

8   Ibid.

9   Ibid.

10   Ibid.

11   Shibli, Aliya. "Who should lead sustainability within a bank?" *The Banker, February 1, 2024. Accessed May 15, 2024,* https://www.thebanker.com/Who-should-lead-sustainability-within-a-bank-1706796310.

Chapter 9

1   US Securities and Exchange Commission. "SEC Adopts Rules to Enhance and Standardize Climate-Related Disclosures for Investors." Accessed May 15, 2024, https://www.sec.gov/news/press-release/2024-31.

2   Butterworth, Lucie. "How does addressing sustainability change how businesses understand value?" IBM, July 26, 2022. Accessed May 15, 2024, https://www.ibm.com/blog/sustainability-value/.

3   Carbon Brief. "In-depth Q&A: What do Rishi Sunak's U-turns mean for UK climate policy?" Accessed May 15, 2024, https://www.carbonbrief.org/in-depth-qa-what-do-rishi-sunaks-u-turns-mean-for-uk-climate-policy/.

4   Morningstar. "SFDR Article 8 and Article 9 Funds: Q1 2024 in Review" Accessed May 15, 2024, https://www.morningstar.com/en-uk/lp/sfdr-article8-article9.

5   European Commission. "The European Green Deal: Striving to be the first climate-neutral continent." Accessed May 15, 2024, https://commission.europa.eu/strategy-and-policy/priorities-2019-2024/european-green-deal_en.

6   European Commission. "EU Taxonomy for Sustainable Activities." Accessed May 15, 2024, https://finance.ec.europa.eu/sustainable-finance/tools-and-standards/eu-taxonomy-sustainable-activities_en

7   European Commission. "Implementing and delegated acts - Taxonomy Regulation." Accessed May 15, 2024, https://finance.ec.europa.eu/regulation-and-supervision/financial-services-legislation/implementing-and-delegated-acts/taxonomy-regulation_en

8   The European Parliament and the Council of the European Union. "Regulation (Eu) 2019/2088 Of The European Parliament And Of The Council of 27 November 2019 on sustainability⬜ related disclosures in the financial services sector," *Official Journal of the European Union*, December 9, 2012. Accessed May 15, 2024, chrome-extension://efaidnbmnnnibpca-jpcglclefindmkaj/https://eur-lex.europa.eu/legal-content/EN/TXT/PDF/?uri=CELEX:32019R2088.

9   The European Commission. "Commission Delegated Regulation (EU) 2023/2772 of 31 July 2023 supplementing Directive 2013/34/EU of the European Parliament and of the Council as regards sustainability reporting standards," *Official Journal of the European Union*. December 22, 2023. Accessed May 15, 2024, https://eur-lex.europa.eu/legal-content/EN/TXT/PDF/?uri=OJ:L_202302772.

10   Ibid.

11   European Commission. "Corporate Sustainability Due Diligence." Accessed May 15, 2024, https://commission.europa.eu/business-economy-euro/doing-business-eu/corporate-sustainability-due-diligence_en

12   Segal, Mark. "China Stock Exchanges Announce Mandatory Sustainability Reporting Requirements for Companies," *ESG Today*, February 12, 2024. Accessed May 15, 2024, https://www.eba.europa.eu/regulation-and-policy/transparency-and-pillar-3.

13   Ibid.

14   Segal, Mark. "Canada Announces Climate Reporting Requirements for Banks, Insurers, Beginning 2024" *ESG Today*, March 8, 2023. Accessed May 15, 2024, https://www.esgtoday.com/canada-releases-climate-reporting-requirements-for-banks-insurers-beginning-2024/

15   Segal, Mark. "Brazil to Require Mandatory Climate Reporting Beginning 2025," *ESG Today*, February 28, 2023. Accessed May 15, 2024, https://www.esgtoday.com/brazil-to-require-mandatory-sustainability-reporting-from-2026/

16   Segal, Mark. "Singapore to Introduce Mandatory Sustainability Reporting from 2026," *ESG Today*, October 25, 2024. Accessed May 15, 2024, https://www.esgtoday.com/singapore-to-introduce-mandatory-climate-reporting-beginning-2025/

17   Prall, Kevin. *Perspectives Paper: ESG and Business Valuation*. London: International Valuation Standards Council, 2021.

18   Koefoed Simonsen, Amanda. "The Green New Deal is a framework of economic transition for financial market participants, companies and for non-EU operators!" LinkedIn, 2023. Accessed May 17 2024, https://www.linkedin.com/posts/amanda-koefoed-simonsen_how-the-corporate-sustainability-reporting-activity-7038138872957935618-dHaC/.

19   Taylor, Alison. *Higher Ground: How Businesses Can Do the Right Thing in a Turbulent World*. Harvard, MA: Harvard Business Review Press, 2024.

20   SRI Connect. "For Companies." Accessed May 15, 2024, https://www.sri-connect.com/for-companies.

21   World Business Council for Sustainable Development. "ESG Disclosure Handbook (2019)." Accessed May 15, 2024, https://www.wbcsd.org/Programs/Redefining-Value/Redesigning-capital-market-engagement/Resources/ESG-Disclosure-Handbook.

Chapter 10

1   Littan, Shari (ed) et al. *Achieving Effective Internal Control Over Sustainability Reporting (ICSR): Building Trust and Confidence through the COSO Internal Control—Integrated Framework*. Committee of the Sponsoring Organizations of the Treadway Commission, 2023.

2   European Commission. "The European Green Deal: striving to be the first climate neutral continent." Accessed May 15, 2024, https://commission.europa.eu/strategy-and-policy/priorities-2019-2024/european-green-deal_en.

3   Council of the European Union. "Environmental, social and governance (ESG) ratings: Council and Parliament reach agreement." Accessed May 15, 2024, https://www.consilium.europa.eu/en/press/press-releases/2024/02/05/environmental-social-and-governance-esg-ratings-council-and-parliament-reach-agreement/.

4   Barnett, Paul. "If what gets measured gets managed, measuring the wrong thing matters." *Corporate finance Review*, February 2015.

5   Légifrance. "Décrets, arrêtés, circulaires" Accessed May 15, 2024, https://www.legifrance.gouv.fr/download/pdf?id=fOTM7ilGbxcYwc159WYE-xxp0eSIBFgHonwOt6OlvQA=.

6   Committee of the Sponsoring Organizations of the Treadway Commission. "COSO Releases New "Achieving Effective Internal Control Over Sustainability Reporting" (ICSR) Supplemental Guidance." Accessed May 15, 2024, https://www.coso.org/_files/ugd/3059fc_c45bb9e3a23448529a65ce-c6e2bc5419.pdf.

7   Committee of the Sponsoring Organizations of the Treadway Commission. "Internal Control – Integrated Framework." Accessed May 15, 2024, https://www.coso.org/guidance-on-ic.

8   Apple. "Environment | Mother Nature." Accessed May 15, 2024, https://www.apple.com/nz/environment/mother-nature/.

9   Global Reporting Initiative (GRI). *GRI 1: Foundation 2021*. Accessed May 17, 2024, https://www.globalreporting.org/how-to-use-the-gri-standards/gri-standards-english-language/.

10   United Nations Global Compact. "Communication on Progress." Accessed May 15, 2024, https://unglobalcompact.org/participation/report/cop.

11   Principles for Responsible Investment. "The Reporting Process." Accessed May 15, 2024, https://www.unpri.org/reporting-and-assessment/the-reporting-process/3057.article.

12   S&P Global. *Corporate Sustainability Assessment*. Zurich: S&P Global, 2014.

13   Global Real Estate Sustainability Benchmark. "Key Dates: GRESB Assessments Timeline." Accessed May 15, 2024, https://www.gresb.com/nl-en/key-dates-gresb-assessments-timeline/.

14   CDP. "Disclosure Timeline for Companies." Accessed May 15, 2024, https://www.cdp.net/en/companies-discloser/how-to-disclose-as-a-company#4dbe1c18fa96f74a3f1517443b741231.

15   Institute of Chartered Accountants in England and Wales. "Technical Audit and Assurance Glossary." Accessed May 15, 2024, https://www.icaew.com/technical/audit-and-assurance/assurance/what-is-assurance/assurance-glossary#section-p

16   Ibid.

17   World Business Council for Sustainable Development and Institute of Chartered Accountants in England and Wales. *A buyer's guide to assurance on non-financial information.* Geneva: WBCSD, 2019.

18   Ibid.

Chapter 11

1   Lindberg, A., Winnman, M. "Här dumpas H&M-kläderna du "återvinner." *Aftonbladet.* Accessed May 15, 2024, https://www.aftonbladet.se/nyheter/a/O8PAyb/har-dumpas-h-m-kladerna-du-atervinner.

2   Ibid.

3   Climate Change Litigation Databases. Accessed May 15, 2024, https://climatecasechart.com/.

4   Laufer, W.S. "Social accountability and corporate greenwashing." *Journal of Business Ethics,* volume 43 (2023): 253–261.

5   Taylor, Alison. *Higher Ground: How Businesses Can Do the Right Thing in a Turbulent World.* Harvard, MA: Harvard Business Review Press, 2024.

6   Building Green. "The Nine Types of Greenwashing." Accessed May 15, 2024, https://www.buildinggreen.com/news-article/nine-types-greenwashing.

7   University College of Estate Management. "What is greenwashing (and how can you spot it)?" Accessed May 15, 2024, https://www.ucem.ac.uk/whats-happening/articles/8-types-of-greenwashing-and-how-to-spot-them/.

8   European Commission. *Proposal for a Directive of the European Parliament and of the Council on Substantiation and Communication of Explicit Environmental Claims (Green Claims Directive).* Brussels: European Commission, 2023.

9   Latham & Watkins. *Focus on Greenwashing: The Latest Regulatory Proposals in the EU and the UK.* London: Latham & Watkins, April 6, 2023.

10   CMS. "CMS Green Globe." Accessed May 15, 2024, https://cms.law/en/gbr/publication/cms-green-globe.

11   GreenBiz. "GreenBiz23 Comms Summit Schedule." Accessed May 15, 2024, https://www.greenbiz.com/events/greenbiz/2023/comms-summit#schedule.

12   Netherlands Authority for Consumers and Markets (Autoriteit Consument & Markt). *Guidelines Sustainability Claims.* The Hague: ACM, 2023.

Chapter 12

1   INSEAD Corporate Governance Centre. "Directors Can Up Their Game on ESG Issues." Accessed May 15, 2024, https://www.insead.edu/insead-corporate-governance-centre/bcg-insead-board-esg-pulse-check

2   Harvard Law School Forum on Corporate Governance. "The Evolving Role of ESG Metrics in Executive Compensation Plans." March 19, 2022. Accessed May 15, 2024, https://corpgov.law.harvard.edu/2022/03/19/the-evolving-role-of-esg-metrics-in-executive-compensation-plans/.

3   The Washington Post. "Despite Spills and Air Pollution, Fossil Fuel Companies Award CEOs For Environmental Records." Accessed May 15, 2024, https://www.washingtonpost.com/business/interactive/2021/fossil-fuel-climate-bonus/.

4   As You Sow. "How Carbon Reductions are Currently Factored into Executive Pay." September 27, 2021. Accessed May 15, 2024, https://www.asyousow.org/our-work/ceo-pay/blog/2021/9/27/how-carbon-reductions-are-currently-factored-into-executive-pay.

5   Harvard Law School Forum on Corporate Governance. "The Evolving Role of ESG Metrics in Executive Compensation Plans." March 19, 2022. Accessed May 15, 2024, https://corpgov.law.harvard.edu/2022/03/19/the-evolving-role-of-esg-metrics-in-executive-compensation-plans/.

6   Semler Brossy. *ESG+ Incentives: 2021 Report*. Los Angeles, CA: Semler Brossy, 2021.

7   Ibid.

8   Investopedia. "What Is the Difference Between Capital and Operating Expenditures?" Accessed May 15, 2024, https://www.investopedia.com/ask/answers/112814/whats-difference-between-capital-expenditures-capex-and-operational-expenditures-opex.asp#:~:text=What%20Is%20the%20Difference%20Between,a%20much%20shorter%2Dterm%20benefit.

9   European Commission. *FAQ: What is the EU Taxonomy Article 8 delegated act and how will it work in practice?* Brussels: European Commission, 2021.

10   EU Taxonomy Info. "Application of the EU Taxonomy for Companies." Accessed May 15, 2024, https://eu-taxonomy.info/info/eu-taxonomy-for-companies.

Chapter 13

1   De Smet, A., Gao, W., Henderson, K. and Hundertmark, T. "Organizing for sustainability success: where, and how, leaders can start." *McKinsey Sustainability*, August 10, 2021. Accessed May 15, 2024, https://www.mckinsey.com/capabilities/sustainability/our-insights/organizing-for-sustainability-success-where-and-how-leaders-can-start#/

Chapter 14

1   Molero, Elisa. "Get Ready To Report: The ESG Reporting Software Market Will Reach $4.5 Billion By 2027." Vertantix. Accessed May 15, 2024, https://www.verdantix.com/insights/blogs/get-ready-to-report-the-esg-reporting-software-market-will-reach-4.5-billion-dollars-by-2027.

2   Fortune Business Insights. "Carbon Accounting Software Market Size, Share & Industry Analysis, By Deployment (Cloud-based and On-premise), By Industry (Energy & Utilities, IT & Telecom, Healthcare, Transportation & Logistics, Retail, Construction & Infrastructure, Food & Beverages, Chemicals, and Others), and Country Forecast, 2024-2032." Accessed May 15, 2024, https://www.fortunebusinessinsights.com/carbon-accounting-software-market-107292.

3   Jung, B. and Lorenz, M. "The bonanza of the ESG software market has started, though the best is yet to come." *Strategy&*, February 2, 2023. Accessed May 15, 2024, https://www.strategyand.pwc.com/de/en/functions/sustainability-strategy/esg-software-market.html.

Chapter 15

1   United Nations. Halfway to 2030, world 'nowhere near' reaching Global Goals, UN warns." July 17, 2023. Accessed May 15, 2024, https://news.un.org/en/story/2023/07/1138777.

2   Stockholm Resilience Centre. "Planetary Boundaries." Accessed May 15, 2024, https://www.stockholmresilience.org/research/planetary-boundaries.html.

3   Copernicus. "March 2024 – 10th consecutive record warm month globally." Accessed May 15, 2024, https://climate.copernicus.eu/march-2024-10th-consecutive-record-warm-month-globally.

4   Climate Trace. Accessed May 15, 2024, https://climatetrace.org/approach.

Printed in Great Britain
by Amazon

47112999R00195